The Right to Transportation

Moving to Equity

Thomas W. Sanchez and Marc Brenman
with
Jacinta S. Ma and Richard H. Stolz

PLANNERS PRESS
AMERICAN PLANNING ASSOCIATION
Chicago, Illinois
Washington, D.C.

Copyright 2007 by the American Planning Association
122 S. Michigan Ave., Suite 1600, Chicago, IL 60603

ISBN (paperback edition): 1-932364-29-3 and 978-1-932364-29-3
ISBN (hardbound edition): 1-932364-30-7 and 978-1-932364-30-9

Library of Congress Control Number: 2007936594

Printed in the United States of America

Tom Sanchez
To Carrie, Nora, and Erin, my greatest sources of joy.

Marc Brenman
To my long-suffering wife, Barbara Bither,
who has tolerated a bi-coastal career.

Contents

Acknowledgments

Tom Sanchez would like to acknowledge Gary Orfield of the Civil Rights Project at UCLA and Chris Edley, Dean of the School of Law–Boalt Hall (both formerly of the Civil Rights Project at Harvard University), Jacinta Ma, Rich Stolz, Lori Kennedy, Amber Ontiveros, Sy Adler, Robert Puentes, Rep. Elijah Cummings and staff, Julie Cunningham, Jeanette Studley, Ben Wiles, Caroline Sanchez, Cynthia Cheski, Sylvia Lewis, and anonymous reviewer(s). He would also like to acknowledge his coauthor for whom he has deep respect for his commitment to civil rights.

Marc Brenman would like to thank his colleagues at the Office of Civil Rights, U.S. Department of Transportation, for the opportunity to learn about transportation equity, and the Washington State Human Rights Commission for the challenge of making some of the concepts in the book operational.

Preface

This book grew out of the report, *Moving to Equity: Addressing Inequitable Effects of Transportation Policies on Minorities*, sponsored by the Civil Rights Project at Harvard University. The objective of the report was to bring more attention to issues surrounding transportation equity and civil rights, especially as they might influence the reauthorization of federal transportation legislation: the Safe, Accountable, Flexible Transportation Equity Act: A Legacy for Users (SAFETEA-LU). Given its objective, the report served more as a summary of the issues than an in-depth discussion of transportation equity. While the report generated much interest, the authors felt that an expanded version would be a useful resource for community groups, planners, policy makers, and elected officials.

Significant civil rights gains have been achieved in the United States since the 1955 bus boycotts in Montgomery, Alabama. Fifty years later, however, the devastating impacts of Hurricane Katrina on the city of New Orleans reminded us of lingering social inequities and the vital role of transportation mobility in our society. Not only can mobility mean the difference between having and maintaining employment or not, but in the case of many low-income New Orleans residents, it can mean losing everything. We feel that a continued and sharpened focus on civil rights and transportation is as crucial today as it ever was.

1

Introduction

Transportation is vital. The Supreme Court has recognized the right to travel as one of the fundamental rights guaranteed by the Fourteenth Amendment to the U.S. Constitution.[1] Given this important role, it would be expected that policy makers would battle over transportation policy. Too often, however, those battles are fought over what specific projects will be funded and in which states or congressional districts, and scant attention is paid to larger social and economic effects.

The history of the civil rights movement provides some evidence of the social importance of transportation to people of color. In 1955, the arrest of Rosa Parks for refusing to give her seat on a bus to a white rider sparked the Montgomery bus boycott. Freedom Riders faced violent attacks to assert the rights of African Americans to ride on integrated buses traveling interstate.

Many past and current transportation policies have limited the life chances of minorities by preventing access to places and opportunities. The expiration in 2003 of the Transportation Equity Act for the 21st Century (TEA-21) provided an opportunity to address some of the inequitable effects that transportation policies have on minority and low-income communities.

Americans have become increasingly mobile and more reliant on automobiles to meet their travel needs, due largely to transportation policies adopted after World War II that emphasized highway development over public transportation. According to Census 2000 data, less than 5 percent of trips to work in urban areas are made by public transit; however, this varies significantly by race and location.[2] Minorities are less likely to own

1

cars than whites and are more often dependent on public transportation. The "transit-dependent" rely on public transportation not only to travel to work but also to get to school, obtain medical care, attend religious services, and shop for basic necessities such as groceries. The transit-dependent are often people with low incomes, and so they face economic inequities as a result of transportation policies oriented toward travel by car.

Surface transportation policies at the local, regional, state, and national levels have a direct impact on urban land-use and development patterns. The types of transportation facilities and services in which public funds are invested provide residents with varying levels of access to meet basic social and economic needs. The way communities develop land dictates the need for certain types of transportation, and, conversely, the transportation options in which communities invest influence patterns of urban development.

While many lament the trend toward "suburban sprawl" as unaesthetic or damaging to the environment, those who support social equity should also be concerned about this trend. Substantial investment in highway development and other transportation programs that encourage private automobile use has encouraged and supported low-density developments that extend increasingly farther and farther from the central city and to residential and commercial areas that are increasingly spread out—edgeless cities.[3] In addition to being costly to state and local governments,[4] transportation policies that encourage these growth patterns play a substantial role in producing some indirect negative social and economic effects, including perpetuating residential segregation and exacerbating the inability of minorities to gain access to entry-level employment that is increasingly found in suburban areas.[5]

Civil rights and transportation have long been linked in the United States, beginning with the involuntary transportation of slaves to the American colonies. In fact, Thomas Jefferson's original draft of the Declaration of Independence included an attack on King George III's policy of slavery in the New World:

> He has waged cruel war against human nature itself, violating its most sacred rights of life and liberty in the persons of a distant people who never offended him, captivating and carrying them into slavery in another hemisphere, or to incur miserable death in their *transportation* thither. . . . Determined to keep open a market where men should be bought and sold, he has prostituted his negative for suppressing every legislative attempt to prohibit or restrain this execrable commerce.[6] (Emphasis ours)

The U.S. Constitution addressed this importation, banning its regulation until 1808. Article I, section 9, reflects the compromise on slavery in the new nation: "The migration or importation of such persons as any of the states now existing shall think proper to admit, shall not be prohibited by the Congress prior to the year one thousand eight hundred and eight (1808), but a tax or duty may be imposed on such importation, not exceeding ten dollars for each person."

Through the years, a number of key Supreme Court civil rights decisions hinged on transportation issues, including ones concerning the right of owners to pursue fleeing slaves across state lines (*Dred Scott v. Sandford*, 1857), and creating the "separate but equal" concept of provision of rights to African Americans (*Plessy v. Ferguson*, 1896).

The Civil Rights Act of 1875 required equal accommodations for blacks with whites in public facilities (other than schools). This represented the last congressional effort to protect the civil rights of African Americans for more than half a century. It stated that "all persons within the jurisdiction of the United States shall be entitled to the full and equal enjoyment of the accommodations, advantages, facilities, and privileges of inns, public conveyances on land or water . . . "[7]

This legislation was effectively voided by the Supreme Court in 1883 through the *Civil Rights Cases*, 109 U.S. 3 (1883). The Civil Rights cases involved the Civil Rights Act of 1875, which required inns, public transportation, theaters, and other places of public amusement to give "full and equal enjoyment" of their services to all individuals regardless of race. Over a strong dissent by Justice Harlan, the Supreme Court held the act unconstitutional as an exercise of Congress's powers under Section 5 of the Fourteenth Amendment to the Constitution. The Court ruled 8–1 that Congress had overstepped its authority to enforce the Fourteenth Amendment with the passage of the act, and therefore it was invalid. It stated that the Fourteenth Amendment applied only to discriminatory action taken by states, not the discriminatory actions taken by individuals in the private sector.

THE MODERN CIVIL RIGHTS MOVEMENT AND TRANSPORTATION

Nearly 100 years after the *Dred Scott* decisions, civil rights and transportation issues persisted. On December 1, 1955, Rosa Parks, a black seamstress and civil rights activist, was arrested for refusing to obey a Montgomery, Alabama, bus driver's order to give her seat up for a boarding white

10,000 Black Men Named George

During slavery, companies purchased slaves to work on the railroads. It is documented that as early as 1838, a southern railroad company purchased 140 slaves for $159,000 to work on the construction of a railroad line in Mississippi.[1]

From their beginning in 1868, plush Pullman train cars (named for George Pullman, owner of the Pullman Palace Car Company) were staffed mostly by black American porters, many of them newly freed slaves. African Americans were concentrated in railroad work because they were excluded from other occupations, while the Pullman Company and the railroad industry actively recruited them to serve their passengers. By the 1920s, the Pullman Company, with 20,224 black employees, was the largest employer of black workers in the U.S. and Canada.[2]

Disrespectfully called "George" by their white passengers, the porters worked in demeaning conditions for shameful wages. In 1911, Floyd Boyd discovered that porters were distributing petitions around the country to raise the wages of Pullman porters. Boyd immediately began trying to persuade St. Paul porters to join the cause. It was an attempt to raise porters' wages from $25 to $50 per month after two years of service. The Pullman Company quashed the effort by raising wages by $2.50 a month.

During World War I, the Chicago, Milwaukee, and St. Paul porters came together to form the Railroad Mens'

Industrial Association.[3] Beginning in 1919 as a fraternal organization, the Brotherhood of Sleeping Car Porters Union was led by Asa (A.) Philip Randolph (1889–1979), who faced racism and political corruption in a 12-year battle to unionize railway porters in the 1920s and 1930s. Randolph got his start publishing a newspaper in Harlem called *The Messenger*. In the 1910s and 1920s, Randolph was a socialist who supported the Russian revolution and the militant working class movement in the U.S.[4] Randolph was successful in getting pay increases and reduced working hours for the porters. In 1925 he was elected president of the union.

The *Washington Post* (August 24, 1997) reported some of the painful experiences of porters who worked on the "fanciest trains during the heyday of rail travel" in the 1930s

Pullman Car Porter

Source: Photographer Jack Delano; Library of Congress Prints & Photographs Division, FSA/OWI Collection; Reproduction # LC-USW3-T01-015550-E.

and 1940s. Workers—paid just $66 a month for 400 hours—were at the beck and call of passengers and at the mercy of supervisors. They "were often chastised without just cause, were fired frequently and at times, had their pay docked. Their reliance on tips forced them to perform onerous jobs and often endure insults and racial slurs—with a smile. The porters hauled luggage, ironed suits, baby-sat children, shined shoes, brought meals to the passenger's berth, tended to the sick and still had to find time to keep the cars clean."[5]

In 1940, 74 percent of American blacks lived in the South. Approximately five million migrated north over the next 25 years. During this northern migration, African American sleeping car porters who worked for railroads were an important link between North and South. Porters traveled the country, had connections in the black communities in the rural South and in northern cities, and facilitated the northern migration. Because of the railroad and Pullman porter jobs, West Oakland, California, had a large and influential African American community long before most western cities did.[6] Oakland today continues to be a heavily African American city.

It is interesting to note that much archeological and historical research has been done as a result of the reconstruction of the Cypress Freeway in Oakland, in part to meet environmental justice demands. An exhibit, resulting from a partnership between Caltrans (the California State Department of Transportation) and the African American Museum and Library in Oakland (AAMLO), is entitled "Holding the Fort," which comes from a song sung by the Brotherhood of Sleeping Car Porters at their West Oakland meetings in the mid-1900s. Here are the first verse and chorus:

> We meet today in Freedom's cause
> And raise our voices high;
> We'll join our hands in Union strong to
> battle or to die.
>
> Hold the fort for we are coming
> Union men be strong.
> Side by side we battle onward,
> Vic-to-ry will come.

Notes

1. A. Philip Randolph Museum, African-Americans in U.S. Railroad History. www.aphiliprandolphmuseum.com/evo_history2.html.
2. Massachusetts AFL-CIO, *A. Philip Randolph and Black Railroad Workers*. www.massaflcio.org/aprandolph.html.
3. Workday Minnesota, Labor Education Service and Minnesota AFL-CIO, October 17, 2003. www.workday minnesota.org/permanent/working_life/history/advocate_series/boyd2.php.
4. *The Messenger*, City College of New York, www.geocities.com/ccnymess/whatis.html.
5. Brotherhood of Maintenance of Way Employees, BMWE Journal, Volume 107, Number 1. February 1998. http://glo.bmwe.org/public/journal/1998/02feb/016.htm.
6. Sonoma State University, California, Cypress Freeway Project Archeology, West Oakland, Historical Background. www.sonoma.edu/projects/asc/cw/history/histhome.htm.

passenger as required by city ordinance. Such municipal and state laws designed to separate the races were common in the South at the time. Outrage in Montgomery's black community over the arrest of Rosa Parks sparked a boycott against the city's bus line—the Montgomery bus boycott, one crucial incident igniting the beginnings of the modern civil rights movement. Working closely with a long-active African American leadership in Montgomery, the Rev. Dr. Martin Luther King, Jr., emerged as the president of the Montgomery Improvement Association (MIA), which organized the boycott. As the MIA's demands expanded beyond more flexibility in bus seating to include more equal access to other municipal services, racial tensions increased. Preaching a course of nonviolence, Dr. King was convinced that the cause could be won through a combination of dignified behavior and economic pressure on the part of the protesters.

The boycott ended in December 1956, over a year after it began. On February 1, 1956, the MIA filed suit in the U. S. District Court to challenge the constitutionality of local bus segregation laws. The District Court ruled in favor of the MIA in June 1956, but the city challenged the ruling, and the case went on to the Supreme Court. This resulted in a Supreme Court ruling on November 13, 1956, that segregation on city buses was unconstitutional. The defendants were represented by Thurgood Marshall (who later became the first African American on the Supreme Court), Robert L. Carter, Fred D. Gray, and Charles D. Langford. The implementation of the Supreme Court's decision, the desegregation of buses, took place on December 20, 1956, after federal injunctions were served on the city and bus company officials, forcing them to follow the ruling. There was also a little-known six-month bus boycott in Tallahassee, Florida, in 1956, which was not successful in desegregating local bus service.[8]

Another famous challenge to racial discrimination and transportation took place when a mixed group of whites and blacks, called Freedom Riders, were sent by the Congress of Racial Equality (CORE) in May 1961 to lead a campaign forcing integration in bus terminals and challenge segregation in local interstate travel facilities. Congressman John Lewis, a pioneer of the modern civil rights movement and one of the original 13 Freedom Riders, has said, "It was almost impossible for blacks and whites to travel together from Washington, D.C., through the South to New Orleans. And you had signs saying, 'White Waiting,' 'Colored Waiting,' 'White Men,' 'Colored Men,' 'White Women,' 'Colored

Women.' Segregation was the order of the day. There was a tremendous amount of fear. So the Ride was going to test this decision, try to desegregate these places, but also to take the civil rights movement into the heart of deep South."[9]

At various bus terminals, the black Freedom Riders would go to the white dining areas and waiting rooms, while the white Freedom Riders would go to the area reserved for blacks. The buses were attacked by mobs in Anniston, Alabama, where one bus was destroyed by a fire-bomb. There were riots in Birmingham and Montgomery, Alabama, when blacks attempted to use facilities reserved for whites; federal marshals and the National Guard were called out to restore order and escort the Freedom Riders to Mississippi. Many of them were arrested in Jackson, Mississippi, for infractions of the state's segregation laws, and a long series of court battles began. These protests led in 1961 to an Interstate Commerce Commission ban on segregation in all interstate transportation facilities.

WHAT IS TRANSPORTATION EQUITY?

Transportation mobility is a hallmark of full membership in American society. The early challenges related to racial discrimination and segregation involved discriminatory practices that directly limited transportation access and mobility of people of color. The effects of limited transportation mobility persist. The lack of mobility helped create ghettos, de facto segregated schools and housing, and social and community isolation. To cure these ills, many promises have been made by the leadership of the dominant society. These promises, together with promises for housing to replace that destroyed in "blight clearing" projects, are often unfulfilled. Whites in suburbs have forgone physical mobility for social cohesion, while destroyed inner-city neighborhoods have been left with neither mobility nor social cohesion.

Efforts to challenge discrimination, segregation, and inequitable transportation policies have become increasingly sophisticated to encompass a broad range of related social impacts. The term *transportation equity* refers to a range of strategies and policies that aim to address inequities in the nation's transportation planning and project delivery system. Across the country, community-based organizations of low-income and minority residents that organized to improve their communities are recognizing the significant role played by transportation in shaping local opportunities and disinvestment. Though the definition of transportation equity may vary from place to place, most of these community residents would agree that an equitable transportation system should:

- Ensure opportunities for meaningful public involvement in the transportation planning process, particularly for those communities that most directly feel the impact of projects or funding choices.
- Be held to a high standard of public accountability and financial transparency.
- Distribute the benefits and burdens from transportation projects equally across all income levels and communities.
- Provide high-quality services—emphasizing access to economic opportunity and basic mobility—to all communities, but with an emphasis on transit-dependent populations.
- Equally prioritize efforts both to revitalize poor and minority communities and to expand transportation infrastructure.

In a broader sense, transportation equity is also about environmental justice, metropolitan equity, and the just distribution of resources. These concepts represent an evolution in how civil rights and transportation are interrelated—especially when we look back on the early cases involving slave transport and the events precipitating the Montgomery, Alabama, bus boycott.

Environmental Justice

The principle of environmental justice grew out of a much broader movement to address the economic and health impacts of environmental racism. Environmental justice is an effective framework for showing how low-income and minority communities face the brunt of negative impacts from transportation investment. Residents understand that toxic dumps and polluting industries are more likely to find their way into low-income and minority communities. Similarly, residents understand that these communities are more likely to face a number of transportation-related burdens.

West Harlem Environmental Action (WE ACT) fought for years to mitigate the high concentration of diesel bus depots in the predominantly minority and low-income communities of northern Manhattan. Research has linked diesel exhaust to asthma and cancer, and WE ACT members were concerned with the potential health impacts of too many bus depots in their community. WE ACT sued the New York Metropolitan Transit Authority (MTA), but lost. The group has continued to collect data on the harmful effects of diesel exhaust and has pressed the MTA to reduce diesel emissions at all bus depots.

Metropolitan Equity

Nationwide, community organizations are also conscious of the impact that transportation investments have on metropolitan growth patterns, particularly transportation's relationship to sprawl. It is not simply a coincidence that economic development tends to follow transportation investment further and further out into suburban communities and exurban areas.

From the perspective of low-income and minority communities, particularly in metropolitan and urban areas, sprawl has particularly pernicious and deleterious impacts. A growing body of research asserts that, in metropolitan areas, the concentrated poverty of central-city communities and the relative affluence of suburban enclaves is not coincidental.

john a. powell of the Institute on Race and Poverty at the University of Minnesota describes sprawl and regional fragmentation and concentrated poverty and social inequity as flip sides of the same dynamic.[10] The same factors that push and pull families away from urban centers to the suburbs trap the families left behind. Those able to leave have the human and financial capital to do so. They leave for better jobs and better schools, and they invest their financial capital in property likely to appreciate in value. Those left behind must deal with struggling schools, less human capital, and fewer financial resources.

Hurricane Katrina in August 2005 demonstrated once again that lack of financial resources and lack of transportation equity go hand in hand and that both have very negative effects on the quality of life and even on life itself. Many low-income African Americans were trapped by the floodwaters of the hurricane. Television showed us people without the necessities of life, left behind by the institutions that were supposed to protect them, and almost completely without the benefits of civic infrastructure. The nation and the federal government were rightfully embarrassed.[11]

The federal government defines concentrated poverty as a census tract with 40 percent or greater of its residents living below the poverty level. This is significant, powell says, because joblessness, blight, crime, and other circumstances destructive to families characterize concentrated poverty. Central-city communities, which are more likely to hold areas of concentrated poverty, therefore carry the burden of having to address more social problems, which serve to push out more families who can afford to leave. As a result, these communities often lack the tax base necessary to address the social ills that plague them.

This metropolitan dynamic has driven a number of organizations into strategies to arrest suburban growth and to create new lifelines to economic opportunity connecting inner-city communities to job-rich suburban centers.

Fair Distribution of Resources

One of the major breakthroughs of the transportation equity movement came when the Los Angeles Metropolitan Transportation Authority (LAMTA) and the Los Angeles Bus Riders Union, a project of the Labor Community Strategy Center, negotiated a binding consent decree as part of a court settlement in 1996. Title VI of the Civil Rights Act of 1964 prohibits recipients of federal funds from discriminating on the basis of race, color, or national origin. In the court case, *Labor Community Strategy Center and Los Angeles Bus Riders Union v. Los Angeles Metropolitan Transportation Authority*, the court was asked to find that LAMTA had wrongfully provided inferior services to Los Angeles's largely minority and low-income bus riders. Furthermore, LAMTA was directing resources to its commuter rail lines, which served a more affluent and primarily white population, at the expense of its bus users. Prior to trial, the judge directed that the parties work to settle the case. This settlement included millions of dollars for new buses, which are ridden primarily by people of color and low-income people.[12]

Welfare Reform

When Congress enacted the 1996 welfare reform law, states were given broad authority to develop their own work-based welfare systems. Millions of low-income individuals, mainly women of color with limited job skills, were pushed into work activities and jobs in order to remain eligible for even a decreased level of benefits. While the strong economy of the 1990s helped to mitigate the impact of existing transportation deficits in many communities, lack of reliable and convenient transportation has remained a significant obstacle to families trying to pull themselves off welfare and out of poverty. Some studies show that up to 96 percent of welfare recipients do not own a car and that two-thirds of the job growth in the nation's metropolitan areas have happened in the suburbs.

While many low- and moderate-income families struggle daily with inadequate public transportation systems, this transportation gap is felt most acutely by welfare recipients struggling to leave welfare for employment. Welfare recipients and employers alike consistently cite transportation as one of the most significant barriers to employment:

- A study in 2000 by the state of Illinois found that 45.7 percent of former welfare recipients were unable to find or retain employment because there were no opportunities nearby. And 40.7 percent reported transportation as a significant barrier to employment.
- A study in 2000 by the state of Kansas found that lack of reliable transportation was the second-biggest obstacle to finding and retaining employment.
- The Welfare to Work Partnership, a coalition of businesses, found that transportation was one of the most significant barriers to employment for their employees. Of survey respondents, 33 percent identified transportation as the top barrier to employment. Even so, only 18 percent of employers surveyed in 2000 were able to provide transportation assistance to employees.

Recognizing these same barriers in their own community, the Interchurch Coalition for Action, Reconciliation and Empowerment (ICARE) in Jacksonville, Florida, initiated discussions in 1998 with members of Jacksonville's local metropolitan planning organization, the local transportation authority, and the local workforce investment board. Jacksonville's traditional hub-and-spoke transportation system helped connect residents from more distant neighborhoods to its central city but failed to readily link residents from one neighborhood to another or to job opportunities in the suburbs. In response to ICARE's recommendations, the transportation authority and the local workforce investment board developed a joint strategy for new and expanded bus service to better connect job seekers to job opportunities.

UPCOMING CHAPTERS

In addition to providing an in-depth discussion of issues, this book includes examples of causes, consequences, and strategies that can be taken to address transportation inequities. The impacts of discrimination on transportation mobility and accessibility pervade our society and have a negative impact on social and economic opportunity. Beyond identifying the problem, the objective is to outline solutions that can be applied by communities, planners, and policy makers concerned with advancing the causes of civil rights and social equity as they relate to transportation mobility.

Chapter 2 discusses a range of demographic trends that relate to inequities in transportation mobility and accessibility. These trends include changes in population and housing characteristics, reflected in urban development patterns.

Chapter 3 focuses on the impact transportation costs have on individuals and families. The availability and cost of transport mobility have direct influence on social and economic opportunity at the local and regional scale.

Chapter 4 examines how transportation policies can create indirect negative impacts that affect the quality of life in neighborhoods and communities. Access to employment, housing, and schools are discussed.

Chapter 5 provides background on policies in the United States that affect transportation equity. Most are rooted in civil rights and environmental justice laws and statutes. The chapter also briefly assesses the effectiveness of these policies.

Chapter 6 argues for expanding how we view issues relating to transportation equity. Equity issues have often been cast from the perspective of race and class only, while there are several other dimensions of transport fairness and distributional equity.

Chapter 7 discusses how the physical disabled and elderly populations face significant challenges in terms of transportation mobility. Barriers limiting access to transport put these persons at distinct disadvantages that can be overcome through several planning strategies.

Finally, Chapter 8 draws some conclusions about the current state of transportation equity and federal transportation legislation, as well as providing some policy recommendations and potential courses of action.

NOTES

1. Shapiro v. Thompson, 394 U.S. 618 (1969).
2. Pucher and Renne (2003).
3. The term "edgeless cities" was coined by Lang (2003).
4. For a description of some studies examining the costs of sprawl, see Katz and Muro (2003).
5. Kain (1968).
6. Thomas Jefferson (June 28, 1776). The rough draft of the Declaration of Independence, Department of Alfainformatica, University of Groningen.
7. *U.S. Statutes at Large*, Vol. XVIII, p. 335 ff.
8. Barnes (1983).
9. CNN Interview (2001).
10. powell (2002).
11. Garcia and Brenman (2005).
12. Garcia and Rubin (2004).

2

Demographic Realities

Shortly after the Los Angeles civil rights protests of the 1960s, the McCone Commission identified inadequate transportation as contributing to high rates of unemployment among the black urban population.[1] In 1968, the National Advisory Commission on Civil Disorders (also known as the Kerner Commission) released its report on the causes and effects of riots in U.S. cities. Among its recommendations to enhance employment opportunities for central-city residents was the creation of improved transportation links between ghetto neighborhoods and new job locations in the suburbs.[2] The increased awareness of transportation mobility needs led to several public transit projects focused on inner-city and reverse commuting.

To consider social equity in terms of transport mobility and accessibility, it is essential to understand the spatial and geographic patterns of residences and their travel destinations. The spatial disbursement of homes, jobs, and other destinations dictates the demand for surface transportation. However, providing transportation service is complicated not only by the fact that persons have wide-ranging travel patterns but also because they have unequal means to actually use the transportation system. Travel patterns are artifacts of urban, suburban, and exurban development patterns, which have direct social equity implications. Demographic trends, land-use patterns, public and private investments, economic inequalities, established planning methods, and historical and institutional racism ultimately shape the landscape of social and economic opportunity. Despite general trends across all metropolitan areas, there are wide variations among metropolitan, urban, and rural areas with respect to transportation access and development patterns.

This chapter focuses on the demographics that shape demand for urban transportation accessibility and mobility, especially as they have been shaped over time by racial and ethnic discrimination and segregation. These patterns coincide with inferior transportation services and low levels of social and economic opportunity. The realities of racism and social injustice shaped—and continue to shape—urban form in which transportation access and mobility are fundamental personal and group needs in the United States. This chapter provides the context and background about the winners and losers that result from inequitable transportation policies and planning.

FACTORS OF CHANGE

Population

Population growth and dispersal have left a lasting imprint on the American urban form. The U.S. population has increased at an average annual rate of 1.1 percent since 1970, with natural increase accounting for nearly two-thirds of this growth (an annualized average of over 1.6 million persons), while net migration contributed the remaining one-third (an annualized average of about 951,000 persons). Rates of natural increase, as well as net migration flows, have fluctuated over time, with the proportion of population growth attributed to natural increase as high as 86 percent in 1989 and as low as 49 percent in 1996.

Population increases have not been uniformly distributed. Since 1970, growth in the West (2.2 percent) and South (1.7 percent) have outpaced that of the Northeast (0.3 percent) and Midwest (0.4 percent) in terms of annual average growth rates. Growth within these regions has also been uneven, with the most substantial population increases occurring in the Mountain and Pacific portions of the West, while the Middle Atlantic region of the Northeast and the East North Central region of the Midwest have experienced the least population growth.

At the regional scale, population changes are reflected in metropolitan development patterns. Overall population change has been relatively small in rural, nonmetropolitan areas, with metropolitan areas absorbing the majority of residential growth. The concentration of population growth within cities, paired with greater efficiency of urban transportation system options, highlights the importance of focusing on, and examining issues and opportunities in, metropolitan areas.[3]

TABLE 1.   FASTEST AND SLOWEST GROWING METROPOLITAN AREAS, 1970–2000

	TOTAL METROPOLITAN POPULATION		% CHANGE
	1970	2000	1970–2000
Ten Fastest Growing Metropolitan Areas			
Las Vegas–Paradise MSA	272,863	1,375,765	404%
Orlando MSA	523,196	1,648,624	215%
Phoenix–Mesa–Scottsdale MSA	1,033,930	3,251,876	215%
Austin-Round Rock MSA	398,646	1,249,763	214%
Riverside–San Bernardino–Ontario MSA	1,135,965	3,248,327	186%
Atlanta–Sandy Springs–Marietta MSA	1,842,951	4,247,981	130%
Miami–Fort Lauderdale–Miami Beach MSA	2,218,372	5,007,564	126%
Tampa–St. Petersburg–Clearwater MSA	1,072,758	2,395,997	123%
San Diego–Carlsbad–San Marcos MSA	1,309,247	2,813,833	115%
Houston–Baytown–Sugar Land MSA	2,199,874	4,715,407	114%
Ten Slowest Growing (Fastest Declining) Metropolitan Areas			
New Orleans–Metairie–Kenner MSA	1,077,287	1,228,445	14%
Rochester, NY	961,226	1,037,831	8%
New York–Newark–Edison MSA	17,022,768	18,331,413	8%
Philadelphia–Camden–Wilmington MSA	5,294,311	5,679,887	7%
Milwaukee–Waukesha–West Allis MSA	1,403,479	1,500,741	7%
St. Louis MSA	2,551,702	2,721,491	7%
Detroit–Warren–Livonia MSA	4,415,161	4,448,517	1%
Cleveland–Elyria–Mentor MSA	2,319,776	2,148,143	-7%
Pittsburgh MSA	2,749,399	2,431,087	-12%
Buffalo–Cheektowaga–Tonawanda MSA	1,347,335	1,170,111	-13%

Source: U.S. Census (2001)

As of 2000, metropolitan areas contained 79 percent of the total U.S. population. This proportion increased from 73.6 percent in 1970, both as a function of metropolitan growth as well as changes in metropolitan area definitions. Rates of population growth ranged from 404 percent for the Las Vegas–Paradise Metropolitan Statistical Area in Nevada to a 13 percent decline for the Buffalo–Cheektowaga–Tonawanda Metropolitan Statistical Area in New York. Table 1 shows the 10 fastest and slowest growing (fastest declining) of the 50 largest U.S. metropolitan areas from 1970 to 2000.

Both population growth and decline are challenges for metropolitan areas. For those experiencing rapid growth, the challenge is to keep pace with outward urban expansion in terms of road building and public transportation needs. In the cases of Las Vegas, Phoenix, and Orlando, Florida, road construction has far exceeded public transportation investments. These challenges have particular consequences for low-income residents who do not own cars and live in areas with inadequate public transit. On the other hand, declining regions like Cleveland, Pittsburgh, and Buffalo struggle to maintain transportation services given weak local economies and diminishing resources for all types of public services.

Patterns of population change are also evident within metropolitan areas, particularly when viewed in terms of urban and suburban differences. Growth patterns from the 50 largest metropolitan areas show that, on average, areas with urban densities (greater than 3,000 persons per square mile) increased by 72 percent. Areas with suburban densities (1,000 to 3,000 persons per square mile) increased by 112 percent, and exurban areas (300 to 1,000 persons per square mile) increased by 31 percent. This urban, suburban, and exurban growth came at the expense of rural zones, which declined by approximately 38 percent per square mile.[4]

Residential and Geographic Patterns

Patterns of population change have a direct racial and ethnic component. Central cities have increasing shares of racial minorities, while the suburbs remain relatively white. Throughout this book, when we refer to "white," we recognize that Latinos can be of any race. We use "white" here as a synonym for "nonminority." Racial minorities are suburbanizing, just not at rates equivalent to those of whites. By 2000, half of all Americans lived in the suburbs.[5] Although more minorities are living in the suburbs than in 1990, whites still have the highest percentage (71 percent) of any racial group living there.[6] In the top 100 most populous metropolitan areas, minorities represented only 27 percent of suburban populations.[7] The concentration of minorities in cities could be seen as beneficial, given higher levels of accessibility to public transportation options. This could be true if employment opportunities and other amenities such as shopping, good schools, and health care were also concentrated in central cities. Instead, as has been extensively documented, employment growth is occurring in the suburbs, away from central cities and the urban core—thus out of reach for those without automobiles. Even basic amenities that suburbanites take for granted, such as large clean supermarkets, can be rare in older inner cities.

Location also dictates the types of transportation options that are available to residents. Although the U.S. population is approximately 69 percent white, 12 percent African American, 12.5 percent Latino, and 3.6 percent Asian American,[8] the composition of major U.S. cities and urban areas is quite different.

According to 2000 Census data, only 52 of the 100 largest cities in the U.S. have a majority white population. The 100 largest cities generally experienced increases in Latinos, Asian Americans, and African Americans and a decrease in whites, with the Latino population growing the most rapidly (see Table 2).

TABLE 2.   CENTRAL-CITY RACIAL COMPOSITION OF THE 10 LARGEST METRO AREAS

METROPOLITAN AREA	% WHITE, NON-HISPANIC	% AFRICAN AMERICAN	% LATINO	% ASIAN AMERICAN
Los Angeles, CA	31	12	44	11
New York, NY	35	26	27	11
Chicago, IL	35	34	26	5
Philadelphia, PA	41	44	10	5
Washington, DC	39	45	10	5
Detroit, MI	20	71	5	1
Houston, TX	32	25	37	5
Atlanta, GA	31	62	4	2
Dallas, TX	38	23	34	4
Boston, MA	56	20	13	8

Note: These cities are in the 10 largest primary metropolitan statistical areas.
Source: Lewis Mumford Center, http://mumford1.dyndns.org/cen2000/

Population growth and resulting geographic expansion are facets of metropolitan development patterns that influence the demand for transportation services. Dense development is more easily served by public transit modes, while low-density development, especially at the urban fringe, relies on high-capacity, auto-oriented facilities. Whether this reliance on the car is desirable is a subject of some dispute, especially from an environmentalist or sustainable development perspective.

The composition of metropolitan areas can be characterized by comparing the proportion of residents living in the central city or urban core to the proportion living outside. An examination of U.S. metropolitan areas shows that, on average, the ratio of central-city to non–central-city (metropolitan) population decreased by approximately 50 percent from 1990 to 2000. Core-oriented metropolitan areas in 2000 included New York City; San Antonio, Texas; and Norfolk, Virgina, which had the highest relative shares of central-city population among large metros. Fringe-oriented metro areas included Atlanta; Orlando, Florida; and Washington, D.C., with the highest shares of non–central-city metropolitan population.

Fringe-oriented growth is not necessarily bad in the context of transportation access, so long as transportation investments maintain connections between fringe and core areas. This has not been the case, however, for Atlanta, Orlando, and Washington, D.C., where public transportation service extensions to the suburbs have been minimal. A significant burden results among those trying to gain access to jobs in the suburbs. Whether this burden resulted from random perturbations of growth and development or was the result, at least in part, of a purposeful intent to segregate will be discussed later.

Metropolitan Racial/Ethnic Segregation

There is a geographic as well as a racial dimension to patterns of metropolitan growth. Metropolitan areas that experienced higher levels of noncore growth between 1990 and 2000 also experienced predominantly "white growth" in these areas and experienced decreases in white residents in their central cities—the outcomes appearing to be what is commonly called "white flight."

On average, African Americans, Latinos, and whites live in neighborhoods with people primarily of the same race.[9] One study employing five different indicators of residential segregation found that overall residential segregation declined between 4 and 11 percent between 1980 and 2000.[10] Trends generally show that, since 1980, Latino–white and Asian–white segregation levels have remained approximately the same.[11] Black–white segregation remains significantly higher than the levels of segregation for other minority groups[12] (see Figure 1). Trends in residential segregation also vary by region. It is unclear whether integration is occurring generally for racial minorities or whether it is isolated to more mobile, middle-class households. It is also important to note that, during the 1990s, the decline in segregation resulted largely from the integration of formerly all-white census tracts, rather than from the integration of formerly majority-black census tracts.[13] Entire counties, such as Prince George's, Maryland, have shifted from predominantly middle-class white to predominantly middle-class black. Economic mobility does not necessarily equate to integration. Residential integration, as opposed to barrier lowering, is not necessarily considered a social good by all African Americans.

Efforts to encourage racial integration can be seen in various state and federal policies over the years. However, opposing forces have reduced their effectiveness, both directly and indirectly. Positive policies include the federal Fair Housing Act, state and local inclusionary housing, and

Figure 1.   Residential Segregation Indices for All U.S. Metropolitan Areas

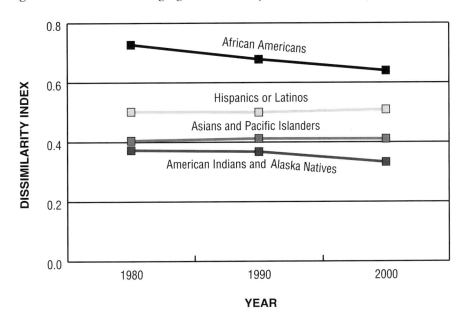

Note: Higher values indicate more segregation; the reference group is non-Hispanic whites.
Source: Iceland, Weinberg, and Steinmetz (2002)

integration maintenance programs (the Shaker Heights, Ohio, project, for example).[14]

These policies have been implemented with the assumption that mixing persons by race and class generates human capital, thus increasing social and economic opportunity. The term *social capital* refers to those stocks of social trust, norms, and networks that people can draw on to solve common problems. Networks of civic engagement, such as neighborhood associations, sports clubs, and cooperatives, are an essential form of social capital, and the denser these networks, the more likely that members of a community will cooperate for mutual benefit. This is so even in the face of persistent problems of collective action (such as the tragedy of the commons or the prisoner's dilemma) because networks of civic engagement:

- foster sturdy norms of generalized reciprocity by creating expectations that favors given now will be returned later;
- facilitate coordination and communication and thus create channels through which information about the trustworthiness of other individuals and groups can flow and be tested and verified;
- embody past success at collaboration, which can serve as a cultural template for future collaboration on other kinds of problems;
- increase the potential risks to those who act opportunistically that they will not share in the benefits of current and future transactions.[15]

The Fair Housing Act of 1968[16] was intended to increase home ownership opportunities for all but fell short in helping low-income populations. In part it could not overcome earlier federal home ownership initiatives, which explicitly required and encouraged residential segregation. Inclusionary housing practices attempt to promote integration through affordable housing requirements intended to support low-income populations, who tend to be minorities. It should be noted, however, that even into the 1990s some public housing, such as that in Boston, remained racially segregated.

At the same time, transportation services within neighborhoods have not supported racial integration. Unsuspecting actions like school busing, while promoting integration "within" schools, can in fact maintain residential segregation because they have not directly influenced residential opportunities that would overcome segregation. The burdens of school integration were almost entirely limited within school districts and not across urban/suburban jurisdictional lines.[17]

There are more than 15,000 largely autonomous public school districts in the United States, and the courts have recognized that the boundaries between them are sacrosanct. Busing largely moved black children from neighborhood schools to nominally better and whiter schools. With court-ordered declarations of "unitariness" (successful desegregation), this social experiment has largely ceased. However, in the process, black neighborhood cohesiveness has been dealt a severe blow. It is important to note that education, housing, and transportation all interacted in a way to create and maintain residential segregation. It was hoped that either direct or indirect benefits of racial integration would lead to less disparity in labor participation rates, household incomes, and other forms of wealth accumulation such as home ownership. There is little evidence, however, to suggest that this has occurred. While metropolitan areas have experienced slight declines in racial segregation since 1970, there have not been corresponding changes in income levels and wealth accumulation for racial minorities. In fact, some recent economic data suggest that class mobility has decreased in the last 30 years. Bernstein (2003) described this as the "inequality wedge" to explain the wage gap between low- and high-income families.

There are several other factors indirectly related to transportation access and mobility. Beyond travel needs to reach job sites, racial minorities suffer from workplace discrimination resulting in unemployment, underemployment, and low wages.[18] Similarly, limited educational opportunities due to the effects of segregation inhibit racial minorities and low-income students from attending good-quality schools. Because they have limited residential mobility, access to affordable housing further constrains locational choices. The combination of these factors contributes to the geographic concentration of poverty characterized by high levels of crime, substance abuse, and political disenfranchisement.

METROPOLITAN INCOME INEQUALITIES

While racial segregation has decreased slightly by some measures, the level of income inequality in the United States continues to increase. In fact, compared with other industrialized countries, the U.S. has consistently ranked at the bottom in terms of income equality.[19] Trends at the national level are symptomatic of income distribution disparities at the state, regional, and local levels and have far-reaching social and economic implications.[20] The Kerner Commission reported that these inequalities played a significant role in fueling the civil unrest of the 1960s.[21] Even during the late 1990s, while the U.S. was enjoying robust economic prosperity with declines in welfare assistance, high employment rates, and record corporate profits, poverty levels increased. Fewer families had health coverage, and real wages declined. Thirty years after the Kerner Commission reported that the nation was becoming "two separate societies," the evidence suggested that the gap between rich and poor was becoming yet more pronounced.[22]

The neighborhood income gap for African Americans and whites increased in absolute and percentage terms in 40 of the 50 largest metros.[23] In 2001, whites had a poverty rate of approximately 8 percent compared with 23 percent for African Americans, 21 percent for Latinos,[24] and 10 percent for Asian Americans.[25] Consistent with these figures are the facts that: (1) The poverty rate in cities is almost double the suburban rate, (2) cities have significantly higher unemployment rates than the suburbs, and (3) there is an income gap between those living in the cities and those in the suburbs.[26]

Household wealth—or assets minus debts—differs significantly by race as well. In 1995, the national median household wealth was $40,200.[27] In comparison, the non-Hispanic white household's median wealth was $49,030, for African American households it was only $7,073, and for Latino households it was $7,255. For those in the bottom 20 percent of income earners, the median wealth by race was $9,700 for non-Hispanic white households, $1,500 for African American households, and $1,300 for Latino households. Forty-four percent of the wealth in the United States was invested in homes and 8 percent in motor vehicles. This highlights the importance of residential location, and especially home ownership, in decreasing the gap between whites and racial minorities. The lack of wealth-building opportunities has hurt racial minorities and contributes to household financial instability. (Chapter 3, Transportation Costs and Inequities, discusses other implications of transportation costs and car ownership for wealth accumulation.)

Residential mobility is very closely related to household economic status. This discussion of segregation, income inequality, and wealth disparities is implicit to land-use patterns and urban form. The next section briefly discusses some of the characteristics, factors, and implications of dispersed urban development and also considers the role of transport mobility.

DEVELOPMENT PATTERNS

Equity Implications of Urban Sprawl

In the debate over the impacts of urban sprawl, social equity conse-quences have received relatively little attention. While sprawl is more commonly referred to as a transportation and land-use issue, the spatial distribution of housing and jobs has inherent civil rights implications. As places grow in population size, demographic variation (by race, ethnic-ity, economic class, and the like) exhibits patterns of greater and lesser degrees of concentration or segregation. These patterns, which indicate social and economic isolation, reflect spatial variations in social and eco-nomic opportunity. Market forces in the form of mortgage lending prac-tices and labor discrimination perpetuate racial and economic isolation along with other social and institutional factors related to racial discrim-ination. These processes are exemplified by what is referred to as the spatial mismatch hypothesis (discussed in Chapter 4), which describes the dynamics of housing and employment discrimination. As will be briefly discussed, these patterns are dynamic and continue to undergo change at the local and regional scale.

Low-density residential development, which prevails in the United States, produces extensive physical separation between residences and jobs. This generates a demand for better linkages by transportation facili-ties serving a variety of travel modes. Dispersed land-use patterns neces-sitate high levels of automobile usage, leading to higher travel costs for individuals and households. Those able to afford reliable automobiles, and the higher levels of mobility that they provide, have higher levels of social and economic opportunity compared with those who cannot.[28] The interaction between land use and transportation then becomes a balancing of accessibility with mobility, where accessibility is the rela-tive connectedness of an area and mobility is the ability to move within or beyond a geographic area or use the transportation system.

Metropolitan location patterns have been profoundly influenced by changing economic and industrial circumstances. In addition, certain federal, state, and local policies have contributed to these trends. Those most often associated with population and employment shifts include significant losses of manufacturing jobs from the urban core, extensive highway building, increasing auto ownership rates, residential lending practices, and exclusionary land zoning policies in the suburbs. With whites having suburbanized at higher rates than African Americans,

Hispanics, or Asians, the combined effect of increasing geographic extent and differences in residential mobility by race and ethnicity produce increasingly concentrated neighborhoods of low-income persons and racial minorities. Each of these will be briefly discussed in the context of transportation and civil rights.

Employment Shifts. A shift in the proportion of jobs in the central city or urban core to the suburbs represents one challenge to maintaining employment accessibility to low-income racial minorities. As racial minorities remain concentrated in the urban core, the problem is not a lack of jobs there but rather suitable jobs given the employment, training, and educational backgrounds of central-city workers. Low-wage and labor-intensive jobs have steadily migrated to the suburbs and exurbs, as well as overseas, with detrimental impacts on low-skilled workers. The challenge for most low-skilled workers with limited transportation mobility is further complicated when employment locations shift with simultaneous labor market changes, making it especially difficult for them to compete.

Highway Construction. Large investments in highway infrastructure are often blamed for facilitating sprawl and white flight. While the interstate system connected cities and metropolitan areas, it provided greater access to suburban areas from downtowns and urbanized areas. The interstates were integral for commerce and freight movement, vital to the economic development experienced throughout the United States in the post–World War II years. Interstates were also viewed as a strategic defense in the event of Cold War aggression. Despite the arguments of some, highways were built to meet several objectives in addition to simply extending the geographic extent of metropolitan areas.

Certain configurations of highways within metropolitan areas are also conducive to outward urban expansion. (See Figure 2 for common urban highway configurations.) Radial highways and beltways increase access to suburban and exurban areas. However, as much research has shown, roadway construction is not the sole determinant of land-use conversions: Highway construction is a response to anticipated land-use change, and land-use change is a response to anticipated changes in transportation accessibility. In other words, urban form is not entirely the by-product of roadway investments but rather the by-product of many local, regional, state, and federal policies that in themselves are influenced by market forces.

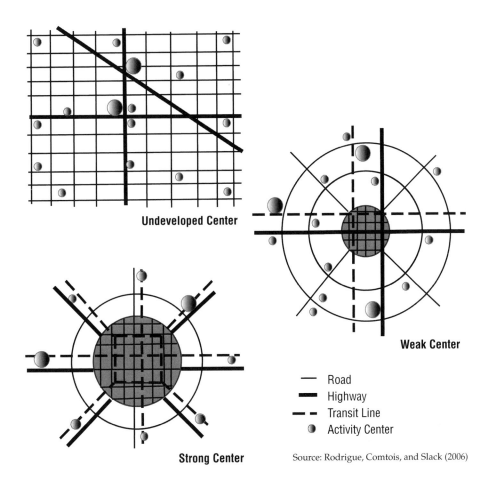

Undeveloped Center

Weak Center

— Road
━ Highway
– – Transit Line
● Activity Center

Strong Center

Source: Rodrigue, Comtois, and Slack (2006)

Figure 2.   Common Urban Highway Configurations

One such force is induced travel, an increase in traffic that is generated not by growth or other demographic forces but by expansion of the road system itself. Most of that additional travel is diverted, not really new. But, over time, adding road capacity can induce longer trips: A new job that is five or 10 miles farther down the freeway may be more appealing if there is less traffic congestion.

Freeway construction also directly destroyed minority neighborhoods by building through them, such as in Salisbury, Maryland. In 1997, residents of the community of Jersey Heights, Maryland, challenged the siting of a new highway adjacent to their neighborhood. They asserted claims against state and federal agencies and officials under the Federal-Aid Highway Act, the National Environmental Policy Act, Title VI of the

Civil Rights Act of 1964, the Fair Housing Act, and the Maryland Environmental Policy Act, as well as the Equal Protection Clause. Maryland intends, with federal funding assistance, to build a new Route 50 bypass around the city of Salisbury in the eastern part of the state. Route 50 is the principal latitudinal artery spanning Maryland's eastern peninsula. Constructed nearly a half-century ago, the highway serves the region's commercial traffic and funnels seasonal vacationers from Baltimore and Washington to the seaside resort of Ocean City. At present, the route also passes directly through downtown Salisbury, where it doubles as a main thoroughfare for local traffic. Officials began as early as 1975 to look for ways to alleviate the resulting traffic and congestion in downtown Salisbury. Their remedy of choice was to construct a bypass around the city.

It was no historical accident that Jersey Heights at the time of the lawsuit was 99 percent African American. Displaced from their downtown neighborhoods by the construction of Route 13 in the 1930s and the original Route 50 in the 1950s, African Americans in Salisbury relocated to Jersey Heights. As a result of widespread steering practices, Jersey Heights was the only area in which Salisbury's African Americans could find available housing. According to one plaintiff, Salisbury has had an "unwritten law"—that "if you were a certain pigm[en]tality you had to live west of this [Wicomico River] bridge." The residents of Jersey Heights were being penalized for the mistakes made by the builders of the original Route 50—the very highway that decimated their former neighborhoods. The placement of Route 50 through downtown Salisbury has resulted in serious congestion and a disproportionate number of accidents, particularly during the summer beach season. The residents' sacrifice this time is for the convenience of the traveling public, particularly vacationers who use Route 50 for access to the ocean beaches on Maryland's Eastern Shore each summer.

First in the 1930s, again in the 1950s, and then again in the past three decades with the bypass project, the residents of Jersey Heights understandably believe they have been treated as if they do not exist. With regard to the bypass project, the Jersey Heights community was essentially excluded from the decision-making processes that led to the key alignment decisions. White residents who lived in the area surrounding Alternate 2—the more northerly route farther away from Jersey Heights—received individual notice about project planning and subsequently raised timely objections to that proposed route. The residents of Jersey Heights, however, received no individual notice and thus were unable to object in any timely way to Alternate 4, which, of the original four proposed alternates, was the route closest to Jersey Heights. Following the path of least resistance, the state highway administration designated Alternate 4 as the preferred route. It was also remarked that, "[A]s often happens with interstate highways, the route selected was through the poor area of town, not through the area where the politically powerful people live."[29]

Urban Distress. Urban distress also has been seen as a major force behind population dispersal and sprawl. The most common form of dispersal occurs when mobile households, typically affluent households, relocate further from the urban core to less dense suburban or exurban residential areas. Critics of the resulting low-density or scattered development argue that these land-use patterns are inefficient because they lead to high infrastructure costs, especially for transportation facilities and public services, and boost energy consumption, degrade air quality, and create health and safety concerns. The social impacts of urban fiscal difficulties and "blight flight" are considered less often than are the impacts on the economic and physical environment. To address current deficiencies, local governments should pay closer attention to the impacts of expenditure and pricing policies on social outcomes. Because demand for public services is correlated with social, economic, and locational characteristics of residential land, inequitable fiscal policies can lead to socially stratified development patterns, as previously discussed. The result isolates the haves from the have-nots, where middle- and higher-income households seek better-quality schools, parks, and high-quality public services.

The Automobile Culture. Along with highways, the automobile, or rather the automobile culture, has been blamed for generating suburban sprawl. As roadway supply increases and automobiles remain cheap, driving has become the more convenient means of transportation.[30] The automobile can be seen as a symptom rather than a cause of low-density development patterns coinciding with large roadway investments. Most U.S. cities are simply too spread out to be adequately served by public transportation systems, with dependence on public transportation sometimes seen as limiting social and economic opportunity. Transport accessibility (roads) and mobility (autos) are nearly essential in the United States, given the geography of our cities and regions. In some cases, automobile ownership programs are promoted to overcome barriers associated with poverty, unemployment, and underemployment and have reemerged as a means to address labor participation challenges. The costs associated with automobile ownership are discussed in Chapter 3.

Transportation Modes. The vast majority of Americans rely on cars to meet their transportation needs. But because personal income dictates the ability to afford an auto, rates of auto ownership vary by race. According to the census, over 93 percent of white households own autos, while 76 percent of African American households, 83 percent of Latino households, and 87 percent of Asian-American households own autos. In part, because persons of color have higher poverty rates, they also have to rely on public transportation for commuting and other transportation needs.[31] Racial differences in transit usage result from housing market discrimination, which relegates minority populations to residential locations where transit is more readily available. Quality and reliability of service are additional factors in determining who uses public transit.

Only 3 percent of whites use public transportation to get to work, compared with 12 percent of African Americans, 9 percent of Latinos, and

Figure 3.   Users of Public Transportation to Travel to Work, by Race

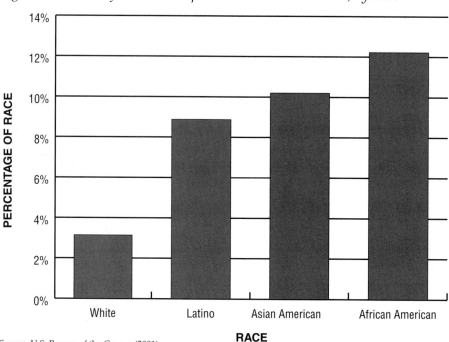

Source: U.S. Bureau of the Census (2001)

10 percent of Asian Americans (see Figure 3).[32] In urban areas, African Americans and Latinos together comprise 54 percent of public transportation users (62 percent of all bus riders, 35 percent of all subway riders, and 29 percent of all commuter rail riders).[33] African Americans also walk to work more than whites.

Housing Policies. Along with substantial highway construction investments, particular housing policies are blamed for promoting sprawl and isolating rich from poor and black from white. Mortgage interest deductions, which benefit those who can afford to own homes, spurred home purchasing in nonurban areas where land was plentiful, making home purchases cheaper in the suburbs. As of 2000, home ownership rates varied significantly by race and ethnicity. At 71.1 percent, the home ownership rate of whites exceeded the national rate of 67.4 percent, with Asian Americans lagging behind at 52.8 percent, African Americans at 47.2 percent, and Latinos at 46.3 percent. These trends do not appear to reflect successful efforts of housing policies and home ownership programs.

Restrictive covenants kept many in the post–World War II generation of African Americans from buying homes in new developments destined to experience rapid value increases, thus depriving them of the potential to build family wealth:

> Long Island's segregated housing patterns have deep structural and institutional roots. The 1934 National Housing Act, which created the Federal Housing Administration (FHA), promulgated policies that created racially homogenous neighborhoods through various devices: deeds with racially restrictive covenants, the manual of home appraisal standards for private home mortgage lending, the underwriting manual for FHA mortgage lending, and other policies. Local housing developers, the banking industry and local governments willingly embraced these devices. The real estate industry on Long Island, as elsewhere, was an active partner in perpetuating racial segregation in housing. In 1950, despite the United States Supreme Court prohibition against enforcement of restrictive covenants in deeds, William Levitt, the famous post–World War II developer who made Long Island this Nation's first suburb, continued to refuse to lease or sell his affordable homes to African Americans.[34]

Even today, Nassau and Suffolk counties comprise the third-most-segregated region in the United States when measuring black–white residential segregation in suburban areas of all metropolitan areas.[35]

Exclusionary Land Use Zoning Policies. Other policies that have implications for race and class are zoning and comprehensive planning. In particular, regulations that dictate residential unit and lot size affect ownership opportunities, which, as previously discussed, have distinct racial characteristics. In many cases these policies act to exclude certain types of housing, many times multifamily, renter-occupied units that would attract low-income households and racial minorities. Reduced housing opportunities in the suburbs exclude racial minorities and contribute to the general separation of races into urban and suburban areas. Just as with the home ownership subsidy provided by the mortgage interest deduction, exclusionary zoning has a disproportionate impact on households that already encounter limited social and economic opportunity.

SUMMARY

Demographic trends and urban development patterns highlight some factors influencing social and economic opportunity in the United States. Race, class, and location are still inextricably linked, giving land-use patterns social implications, and, in turn, giving social circumstances an impact on land-use activities. Low-density land uses are not conducive to efficient public transportation systems and effectively require autos for travel needs. This requirement, in the form of additional household expense, is more burdensome for low-income households struggling to afford housing, health care, education, and other important costs. The form of our communities and regions, as well as their social and economic composition, is greatly influenced by travel needs and patterns.

NOTES

1. Kain and Meyer (1970).
2. National Advisory Commission on Civil Disorders (1968).
3. A metropolitan area is defined by the U.S. Census as having "a core area containing a substantial population nucleus, together with adjacent communities having a high degree of economic and social integration with that core." County boundaries tend to be the building blocks for metropolitan area boundaries.
4. Nelson and Sanchez (2005).
5. Hobbs and Stoops (2002).
6. Logan (2001). Only 39 percent of African Americans, 49 percent of Latinos,

and 59 percent of Asian Americans lived in suburbs.
7. Frey (2001). Suburban diversity is complex, and these overall statistics conceal the significant variations across metropolitan areas and racial or ethnic group. Also see Frey (2002) and Logan (2002b) for more details about these variations.
8. U.S. Bureau of the Census (2001).
9. Lewis Mumford Center (2001). "The typical white lives in a neighborhood that is 80.2% white, 6.7% black, 7.9% Hispanic, and 3.9% Asian. . . . [T]he typical black lives in a neighborhood that is 51.4% black, 33.0% white, 11.4%

Hispanic, and 3.3% Asian. The typical Hispanic lives in a neighborhood that is 45.5% Hispanic, 36.5% white, 10.8% black and 5.9% Asian."

10. Iceland, Weinberg, and Steinmetz (2002), using five indicators introduced by Massey and Denton (1988).
11. Lewis Mumford Center (2001).
12. Lewis Mumford Center (2001).
13. Glaeser and Vigdor (2001).
14. The Institute on Race and Poverty (1996).
15. Putnam (1995), p. 67.
16. 42 U.S.C. §§ 3601–3631.
17. Carter, Flores, and Brown (2004).
18. Fichtenbaum and Blair (1989), Jargowsky (1997).
19. McFate (1991).
20. Galbraith (1998).
21. National Advisory Commission on Civil Disorders (1968).
22. Milton S. Eisenhower Foundation (1998).
23. Logan (2002a).
24. Latinos may be of any race.
25. Proctor and Dalaker (2002).
26. Logan (2002a).
27. Luckett (2001).
28. Sanchez, Stolz, and Ma (2003).
29. Triangle Improvement Council v. Ritchie, 402 U.S. 497, 502 (1971).
30. While it is relatively inexpensive to obtain a car, the overall costs to households are quite high. See discussion in Chapter 3.
31. The census definition for public transportation includes bus or trolley bus, streetcar or trolley car, subway or elevated railroad, ferryboat, or taxicab.
32. U.S. Bureau of the Census (2001).
33. Pucher and Renne (2003).
34. Education Research Advocacy & Support to Eliminate Racism (2005)
35. Education Research Advocacy & Support to Eliminate Racism (2005).

3

Transportation Costs
and Inequities

Transportation costs are frequently identified as having inequitable effects. The concerns are that transport costs, and especially cost increases, are regressive and result in greater burdens on low-income persons. This chapter discusses aspects of household costs; issues related to car ownership, transit fares, and road tolls; and ways in which federal funding produces geographic inequities.

Transportation is the second-largest expenditure category for American families, accounting for 18.6 cents of every dollar spent annually.[1] Only shelter, at 19.2 cents per dollar spent, exceeds transportation (see Figure 4). Transportation has not always consumed such a high percentage of the family budget, but as public investments in transportation began to emphasize roads and highways over public transit, private spending on transportation increased dramatically. This has resulted in shifting household spending more toward private transportation, due to the lack of public transportation options. Families living in sprawling metropolitan areas, with little public transportation and destinations so spread out as to be unreachable by foot or bicycle, must spend even more on transportation, in some cases spending more than they do on rent or mortgages.

Families forced to spend thousands of dollars annually on owning and operating cars and trucks (which are rapidly depreciating assets) have less money to invest in home ownership, hindering wealth creation and

Figure 4.   How Families Spend Each Dollar

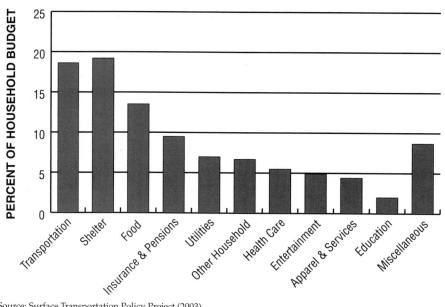

Source: Surface Transportation Policy Project (2003)

the ability to enjoy home ownership. The poorest Americans are especially hard hit, spending nearly 40 percent of their take-home pay on transportation costs, an expense that may require those families to dip into savings, borrow from relatives, and look for nontraditional sources of income to make ends meet.

HOUSEHOLD TRANSPORTATION COSTS

There are some conflicting perspectives on the amounts and proportions of household income expended on transportation by different income groups.[2] Despite the variation in estimates, it is undeniable that transportation costs are high. Data from the Consumer Expenditure Survey (CES) show that low-income households devote a greater proportion of their incomes to transportation-related expenses, regardless of whether they use public transportation or own automobiles. A Surface Transportation Policy Project (STPP) report from 2001 found that those in the lowest income quintile spent 36 percent of their take-home pay on transportation, compared with those in the highest income quintile, who spent only 14 percent on transportation. Figure 5 shows the level of household spending for transportation both in terms of proportion to income and in proportion to total household expenditures.

Figure 5.   Household Transportation Spending, by Income Group

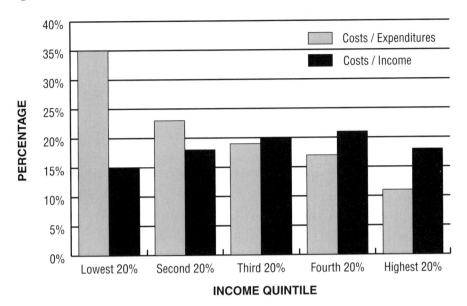

Source: U.S. Consumer Expenditure Survey

Using CES data, Rice (2004) found that the poorest households in California spend smaller shares of their total household budgets on transportation compared with low-income or high-income households. Rice acknowledged that these results can be interpreted in different ways and that lower expenditures on transportation cannot be equated with different levels of transportation affordability. As poor or low-income households spend less on transportation, other factors such as time costs, quality of service, and consumer trade-offs fail to be accounted for. In addition, the figures on average household expenditures on transportation do not control for household size or life cycle (age of household members and presence of children). Rice also found that these patterns of costs were similar to those of the United States as a whole.

Drawing the same conclusion as Rice, and also analyzing CES data, Blumenberg (2003) concluded that, despite the findings of the STPP report, lower-income households do not suffer a disproportionate impact from transportation costs compared with higher-income households. Blumenberg reported that there is a slight variation in transportation costs by income quintile, with the lowest quintile spending 17 percent of its household income, followed by 19 percent, 21 percent, 20 percent, and 18 percent, respectively. These compare to Rice's 11 percent, 14 percent, and

16 percent reported for poor, low-income, and high-income households (terciles). It is unclear why there is a discrepancy in their results despite using the same data source; however, they indicate the same general point: Transport costs are relatively constant across income groups.

While not reporting specific quantitative results, Deka (2005) refers to the higher proportional costs of transportation for poor households compared with "rich" households; he argues that an even more significant issue is that, over time, the proportion of household expenditures on transportation for poor households is increasing at a faster rate relative to that of rich households. In other words, not only will the poor be paying more than the rich for transportation, but the gap between income groups is increasing. The implication is that lower-income households will have decreasing amounts of disposable income available for home ownership, food, utilities, education, health care, and other household requirements.

In light of these discrepancies, what is the appropriate way to compare transportation expenditure levels across household income levels? Both Rice and Blumenberg briefly discuss the differences between transportation costs as a proportion of household income and total household expenditures. When comparing results from these two methods depicting transportation cost burdens, an important factor to consider is the inelasticity of transportation costs. With the total household expenditures as the denominator, the proportions of expenditures devoted to transportation remains relatively constant across income groups because transportation is an inelastic consumption item.[3] Despite households devoting about the same proportion of their total expenditures to transportation, the lowest income quintile travels about one-third as much as households in the highest income quintile. In addition to total *distance*, total travel *time* must be considered. Households in the lowest income quintile average nearly four minutes per mile traveled compared to three minutes per mile for households in the highest income quintile—much of this being explained by high rates of public transit ridership by low-income persons. While it may be true that low-income households pay similar proportions of their overall budgets for transportation compared with high-income households, they also consume far less in terms of overall travel distance resulting in a higher per-unit time cost. It can be argued that higher time costs are useful indicators of poor service quality or convenience.

On the other hand, when comparing transportation expenditures as a proportion of income, low-income households pay significantly higher levels than do higher-income households.[4] Using this approach also highlights the significant burden that lower-income households realize and the difficult trade-offs they make to satisfy their travel needs. Using household income as the denominator for estimating the financial burden of transportation costs (as opposed to total household expenditures, as done by Rice and Blumenberg) better illustrates the impact of high travel costs on lower-income households. As shown in Figure 6, according to the CES, overall annual expenditures by the lowest income groups exceed their annual incomes, contributing to higher levels of debt and financial liabilities. In 2001, annual household expenditures were 225 percent of household income for the lowest income group but only 64 percent for the highest income group. Possible explanations include underreporting of income or underreporting of debt. In either case, it is not likely that they are systematically overreporting their transportation costs.

Another measure of the impact of transportation costs on low-income households is the rate of increase in transportation expenditures. Between 1993 and 2003, households in the lowest income quintile saw the amount of their income spent on transportation increase by more than 4 percent. While not a dramatic increase, this was the highest rate of change among household income quintiles. By comparison, households in the highest income quintile spent about 11 percent *less* on transportation in 2003 than they did 10 years earlier. These trends suggest not only that low-income families are spending more of their incomes on transportation but also

Figure 6.   *Household Expenditures as a Percentage of After-Tax Income*

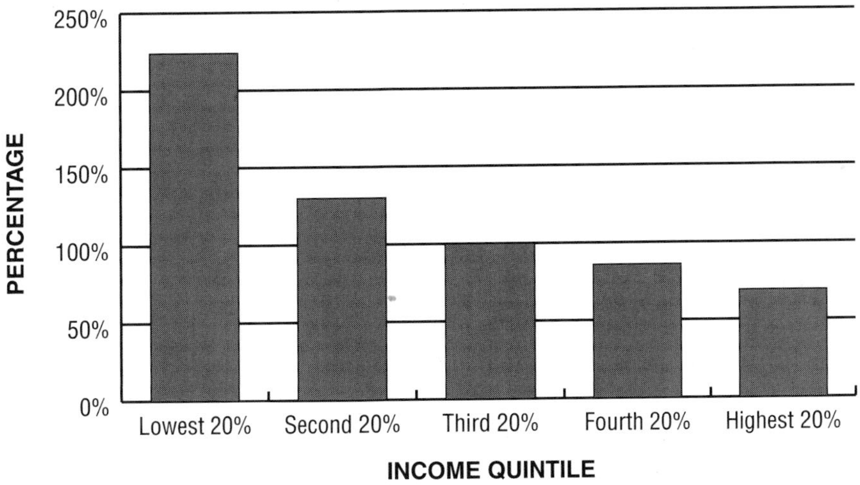

Source: U.S. Consumer Expenditure Survey

that transportation costs are increasing at a faster rate for them. The increasing burden of transportation costs compounds the financial challenges that lower-income households face. Increasing costs and growing debt problems further reduce the lower-income population's ability to pay for other needs, further removing this population from the possibility of home ownership and wealth accumulation. Other evidence suggests that the debt incurred by families related to car ownership makes it more difficult to buy a home, which is the primary means of wealth accumulation among low- and middle-income households.

Considering the previous discussion about household transportation costs, it is important to look in further detail behind the numbers. Each income quintile, for instance, has households that range in size as well as mobility levels (that is, car ownership). These two particular characteristics have significant impacts on transport burden because the number of persons in a household (as well as their ages) influences travel demand, and vehicle ownership levels influence the ability to meet travel needs.

Analyzing household transportation costs along with travel activities helps to illustrate travel costs versus benefits. Thus far, most previous analyses have focused on either one or the other—and not the cost per unit of transport consumed. Highly mobile persons or households are those paying relatively lower amounts per unit of travel. The most significant costs of auto ownership and operation are monthly finance payments, insurance, and in some cases state vehicle registration and taxes. However, the most visible costs are for fuel, parking, maintenance, and repair. Despite the fact that these costs are much higher per unit traveled compared with public transit, auto owners are not bound by service schedule restrictions or physical route coverage limitations—transport mobility is essentially unlimited. Shen illustrates this point when analyzing regional employment access by public transit versus autos for the Milwaukee metropolitan region. Figures 7 and 8 show the differences in employment accessibility for auto versus transit users.[5]

Car Ownership

There is a strong correlation among not owning a car, poverty, and the infirmities associated with aging. Not owning a car is most prevalent among the poor—including the elderly poor, the working poor, and the unemployed. Physical disabilities associated with aging are a significant correlate of not owning a car. Physical disabilities that require wheelchair use are widely recognized as a powerful correlate of mobility

Figure 7.   Accessibility for Job Seekers Commuting by Car

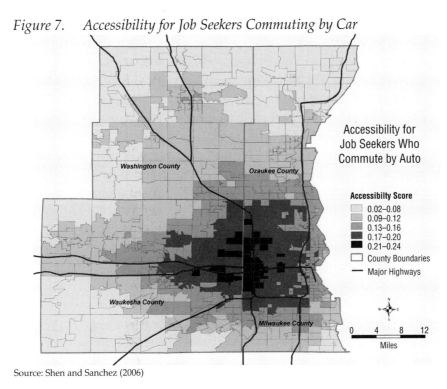

Source: Shen and Sanchez (2006)

Figure 8.   Accessibility for Job Seekers Using Transit

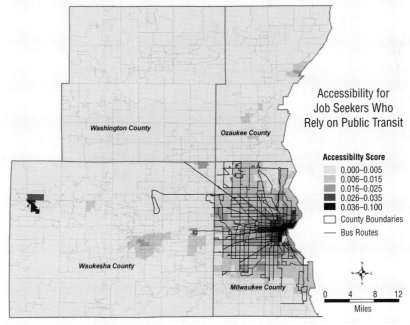

Source: Shen and Sanchez (2006)

disadvantage, but these affect a much smaller population than the low rate of car ownership associated with poverty and/or aging. Not owning a car is also strongly correlated with urban location. Lack of car ownership is most isolating for those who live alone in suburban communities. Not owning a car seems to be least isolating for those with a large network of family and friends and least immobilizing for those who live in urban settings suited to walking and the use of public transportation. The mobility available to those who do not own cars hinges on the ability of others to provide transportation when and where it is needed. These "others" include transit agencies, taxi companies, paratransit providers, family, friends, coworkers, neighbors, schools, churches, senior centers, and social service agencies.

Some have suggested that a way to overcome disparities in transport costs and mobility levels is to increase car ownership levels among low-income households.[6] It has been argued that this would provide low-income persons with improved accessibility and social and economic opportunity. Others also argue that increasing transit access for low-income persons (instead of to cars) relegates them to inferior transport modes and fails to put them on equal footing with those of greater economic means. A 1999 study by the Progressive Policy Institute, *Working Far from Home: Transportation and Welfare Reform*, stated,

> The shortest distance between a poor person and a job is along a line driven in a car. . . . Too often policy makers . . . are willing to consign poor people to barely functional public systems from which higher-income citizens routinely withdraw. People who point to mass transit as the environmentally sound alternative to cars for the working poor would subject them to inconveniences they themselves would never tolerate.[7]

As discussed earlier, car ownership can be quite expensive, especially for low-income persons. The notion that a bias exists in providing better transport mobility for low-income persons with transit is inaccurate. In fact, cases where urban planners and transit activists are trying to increase ridership levels among all income classes—including higher-income "choice" riders—can be seen across the country. For example, tenets of "smart growth," neotraditional design, and new urbanism that promote integration of non-auto modes of travel include support for transportation alternatives.[8] Instead of lowering levels of transport mobility for essentially middle- and upper-income persons, the push for public transit is broadening its scope to encourage higher-income users to take advantage of public transportation options. Increased transit ridership is a goal targeted more broadly than just at those at the lower end of the economic scale.

The Equity Costs of Fare Increases

The emphasis on highway and road construction in federal and state policy shifts resources away from public transportation options for low-income families. According to survey results released by the American Public Transportation Association (APTA) in 2002, more than 50 percent of the transit agencies that responded to the survey had implemented, or were planning to implement, fare increases (almost 90 percent of the large systems), and 34 percent said they were cutting back on transit service.[9] These fare increases and service cuts are being driven primarily by municipal, county, state, and transit agency budget crises brought on by the nation's economic downturn.[10] Those who are dependent on public transportation often have difficulty meeting fare increases.

Although more research is needed in this area, it is likely that fare increases create a greater economic burden on minorities because they are disproportionately poor and more frequently rely on public transportation. An APTA report in 1992 found that nationwide, on average, users of public transportation are 45 percent white, 31 percent African American, and 18 percent Latino/Hispanic, even though their general populations are approximately 69 percent, 12 percent, and 12.5 percent, respectively.[11] Public transportation users also tend to have lower incomes. Nationally, approximately 38 percent of transit users have incomes of $20,000 or less, while 41 percent have incomes between $20,000 and $75,000. Only 21.5 percent have incomes above $75,000.[12]

APTA research and other sources suggest that fare increases can have very negative consequences for transit agencies.[13] Some estimates show that transit ridership decreases between 2 and 4 percent for every 10 percent increase in transit fares. These trends also tend to be more pronounced in smaller population centers. By increasing fares, public transit agencies run the risk of losing ridership, particularly riders with other transportation options. Those who remain—riders who lack other options—bear the burden of higher fares and service cutbacks that may result from ridership decline and that may have a severe impact on their economic livelihoods and ability to have access to basic services.[14] Some evidence shows that reducing fares can dramatically increase ridership.[15] More research in this area would provide a clearer understanding of the effect of fare increases on minority and low-income populations.

Bus-fare Blues

"Another quarter, please." The bus driver was glaring at me and my 17-month-old son as I fumbled for an additional quarter. My fingers clawed their way into the dark recesses of my backpack. Brushes, crumpled receipts, paper clips, pens, old address books intertwined with new address books, erasers, old watch bands, and . . . oh, ahhh, could it be true? A quarter? Clutching the sliver of metal, my fingers climbed back up through a hidden passage of Mt. Backpack. But alas, it was just a nickel. "Would a nickel be OK? It's all I have right now?" I plead.

"No, it's $1.25; you can get off at the next stop."

Since I started school in January, I've been taking Muni more than usual, and a bus pass was too rich for my meager, working-poor single-parent budget, so every week I begged, borrowed, or stole my way onto San Francisco's main transportation system.

Until now.

The Municipal Transportation Authority is proposing a rate hike to $1.50 a ride to offset its $24 million budget deficit. This fare increase would make it almost impossible for very-low-income folks like me to ride the bus at all. And considering that we make up the majority of bus riders, I have to ask: Who is the MTA targeting for these rate hikes?

Yes, it's true that in San Francisco, conscious, privileged people with homes and high-paying jobs ride the bus because they want to—after all, it's better for the environment—but so do poor immigrants, fixed-income elders, youths, poor workers, and disabled and houseless folks. We all have different reasons, but we all ride.

"All services are hurting because of California's budget" was MTA's statement about the 2003 Muni rate hikes from $1 to $1.25. At that time Muni cited the fact that the system needed to offset a then-$55 million deficit.

Of course, all public services in California are facing budget deficits—but let's take a moment to connect the dots, or rather, the corporate welfare recipients. We could start with Enron, which stole all of California's surplus with its fake energy crisis, and the Governator, who didn't go after Enron for that stolen revenue (he also owns interests in energy stocks) and who decided owners of expensive cars like his Hummer needed to pay less taxes, which took a major local revenue source away from desperately needy city budgets.

Corporate-esque MTA board members like Ted Tedesco, previously with American Airlines, and bank executive Thomas O'Bryant are voting against their own best interests when they make public transportation increasingly costly for poor workers. Cheap transportation enables the urban/suburban apartheid they rely on to get through their daily lives. If it weren't for cheap public transit, the poor service workers like maids and dishwashers couldn't get from the poor areas of the city to the wealthy neighborhoods across town, where people like those MTA board members reside.

Last week a new coalition representing some of the poorest citizens of San Francisco presented its own "Platform for Transit Justice" to the MTA, declaring public transportation to be a human right.

The coalition believes that as a transit-first city, San Francisco should encourage use of public transit instead of cars and proposes a variety of revenue-raising measures that would eliminate the deficit.

As the Muni bus doors close on me and my son with an extra wumph, I consider illicitly entering through the back door of the next bus without paying the fare. Then I remember that when they hiked the rates in 2003, they also jacked up the issuing of tickets to people trying to ride without paying the fare—criminalizing the poor while targeting the poor. Without options, I gather our stuff, and we begin the long walk home.

The author, Tiny, is an editor at POOR *magazine. Originally published in the* San Francisco Bay Guardian, *February 9-15, 2005. Reprinted with permission.*

TRANSPORTATION POLICY FAVORS HIGHER-INCOME PUBLIC TRANSIT RIDERS

Some research also suggests that low-income riders of transit tend to subsidize their higher-income counterparts. Fare structures are often designed in such a way that short trips subsidize longer trips, and low-income and central-city riders generally make short trips compared with higher-income suburban users who make long trips.[16] One researcher noted that a user who travels one mile pays more than twice the true cost of the trip, whereas a user who travels 20 miles pays only 20 percent of the cost.[17] In addition, the amount of revenue gained from passenger fares, including passes, tends to be higher on central-city transit routes than suburban routes, and more low-income transit riders tend to make trips on central-city routes.[18]

One notable example of this subsidization can be seen by comparing bus and rail service.[19] Data from the 2001 National Household Travel Survey show that in urban areas, households earning less than $20,000 comprised 47 percent of bus riders, 20 percent of subway riders, and 6 percent of commuter rail riders.[20] On the other hand, households earning $100,000 or more comprised 42 percent of commuter rail riders, 27 percent of subway riders, and only 7 percent of bus riders.[21] Clearly, more individuals with low incomes rely on bus service, and more high-income individuals rely on rail service (see Figure 9).

Figure 9.   Modes of Transportation by Household Income

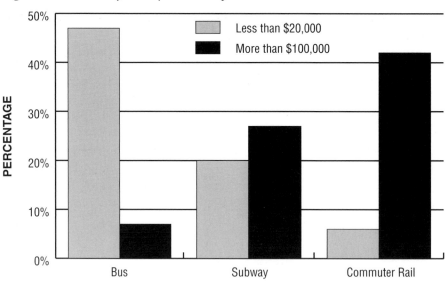

TRANSPORTATION MODE

Source: Pucher and Renne (2003)

Bus transit receives only 31 percent of the capital funds spent nation-wide for transit, although it carries more than 60 percent of the trips.[22] This disparity is exacerbated by requirements that federal funding for transit generally must be used only for capital expenditures, not operating expenses. Because rail transit is capital intensive and bus transit is labor intensive, a greater emphasis on capital subsidies favors rail service over bus service and consequently generally favors higher-income over lower-income riders.

Los Angeles is one example of a city where there were disparities in funding for bus compared with rail transit. Community activists and attorneys alleged in a lawsuit[23] in the early 1990s that the Los Angeles Metropolitan Transportation Authority (LAMTA) spent only 30 percent of its resources on bus transit, even though almost 94 percent of its riders used the buses, and 80 percent of them were people of color. Of LAMTA's resources, 70 percent went to rail, even though only 6 percent of its riders used rail. Rail riders were primarily white.[24]

The gulf between governmental financial and political support for rail compared with bus service, however, is not nearly as great as that for highway systems compared with public transit systems.

ROAD TOLLS

Tolling of roads and lanes has become popular in the United States. This involves charging an extra fee to users for the privilege of driving on a dedicated lane or road with anticipated benefits from reducing congestion and speeding traffic. The topic is a favorite among many transportation planners and economists. However, for jurisdictions considering instituting tolls, there are fears that the tolls will have a regressive economic effect on low-income drivers. Regressivity means that lower-income consumers pay a greater share of their budget or receive less benefit than consumers with higher income. For example, sales taxes are generally labeled regressive because they are paid on many items considered necessities, which the rich and the poor use in equal amounts. The example often given is toilet paper. Although the rich and the poor theoretically use equal amounts of this product, the percent of discretionary income spent by low-income persons is much higher than the percent spent by higher-income persons.

If a low-income person cannot afford to use a tolled lane or road, he or she will take a longer time to get to work. Studies have shown that distance to a job is one determinant of whether people will move from welfare to work.[25]

The regressivity argument is a difficult one, often hinging on the questions: Who benefits, how, and how much? Are people's needs being met? Should they be? Which needs? What is society's obligation to low-income people? Martin Wachs has encapsulated some of these arguments in the context of an iconoclastic essay on why fuel prices should be raised. Wachs noted that only poor people who drive pay the fuel tax, that some fuel tax revenues may be diverted to transit expenditures, and that sales tax as an alternative to fuel taxes would be just as regressive as fuel taxes. He also noted that jurisdictions interested in transportation improvements may well raise sales taxes to pay for them. However, increasing fuel taxes may be more politically feasible than increasing sales taxes.[26] It is interesting to note that Wachs's argument was borne out in Washington State, where the legislature's increase in the state gasoline tax to pay for transportation improvements was challenged by a citizen initiative. It failed at the ballot box on November 8, 2005.

Advocates of tolling state that studies have shown that people of all income levels use tolled lanes and roads.[27] However, these studies define "low income" as being below $40,000 per year. Thus, they exclude very-low-income persons, who may be tolled off the road.

Tolls are the oldest form of road charges.[28] They are a user-pays system. Turnpike tolls have been used in America since colonial days, and toll roads make up as much as 9 percent of all highway mileage today. In addition to equity concerns, there is opposition to tolling because of "double taxation" issues, in which opponents feel that they are already paying for roads through gasoline taxes. In the United States, we nominally have a progressive income tax system, but many of our other taxes are regressive. Such regressive taxes act to limit opportunity and prevent social mobility. Tolls can ultimately prevent the travel and mobility of low-income people altogether.

There are federal restrictions on tolling on freeways that date from the 1950s, when tolls meant delays due to queuing at toll plazas. The lingering bias against tolling in important sections of federal highway law dates back to the beginning of the interstate highway system in 1956. A major idea in 1956 was to fully finance the interstate highway system using fuel taxes and make the entire system toll free. Section 301 of the U.S. Code is titled "Freedom from tolls," and reads: "Except as provided in section 129 of this title with respect to certain toll bridges and toll tunnels, all highways constructed under the provisions of this title shall be free from tolls of all kinds."[29]

Current surface transportation bills may replace the anti-toll provisions in Title 23. Toll roads constitute about 4,900 miles (9 percent) of America's 56,000 miles of interstates and other freeways and expressways. As revenue from gasoline taxes declines, road builders and maintainers will be seeking different sources of revenue. One place they are looking is new and increased tolling.

There are other road-pricing options being explored, some of which have equity implications. Road pricing is defined to include usage-based vehicle charges such as pay-as-you-drive insurance, "cash out" strategies such as parking cash out, mileage-based car leasing and vehicle taxation, and car sharing. Road pricing has the potential for creating the most fundamental change in our methods for planning and funding our transportation system since the 1950s. Modern implementations of road pricing include congestion pricing or value-priced tolls collected electronically that vary with the level of congestion. However, the approaches to road pricing can encompass a variety of market-based approaches to respond to congestion problems.

Proposed solutions to equity concerns include using some of the newly generated revenues to pay for enhanced public transportation, offering subsidies for low-income drivers, and waiving tolls for low-income drivers. Road pricing theoretically can generate revenues that can be used to enhance urban mobility. In an article on congestion pricing, Lauren Smith states, "The equity of congestion pricing depends on how the collected revenues are redistributed to travelers and on whether travel alternatives are available."[30] Congestion-pricing schemes need to somehow compensate low-income drivers to avoid being inequitable and regressive. Under a fair redistribution policy, drivers across income groups should be made better off.

Tolled lanes are sometimes referred to by critics as "Lexus Lanes." But at least one study, by Marlon G. Boarnet and colleagues, stated, "Perceptions about equity were more fluid than previously thought, and frequently hinged on alternatives to the project, as well as perceived value relative to the cost."[31] Theoretically, these problems are solvable. For example, some believe that the public is as concerned about efficiency as it is about equity. In theory, market signals and public response will shape tax systems. Drivers can essentially vote with their cars and choice of travel activities.[32]

METROPOLITAN PLANNING ORGANIZATIONS AND DISPARITIES IN FEDERAL FUNDING BY GEOGRAPHIC AREA

The negative consequences of funding policies that favor spending on highways over transit are exacerbated because metropolitan planning organizations (MPOs) receive only a small percentage of federal funds. MPOs have a better understanding of the transportation needs of metropolitan areas where many minorities and low-income individuals reside and would be more likely to invest in public transit. Currently, MPOs have direct control over only 6 percent of federal transportation funds. This distribution formula discourages establishment of integrated transportation and land-use policies. Although states have the ability to provide more funding to local transportation agencies, few states actually do. One notable exception is California, which gives 75 percent of its federal and state transportation program funds to regional and metropolitan transportation agencies. These local agencies have pioneered innovative programs such as providing incentives to develop denser housing within walking distance of mass transit. Increased funding for MPOs would have the potential of allowing them to make major multimodal investments that address air quality, traffic congestion, and other priority concerns of their specific communities.[33]

MPOs are organizations of local governments legally charged with the task of coordinating short- and long-range transportation planning for all urbanized areas in the country with more than 50,000 residents.[34] MPOs exist in numerous forms but generally operate as a function of regional councils of government (COGs) or as subdivisions of state departments of transportation (SDOTs). Although a few regions around the country established MPOs as early as the 1950s, it was not until the early 1970s that the federal transportation bill demanded the creation of regional entities to carry out metropolitan transportation planning. Though the degree of authority given to MPOs did wax and wane in ensuing decades, their overall power remained quite limited until the 1990s.[35]

MPOs received a significant lift under the Intermodal Surface Transportation Efficiency Act of 1991 (ISTEA), which gave MPOs unprecedented authority and flexibility over the allocation of funds for different types of surface transportation projects, such as the Surface Transportation Program, Transportation Enhancements, Congestion Mitigation and Air Quality, and Metropolitan Planning funds.[36] ISTEA made MPOs primarily responsible for planning and allocating transportation funding in these metropolitan regions by sending certain funds directly to them. ISTEA also broadened the membership of the policy-setting boards of MPOs governing large areas and required that they include representatives from local governments in the region, agencies operating major transportation systems, and state officials.[37]

Though ISTEA and the Transportation Equity Act for the 21st Century (TEA-21) gave MPOs direct control over only a portion of total federal transportation funds, they made MPOs much more influential than they had been previously and helped to standardize their function by giving them uniform responsibilities.[38] Still, substantial differences among MPOs remain, as states maintain significant discretion over the delegation of authority to MPOs within their bounds. In California, the state DOT channels 75 percent of its federal and state transportation program funds directly to MPOs for programming and planning, whereas in North Carolina and Wisconsin, the state DOT retains a much greater share of these funds. Though federal requirements do hold MPOs accountable for meeting basic representational criteria, the specific structure of MPO boards and decision-making processes are left to the discretion of the states and local governments.

Although most of the nation's population is located in metropolitan areas, generating substantial revenues for highway spending and having significant transportation infrastructure needs, some evidence suggests that states spend more on serving transportation needs in nonmetropolitan areas than in metropolitan areas.[39] A study of transportation spending in Ohio found that, while urban counties generated more local revenues for highway spending than other areas, there was not a corresponding level of spending in urban areas.[40] Studies examining metropolitan areas and counties are informative. An analysis of per capita spending between cities and other areas, however, would provide us with a better understanding of how transportation funds are being spent.[41] This type of analysis is difficult to perform because the data on how federal transportation funds are spent are provided only on a county-level basis, and county boundaries do not always coincide with city limits.

In Baltimore, however, city and county boundaries coincide. Thus, it is possible to determine the per capita distribution of funding by county and determine how funding for Baltimore ranks relative to other counties. An unpublished analysis by the Surface Transportation Policy Project shows that Baltimore receives the lowest federal highway funding per capita in the state—$121 per person—showing a clear preference in funding for suburban and rural counties.[42] Interestingly, the distribution of this $121 per person is fairly even, with the largest amount spent on bridge repair and a significant portion directed to bicycle and pedestrian facilities, transit, and road repair. This type of analysis can be performed only if more data are collected that are geographically coded for geographic units smaller than counties. It is also difficult to analyze whether there are any funding disparities between minority communities and nonminority communities for the same reason; DOT data are available only for counties.

ECONOMIC IMPACT OF TRANSPORTATION POLICY ON LOW-INCOME AND MINORITY HOUSEHOLDS

Transportation policies have a direct impact on low-income, minority communities by making accessibility difficult. Federal, state, and local transportation policies emphasizing highway construction lead to dependency on automobiles and rising transportation costs. Generally, 80 cents of every dollar spent on federal surface transportation programs is earmarked for highways, and 20 cents is earmarked for public transportation (which includes both bus and rail transit). Even so, states are unlikely, for various reasons, to be devoting 20 percent of their overall transportation expenditures to public transportation.[43]

Thirty states restrict use of their gasoline tax revenues to funding highway programs only.[44] Revenues from gas taxes are the single largest funding source for transportation programs. Several other states allow only a small portion of gas tax revenues to be spent on transit. For example, Michigan allocates 10 percent or less of its state gas tax and related transportation revenue for public transportation.[45] In Alabama, the Birmingham metropolitan region has struggled to raise state and local revenue to match more than $80 million in federal grants for public transportation largely because the state constitution prohibits the use of gas tax revenue for this purpose.[46] At the local level, funds spent on bus transit capital and operating expenses sometimes add up to a small percentage of funds spent on all different types of transit and may be much less than the 20 percent allocated by federal policy.[47] Policies that restrict allocation of public funds to public transit contribute to increasing household transportation expenses, particularly for low-income families.

SUMMARY

The economic cost of transportation is one factor that influences mobility. An accounting of transportation expenditures does not directly reveal the trade-offs that are made by households as they balance financial and time costs associated with their travel needs. Whether low-income persons pay the same amount or more for transportation compared with higher-income persons sidesteps the real issue of whether a dollar spent by low-income persons purchases an equivalent amount and quality of transportation mobility and accessibility. In other words, the question should not be limited to how much is spent, but should address what they got for their money. Such social cost accounting is difficult to perform, which likely explains why so little of it is performed when analyzing household travel behavior.[48]

Other evidence suggests that transit fares, road tolls, and federal transportation funding programs have also produced inequitable outcomes. Many of these outcomes result from a bias toward auto modes of travel, which have inherent consequences for those who cannot afford cars. In addition, policies that over-invest in auto modes and under-invest in public transportation also have direct implications for urban areas, which is where the majority of low-income, racial minorities reside.

NOTES

1. Surface Transportation Policy Project (2001).
2. See Rice (2004), Blumenberg (2003), Surface Transportation Policy Project (2001).
3. See Rice (2004).
4. See Surface Transportation Policy Project (2001).
5. Shen and Sanchez (2006) used a sophisticated measure of employment accessibility that accounted for travel time, mode, and employment competition.
6. See Ong and Blumenberg (1998), Taylor and Ong (1995), Waller and Hughes (1999).
7. Waller and Hughes (1999), p. 1.
8. Principle No. 8 from the *Charter of the New Urbanism* (Congress for the New Urbanism, 2000) states, "The Physical organization of the region should be supported by a framework of transportation alternatives. Transit, pedestrian, and bicycle systems should maximize access and mobility throughout the region while reducing dependence on the automobile." See Talen (2002) for a discussion about new urbanism and social equity.
9. American Public Transportation Association (2002). Three hundred and fifty systems were surveyed, and 33 percent responded. Twenty-three large, 31 medium, and 60 small systems (defined by number of unlinked trips per year) responded.
10. American Public Transportation Association (2002).
11. American Public Transportation Association (1992).
12. Pucher and Renne (2003).
13. American Public Transportation Association (1991).
14. See American Public Transportation Association (1991) and Rubin (2000).
15. Rubin (2000).
16. Deka (2004).
17. Deka (2004).
18. Deka (2004).
19. The demographics of a community and amount of subsidization are likely to vary by locality, and there may be some communities in which this type of subsidization may be appropriate, but not enough data exist to make that determination.
20. Pucher and Renne (2003).
21. Pucher and Renne (2003), Table 10.
22. Deka (2004).
23. The Los Angeles Bus Riders Union was the lead plaintiff in the case brought by the NAACP Legal Defense and Educational Fund. The case was settled and included provisions requiring LAMTA to reduce bus pass fares, purchase new buses, and expand bus service (see Mann, 1997).
24. See Rubin (2000); Labor/Community Strategies Center, Bus Riders Union v. L.A. County Metropolitan Transportation Authority, Plaintiffs' Revised Statement of Contentions of Fact and Law, No. CV-945936 (C.D. CA, October 24, 1996).
25. Waller and Hughes (1999), pp. 1–2.
26. Wachs (2003).
27. For example, see Dornan and March (2005).
28. U.S. Federal Highway Administration (2003).
29. 23 U.S.C. § 129.
30. Giuliano (1994); Litman (1996).
31. Boarnet, DiMento, and Macey (2002).
32. Stiglitz (2005).
33. See Kinsey (2003).
34. 23 U.S.C. § 134(b)(1).
35. See Puentes and Bailey (2005) for detailed discussion of metropolitan transportation planning and funding.
36. Puentes and Bailey (2005).
37. Intermodal Surface Transportation Efficiency Act of 1991, H.R. 2950, 102nd Cong., 1 sess. (1991). Title I, § 1024, subsection 134(b)2.

38. See Puentes Linda Bailey (2005) for detailed discussion of metropolitan transportation planning and funding.
39. Puentes and Prince (2003).
40. Hill et al. (2003).
41. This type of analysis would provide a better understanding of transportation spending in states with large minority populations in rural areas as well as in states with large minority populations in cities.
42. Ernst (2003).
43. Puentes and Prince (2003).
44. Puentes and Prince (2003).
45. Stolz (2001b).
46. Niolet (2003).
47. Interfaith Federation (1999).

4

The Indirect Economic and Social Effects of Transportation Policies

The previous chapter was about some of the *direct* effects of transportation policies on low-income people and minorities and their ability to travel. Direct effects are typically associated with visible transportation costs and benefits that are easily identified at the individual, household, or community scale. There are also associated indirect effects that result when access to transportation itself is limited to the point of adverse impact on social and economic opportunities. This chapter discusses several indirect effects, including some related to employment outcomes, access to housing, and access to education, as well as health and safety issues.

SPATIAL MISMATCH

Of all the issues related to transportation and civil rights, the perceived mismatch between the residential location of low-income urban (and often minority) households and the location of low-skill jobs has received the most attention in the academic literature.[1] Some argue that, as a result of racial discrimination, a spatial mismatch results when suitable jobs in the suburbs are inaccessible to persons who rely mostly on public transportation. As discussed earlier, these people tend to be disproportionately low income and people of color. The mismatch is partly the result of the growth of new jobs in areas outside the city, especially in outer-ring suburbs, exurbs, and outlying industrial parks. With spatial mismatch there is concentrated poverty in the historic center of cities but growing employment opportunity toward the edge of the metropolis, especially in areas poorly served by public transportation. Despite the trend of businesses relocating to suburban areas, a large proportion of metropolitan employment remains in downtowns. Managerial and information-processing services have remained in downtown areas, while entry-level, low-skill jobs flowed to the urban fringe and beyond. High-tech jobs have become located in campus-like suburban office parks. Some have been located along metropolitan ring roads, such as around Boston and Washington, D.C.

Chambers of commerce and real estate agents sell themselves and their locations to prospective companies on this basis. These businesses tend to cluster. Such suburban and campus-style development is very different from the redevelopment of brownfields, which are often located in older urban areas with ready access to existing public transportation service. Another possible reason for location of new jobs remote from where people of color live is racial discrimination. Just as white flight was a phenomenon of nonminorities moving out of older inner cities via new freeways to find better homes and schools, businesses may flee to seek a workforce whom they see as better trained and educated. Businesses move for many reasons—to avoid unionization of a workforce, to pay fewer taxes, to gain the benefits of transportation facilities, to pay lower wages, to pay less for expansion and real estate. Many of the new businesses being formed are high tech and employ fewer people of color. The first businesses to be outsourced offshore include those in manufacturing, which used to be a source for minority employment in the North, such as the automakers in Detroit. George J. Bryjak has stated, "Fewer good-paying jobs will await college and technical school graduates as the societal opportunity structure is diminished. The upward mobility of African-Americans, Latinos and other minority groups playing catch-up will be slowed."[2]

Some research suggests that the average distance between a central-city resident's home and potential employment locations has been increasing over time.[3] As this distance increases, low-skilled workers with few transportation options are unable to travel to these new, dispersed locations. In theory, when job locations are concentrated, commute times and distances are shorter than when jobs are located in dispersed locations—that is, commuting to jobs in dispersed locations is inefficient. Some argue, however, that dispersing residences and jobs leads to *more* efficient transportation because the negative effects of transportation will also be dispersed, resulting in less congestion.[4] Such theories ignore the fact that transit-dependent populations have limited overall travel mode options.

Related to the spatial mismatch between jobs and central-city residents are reverse-commuting travel patterns. While a majority of commute trips flow to central cities from outlying areas, a portion of trips also flow in the opposite direction to connect workers with job opportunities located in the urban fringe and suburbs. In 2000, 1.6 million people per day made reverse commutes in the 10 largest metropolitan areas. Data from the U.S. Bureau of the Census on county-to-county commute flows in the 10 largest metropolitan areas show that the volume of reverse commuting increased from 3.4 percent to 4.0 percent of all commute trips.[5] While this may not appear to be a significant increase in reverse commuting, compared with other commute trip types, reverse commutes represented nearly 13 percent of new commute trips from 1990 to 2000. Also, these figures provide no insight into the number of additional reverse commute trips that might be taken if there were better transportation options serving these travel patterns. Because it is difficult for public transportation to serve dispersed suburban locations from the central cities, workers who were transit dependent and faced with reverse commuting were put at a distinct disadvantage.[6]

It is likely that the vast majority of reverse commute trips require a car, especially if travel is required during off-peak periods (evenings and weekends). Without reliable transportation options, transit-dependent workers are often excluded from suburban employment opportunities. Urban public transportation systems operate most efficiently in concentrated, densely developed urban areas. Because of this, transit systems tend to be oriented toward downtowns and do a poor job of serving dispersed trip origins and destinations.[7] Consequently, transit systems often do not adequately serve the needs of minorities and low-income individuals due to residential segregation and nontraditional work hours.

Analyzing residential location and employment location patterns is complex. The simple ratio of total jobs to total working-age persons in a specific geographic area is an inadequate indicator associated with mismatch. Workers' job skills, educational background, gender, race, and mobility are significant factors in determining the numbers and types of jobs that a worker is selected to hold. While gender and race are almost never legally permitted exclusionary criteria, the reality is that discrimination continues to exist and has an effect in the job market. It can be argued that, controlling for "skills" and "mobility" matching, the disparity in employment levels by race and gender can be attributed to historic or contemporary patterns of discrimination.[8] Some research suggests that higher levels of access to public transit service are associated with higher levels of labor participation and lower levels of regional wage inequality.[9] However, further research is needed that focuses on the relationships among residential location, housing affordability, transportation mobility, and employment outcomes to inform appropriate public policies.

Some argue that transportation policies, funding priorities, and people's preferences are so strongly in favor of traveling by automobiles that mobility benefits from public transportation are negligible.[10] Some also argue that public transit is not a viable alternative to the personal automobile due to the geographic imbalance between housing and job locations.[11] The fact that small investments are made in transit (relative to roads and highways) while metropolitan areas continue to sprawl leads to further auto dependency that imposes a disproportionate burden on low-income persons.[12] Many low-income and minority households lack access to an automobile and thus depend on poor-quality public transit, which limits the location and types of employment that are available to them.[13]

Other research suggests that increased automobile ownership rates may have beneficial impacts on low-income workers and their families.[14] Autos improve not only job search activities, but also job retention, especially in cases where (or when) public transit service is unavailable.[15] In addition, autos provide flexibility beyond work-related trips, so that individuals can meet other daily needs related to child care, education, shopping, health care, and the like. The role of cars should be a consideration in transportation mobility strategies for low-income and minority people. The challenge, however, is to devise public policy that effectively increases auto access in cases in which other modes are infeasible. In addition, programs to increase automobile ownership among minorities run into opposition from environmental groups, which never see increased car ownership or use as a solution to any problem. One of the essential tensions in dealing with transportation equity issues is the lack of interest or understanding by environmental groups. As discussed elsewhere in this book, steps have been taken to resolve this tension through the environmental justice movement. In addition, one of the core belief structures in environmentalism, sustainable development, includes equity as a primary concept. Nevertheless, the concept of equity rarely appears in sustainable development documents in anything other than a hortatory form.

Several spatial mismatch analyses leave open the question of whether public transportation significantly affects employment levels and commuting activities in urban areas. With more detailed data and analysis, these effects can be better understood, providing tangible evidence of the relationship between increasing and improving public transportation and solving metropolitan unemployment and commuting problems. This type of research could be useful to clarify or redirect current policies attempting to overcome the spatial mismatch between low-income persons and employment opportunities. Unfortunately, what we learn as a result of research and experience is not often put into practice in a way that reduces transportation, social, and economic inequality. The link between theory and practice is not unique to transportation equity research, but it must become a priority to bring about meaningful improvements.

TRANSPORTATION POLICIES AND ACCESS TO HOUSING

One significant indirect effect from biased transportation policies is residential segregation. Examples of residential location patterns as a product of both land-use and transportation investment decisions are highway investments in combination with federal housing and lending policies leading to post–World War II suburbanization, which played a significant role in white flight from central cities to suburbs. This had profound impacts on shaping urban form and racial segregation patterns.[16] Highway investments encouraged geographically dispersed development located increasingly farther away from central cities and have played an important role in fostering residential segregation patterns and income inequalities.[17]

Displacement and gentrification are two related examples of the potentially negative impacts on low-income neighborhoods of color. The term *gentrification* refers to changes from investments that bring new businesses, housing stock, street character, and higher-income residents to low-income communities. Gentrification and displacement can result when new investments in communities occupied by low-income people and people of color produce new businesses and new and renovated housing stock that is occupied by higher-income and whiter people. There is tension between this displacement and improved community and economic services, which are highly sought goals in communities where there has been a lack of private investment. These investments result in rising property values and improved community institutions like schools and parks but also can result in the displacement (or involuntary relocation due to neighborhood affordability) of long-term, lower-income residents. Residential location and housing are directly related to the need for equitable and efficient transportation systems, especially for persons with limited mobility. When housing is destroyed for freeway projects in minority and low-income communities or becomes unaffordable, the displaced individuals have fewer options for seeking alternative housing and may end up living farther away from their jobs and social networks. Social cohesion is damaged or ruined. This will be especially burdensome if their transportation options are limited. An individual's residential location is crucial and encompasses not only issues of affordability but also issues of access to public schools, police and fire protection, and public transportation.[18]

Displacement

Transportation policies and practices of locating freeway projects in minority neighborhoods have, in a number of cases, impeded the ability of minorities to gain access to housing opportunities. Freeway alignments and expansions in urban areas typically occur where land prices are depressed—which usually corresponds with the residential neighborhoods of low-income and minority households. Such neighborhoods have little political power and experience institutional forms of discrimination, such as low-quality schools, waste transfer stations, bus barns, differential policing, lack of housing code enforcement, poor shopping opportunities, poor health care facilities, and sources of pollution. In some respects, freeway locations in cities are the progeny of "Negro removal" or "urban renewal" programs that were thought to cure "urban blight" by tearing down minorities' homes.[19]

Some freeway construction projects have destroyed thousands of residential units occupied by minority and low-income households. In some cases, community objections to proposed projects have prevented widespread displacement and other inequitable effects. For example, in 1972, individuals and organizations concerned about people who would be displaced by the proposed I-105 "Century Freeway" construction in Los

Angeles brought a lawsuit against state and federal government officials seeking injunctive relief. In 1982, the U.S. District Court approved a final consent decree requiring the state and federal defendants to provide 3,700 units of decent, safe, and sanitary replacement housing to residents who were displaced by the freeway.[20]

Another example was the proposed extension to the Long Beach Freeway (I-710) in California. In 1994, the original proposal to extend the freeway provided more measures to lessen the impact of the proposed freeway in the predominantly white communities of South Pasadena and Pasadena and fewer measures in El Sereno, an almost completely Latino neighborhood in East Los Angeles.[21] The original plan was to place mostly below-grade freeways in Pasadena and South Pasadena but not in El Sereno. Also, it would have built five tunnel sections in Pasadena and South Pasadena to "mitigate the perception of a divided neighborhood" and only one tunnel in El Sereno (including a tunnel near the South Pasadena High School, but not one near the Sierra Vista Elementary School in El Sereno). Community members objected to the extension as proposed and, through a lawsuit, were able to make the project more equitable.

CASE STUDY

In addition to disrupting otherwise thriving neighborhoods, some freeway construction has posed physical hazards to the minority and low-income individuals living near them. In Miami–Dade County, Florida, community residents remember well the detrimental impact that the construction of Interstate 95 had on vibrant African American communities and business districts in the 1950s and 1960s. The decision to widen I-95 in the 1990s exacerbated the negative impact of the highway on local residents. Not only had the community never recovered from the original highway construction—the neighborhood's property values had declined significantly over the past couple of decades as blight crept into the community—but the highway is within feet of residents' houses. The only barrier protecting homes from the noise, vibration, and danger of potential accidents was a wire fence. On several occasions, local residents reported cars, tires, and other debris flying into their yards from the freeway, and many residents were afraid to be in the rear of their houses for fear of their lives.[22]

Local residents, who were predominantly minority and low-to-middle income, argued that the placement of the freeway and the proposed expansion constituted a clear case of discrimination and environmental injustice. Their accusations were further supported by the observation that other stretches of I-95 in Miami–Dade County in areas that were typically affluent and less likely to be predominantly minority had well-built and sturdy sound mitigation walls protecting property from the highway. In response to the residents' concerns and allegations of discrimination, Florida officials quickly pulled together the financial resources to build a mitigation wall.[23]

Another example of how transportation decisions can have a negative impact on minority communities is the controversy over a proposed major road that threatens to destroy a sacred American Indian site just outside of Albuquerque, New Mexico. Community leaders there are struggling to protect the petroglyphs, a place for prayer and culture for the many Native American tribes (primarily Pueblo Indians) in that region of the country. Despite the petroglyphs' designation as a national park in 1998, developers and local politicians have repeatedly attempted to build roads through the park to facilitate access to new suburban growth farther out into the areas around Albuquerque. Through political and community organizing and legal advocacy, the Sacred Alliances for Grassroots Equality Council has succeeded in slowing efforts to develop portions of the Petroglyph National Park. Whether they will be able to completely prevent road construction through the petroglyphs remains in question because powerful interests continue to advocate for road construction.[24] Although proposed road projects would not destroy the community in which the Native Americans reside, they would be just as harmful because they would destroy a sacred site that is an integral part of their sense of community, despite a presidential Executive Order requiring federal agencies to be cognizant of adverse impacts on Indian sacred sites and to avoid them whenever possible (see Appendix II for Executive Order No. 13007: Indian Sacred Sites, May 24, 1996).

In other large construction projects—such as I-670 in Columbus, Ohio; I-94 in Detroit; I-5 in Portland, Oregon; and I-43 in Milwaukee—anecdotal evidence suggests that minority and low-income communities have been unable to prevent the displacement of large numbers of individuals and the resulting disintegration of their communities.

GENTRIFICATION

Another housing-related impact of transportation policies is gentrification. Gentrification is commonly characterized as a transformation of neighborhood conditions that encompasses physical, economic, and demographic dimensions and can be defined as "the process by which higher-income households displace lower-income residents of a neighborhood, changing the essential character and flavor of that neighborhood."[25] It occurs for a number of reasons, including increased desirability of an area due to transportation investments such as extension of commuter rail lines, new or improved train services or stations, or new highway ramps or exits. Most commonly, gentrification has been portrayed in terms of residential location patterns, such as "back to the city" relocations of middle-income households from the urban fringe, suburbs, or elsewhere within a metropolitan region.

Gentrification, however, manifests itself through reinvestment and rehabilitation of previously degraded neighborhoods, improving the physical condition and appearance of both residential and commercial properties. Due to the perception that increased property values, increased safety, and improved neighborhood amenities signal neighborhood revival, middle-income households upgrade housing conditions for their personal consumption. While owner-occupied single-family residences replace renter occupancy, businesses that target the demographic group of middle-income homeowners transform older, traditional commercial locations through reinvestment and rehabilitation of structures. Thus, the gentrification process entails physical property improvements, a demographic change to higher income levels, more "yuppie" (young, urban professional) households, and increases in property values. Some neighborhood gentrification processes absorb vacant properties, while others involve replacement (or displacement) of households no longer able to afford housing due to housing cost (price/rent) appreciation.

While some consider property value increases resulting from gentrification to be positive, such changes have also been criticized for worsening the well-being of low-income persons, especially in neighborhoods of color. Some have argued that increases in property values are capitalized in rent increases, which then push households that are less able to pay to other neighborhoods or to undesirable housing arrangements.[26] In particular, some argue that certain antisprawl land-use policies that direct housing development away from the urban fringe reduce housing affordability and limit housing choice, especially for low-income households. Others have argued, in addition to causing displacement, that gentrification is undesirable because it leads to homogenous neighborhoods that are not socioeconomically or culturally diverse.[27] However, there are insufficient data to draw specific conclusions about the net social and economic impacts of transportation investments on gentrification and displacement.

ACCESS TO EDUCATION

Creating barriers to education is another indirect effect of transportation policies. Following the U.S. Supreme Court decision in *Brown v. Board of Education*,[28] "busing" and yellow school buses became well-known symbols of the fight for equal educational opportunities for African Americans. The significance of these symbols is diminishing because more and more school systems are returning to the idea of neighborhood schools, and courts are declaring school districts "unitary," meaning, in the view of federal court judges, that they have eliminated the effects of past segregation as far as they are able. Today's transportation policies, however, still have an effect on access to educational opportunities for a number of minorities and individuals from low-income communities.

No longer do most students rely on yellow school buses to get to school. Many students depend on public transportation to attend school and college as well as to participate in extracurricular activities. Many students are driven or drive to school. A recent study of this issue estimated that nationally, during normal school hours, the majority—60 percent—of all student trips were made by car and that these were primarily trips to and from school.[29] One study found that students traveling to or from school in cities of more than 500,000 accounted for 15 percent of all public transportation trips.[30] It was estimated in 1996 that 20 percent of school children in California were using public transportation or other special transportation service to go to school and that growing numbers of students were relying on public transportation in other states such as Ohio.[31]

The National Academies' Transportation Research Board stated, "transit services in large urban areas have long been used to transport students, particularly those in high school and junior high school."[32] While there is no research documenting how many of these students taking public transportation are minorities, it stands to reason that many of the K–12 (kindergarten through 12th grade) students who depend on public transportation are minorities located in urban areas with a developed public transportation system. Supporting this idea is the fact that Los Angeles,[33] Houston,[34] and Washington, D.C.[35]—cities with significant minority populations—provide discounted public bus fares for students.

Although a large proportion of K–12 students do not need to rely on public transit to get to school, for those who do, access to that transportation may mean the difference between attending and missing school. For instance, during efforts to obtain free student transit passes from the Metropolitan Transportation Commission serving the San Francisco Bay Area, evidence was presented that students without access to public transportation would not attend school.[36] A number of high school students in Oakland and El Cerrito, which have significant minority populations, testified that they needed free transit passes because their families sometimes had to decide between food and bus fare.[37] In Portland, Oregon, the school district does not provide bus service for students living within 1.5 miles of a school. Sisters in Action for Power, an organization focusing on the interests of low-income girls and girls of color, pressed for free rides to high school on public buses after its survey of more than 2,000 students found that 11 percent reported missing school due to their inability to meet transportation costs.[38] An informal survey of more than 500 high school students in Providence, Rhode Island, found that a number whose families were unable to afford bus passes stayed home and missed school, especially during harsh winter days, and others got detention for being late because of the amount of time it took them to walk to school.[39] Currently, students attending Providence public high schools who live within three miles of their school must walk or provide their own means of transportation.

Limited funding for schools makes it difficult for school districts to transport all children in school buses. Recent severe cuts in school budgets make it likely that more school districts will need to reduce the transportation services they provide and that more children will need to rely on public transportation to attend school. Transportation policies should recognize and address this growing need.

In addition, education reform laws do not always consider the impact of access to transportation. For example, states authorizing charter schools do not always require that the schools provide transportation to students.[40] Some states that require charter schools to provide transportation to students require only that they follow the same standards of other schools in the district, such as providing transportation only to those residing in the school district in which the charter school physically exists, even though charter schools generally can enroll students from surrounding districts. This is especially ironic, because under busing for desegregation purposes, the federal courts did not require busing across school district lines. Once again, the division between suburb and central city worked against minority interests. Failure to provide transportation may reinforce the segregative effect of charter schools by limiting the ability of low-income minority students to enroll because of a lack of transportation.[41] Another education reform law, the No Child Left Behind Act,[42] allows students to transfer from "failing" schools, which are often schools with predominantly minority populations. It does not require that transportation be provided to students who wish to transfer. Although this provision has the potential to reduce segregated schools, not providing transportation to nonfailing schools means that many minority students will not be able to take advantage of this option.

Lack of access to transportation also affects access to higher education. Many people of color, for financial and other reasons, attend local community colleges or do not live on campus, often requiring that they find transportation other than walking. For example, minority students make up 30 percent of community college enrollment nationally, and their enrollment is often higher in urban areas.[43] It is likely that at least some of these students rely on public transportation. These students are likely to experience long or inconvenient commutes, as many colleges were designed to serve a region and not necessarily to be accessible by public transportation. It is not known how many students who cannot afford a car decide not to go to college or drop out in the face of an overly arduous commute on inadequate public transportation. Federal and local transportation policies must find ways to better serve the transportation needs of those most dependent on public transportation, or the dream of equal access to educational opportunities will remain deferred for many students of color.

TRANSPORTATION POLICIES AND HEALTH EFFECTS

Historically, public health concerns emerged out of the industrial revolution, as new technologies and processes were found to have deleterious effects on workers and society at large. Issues of social justice are implicit in poor public health and inequalities caused by hazards faced especially by women, children, and racial minorities. Legislation established to improve workplace conditions has dramatically improved the living conditions for millions of people.

There are great inequities in public health in the United States. Little progress has been made to narrow this gap, and by many accounts the inequities are growing. A wide range of research provides evidence that poverty, racism, sex discrimination, and low socioeconomic status are major factors contributing to poor public health and health inequalities. Other social, economic, and environmental conditions have negative consequences and contribute to pollution, lack of affordable housing, inadequate public transportation, and disparity in educational and employment opportunities. Income and social class remain strongly linked to health status in the United States, where low-income persons are more than five times as likely to suffer from poor health as are those living in high-income households.

Beyond creating obstacles to social and economic opportunities, transportation policies can also create or help to perpetuate health disparities. That racial minorities face health disparities compared with whites is widely recognized. Health professionals also recognize that addressing these inequities requires health treatment and prevention programs for individuals as well as social policy changes to address the root causes of inequity.[44]

The following discussion focuses on select significant health impacts that are directly related to inequitable transportation policies. The first is the impact of air pollution resulting from vehicle emissions. While auto travel is virtually ubiquitous throughout urban areas in the United States, in many cases the highest concentration of emissions has been shown to exist near neighborhoods with predominantly low-income, racial minorities. The incidence of poor air quality is exacerbated by residential segregation, which serves to concentrate exposure levels with elevated levels of noise, water pollution, and cancer the possible results. Epidemiologists have yet to find a causal connection between proximity of transportation facilities and disease. However, there is a firm perception among advocates for people of color that such a connection exists. Another major health issue related to transportation is personal safety, most closely related to pedestrian injuries.

The location of transportation facilities, whether roads, rail, or terminals, is influenced by the surrounding demographic and land-use characteristics. In cases where new facilities are being sited, areas with the cheapest land and other location costs are targeted. Residents in these areas are nearly always low-income or racial minorities. Negative impacts come in the form of residential displacement, as well as other negative effects on environmental quality.[45] Much of the environmental justice movement has been driven by the siting in minority areas of undesirable land uses such as industrial plants and transportation facilities.

One example is the American Marine transload facility, Hunts Point, in the Bronx, New York. This is one of the more significant environmental justice cases in New York. American Marine Rail proposed building a transload facility to handle 5,200 tons of trash per day. This facility would transfer the trash from one mode to another (truck to barge, truck to train, etc.). It was projected that the facility would receive most of New York City's waste once the Fresh Kills Landfill was closed. Local environmental groups and congressional representatives from the Bronx and Brooklyn challenged the permit after it was issued. They claimed that there was willful clustering of solid waste facilities in their neighborhoods. A New York City judge reversed the permit and demanded it back to the Department of Environmental Conservation (DEC) on the ground that the earlier ruling by the DEC did not take into account that this was a community of over 90 percent people of color with 10 already-existing waste transfer stations, a sewage treatment plant, and two contiguous parks. The issue of PM2.5[46] and the attendant health impacts were also discussed in the case. The judge concluded that it was a travesty that the DEC issued this permit without conducting an environmental impact statement (EIS).

The issue of residential mobility and segregation is directly linked to issues of environmental racism. Low-income households have little choice when it comes to locating or relocating relative to undesirable land uses. The resulting residential immobility is reinforced by transportation immobility in the form of low auto ownership rates. Low-income racial minorities end up facing relative social, economic, and spatial isolation. Again, these obstacles confound other public health issues that have explicit social justice implications. Transportation mobility is only a contributing factor to these problems along with other institutionalized structures that influence unfair land-use and public investment decisions. Other research has identified cases where public decision-making bodies are not geographically and demographically representative.

Air Pollution

Several scholarly articles in the field of public health have suggested that residential racial segregation is a primary cause of racial disparities in health.[47] One example is the link between segregation and health disparities in Detroit,[48] which has a population that is approximately 83 percent African American.[49] The evidence suggests that the transportation policies of the 1950s and 1960s—which supported highway system expansions and location of heavily traveled roads in impoverished neighborhoods in Detroit—led to residents' higher risks for a variety of diseases.[50] As mentioned earlier, a direct causal link has not been established by scientists; however, there remains a strong statistical correlation.

Like Detroit, many urban areas have significant pollution, much of which can be traced to transportation policies that favor highway development and automobile travel over public transportation. In addition, these transportation policies, combined with land-use or zoning policies, lead to more toxic usage of land in poor and minority neighborhoods than in affluent areas and areas with fewer minorities.[51] Higher percentages of African Americans (65 percent) and Latinos (80 percent) compared with whites (57 percent) live in areas with substandard air quality.[52] Research suggests that these polluted environments in turn result in higher rates of respiratory disease, such as asthma.[53]

It is known that the occurrence of asthma and asthma-related deaths is higher for African Americans and Latinos than for whites.[54] Asthma is almost twice as common among African Americans as it is among whites. Even more disturbing are the disparities in asthma deaths. While African Americans make up approximately 12 percent of the U.S. population, they account for about 24 percent of all asthma deaths.[55] A report by the EPA found that non-Hispanic, African American children who live in households with incomes below the poverty level have the highest rate (8.3 percent) of asthma of all racial groups.[56]

While it is not known to what extent these disparities are due to outdoor pollution, research studies have found a strong and significant correlation between residing near heavy automobile or truck traffic and increased difficulties with respiratory function and higher incidence of disease, such as asthma, in children.[57] Specifically, several studies have found that high concentrations of emissions from vehicles are linked to the incidence of asthma.[58] Other studies have found causes of asthma in cockroaches, thunderstorms, dust, genetics, and dirty houses, among others. Proximity to health care may cause overreporting. This can indeed be a transportation issue, in part because it may be physically difficult to get to health care facilities. A study of Atlanta during the 1996 Summer Olympics, when alternative transportation strategies were implemented[59] found that hospitals and doctors saw significantly fewer children for serious asthma problems.[60] A study examining the effect of daily air pollution levels on asthmatic children living in the Bronx and East Harlem, New York; Baltimore; Washington, D.C.; Detroit; Cleveland; Chicago; and St.

Louis found that increased exposure to certain air pollution was associated with asthma.[61]

The neighborhoods of Harlem and South Bronx in New York City have received attention because of high rates of asthma. Central Harlem's population is approximately 88 percent African American and 10 percent white.[62] South Bronx has a population of approximately 79 percent Latino and 19 percent African American.[63] Neither of these communities has been meeting air quality standards.[64] Most of the area's bus depots were sited in Harlem[65] and, like the South Bronx, it contains or is surrounded by heavily traveled commuter highways.[66] One study of these communities found that the rates of developmental and respiratory diseases (such as asthma) are disproportionately high.[67]

Personal Safety

Transportation policies that favor reliance on automobiles and result in busy roadways in minority communities also raise another public health concern: personal safety—particularly that of minorities and low-income individuals who live in urban areas. Overall, African Americans and Latinos have a pedestrian fatality rate that is almost twice as high as that of whites,[68] and they have a higher likelihood of pedestrian fatalities compared with the general population in the United States.[69] One study found that the most dangerous metropolitan areas for walking were Orlando, Tampa, West Palm Beach, Miami, and Jacksonville, Florida; Memphis and Nashville, Tennessee; Houston and Dallas–Fort Worth, Texas; and Phoenix, all areas with significant minority populations.[70] A study of Atlanta pedestrian fatality rates from 1994 to 1998 found that whites had a significantly lower pedestrian fatality rate of 1.64 per 100,000 than Latinos (3.85) and African Americans (9.74).[71] Newspaper accounts have reported that in Orange County, California, and in the Virginia suburbs of Washington, D.C., Latinos suffer a greater percentage of pedestrian fatalities than their population in those areas.[72]

Disparities in the number of pedestrian deaths are certainly related to the fact that higher percentages of people of color compared to whites do not own cars and must rely on walking as a primary mode of transportation. An analysis of 2000 census data shows that these minorities are much more likely than whites to walk to work. While 2.6 percent of non-Hispanic white workers walked to work in 2000, 3.2 percent of African American workers, and nearly 4 percent of Latino and Asian American workers, walked to work.[73]

One study found that children who are pedestrians are at increased risk for serious traumatic brain injury and lifelong disability if they live in poverty, face a large traffic volume and traffic moving at high speeds, and lack space to play other than sidewalks and streets.[74] National Highway Traffic Safety Administration (NHTSA) data show that the most dangerous roads for pedestrians are those that have multiple lanes, high speeds, no sidewalks, long distances between intersections or crosswalks, and roadways lined with large commercial establishments and apartment blocks.[75]

Relying on walking for transportation may have other negative effects. One study found that low-income mothers relying on walking as a primary mode of transportation suffered physical fatigue and stress from having to manage walking long distances with young children in all types of weather and on busy roads.[76]

Walking and bicycling have been widely promoted as efficient, low-cost ways to increase physical activity and thus improve overall health.[77] However, minorities and those who live in areas of poverty do not live in areas conducive to walking and bicycling despite high-density street networks in urban core areas. The Centers for Disease Control (CDC) identified the most common barriers preventing children from walking and bicycling to school as dangerous motor vehicle traffic and long distances.[78]

States are spending very little federal transportation funding to improve conditions for walking.[79] As documented by the Surface Transportation Policy Project, a national organization concerned with improving the nation's transportation system, "less than one percent (0.7 percent) of federal transportation construction, operations, and maintenance funds are spent to ensure a safe walking environment."[80] Transportation policy should support both public transit and safe environments for pedestrians.

SUMMARY

While examining the equity of transportation costs and benefits, it is important to consider both direct and indirect effects. Direct effects such as those from fares or taxes, which can have immediate impacts on travel behavior, can lead to longer-term, secondary impacts that can be more far reaching. The challenge then becomes to decide which aspects of equity to include and the metrics by which to evaluate them. Litman (2005) illustrates the complexity of equity analyses in his discussion of transportation equity evaluation variables shown in Table 3 below.

TABLE 3.   EQUITY EVALUATION VARIABLES

TYPES OF EQUITY	CATEGORIES	IMPACTS	MEASUREMENT UNITS
Horizontal	Demographics (including age, gender, race, ethnic group, family status)	Price or fare structure	Per capita
Vertical with respect to income and social class	Income class	Tax burdens	Per vehicle-mile or kilometer
Vertical with respect to need and ability	• Geographic location • Ability (for example, people with disabilities and licensed drivers) • Mode (walkers, cyclists, motorists, bus users, and the like) • Vehicle type (such as cars, trucks, buses) • Industry (including truckers, transit, taxis, vehicle manufactures) • Trip type and value	• Transportation service quality • External costs (including crash risk, congestion, pollution) • Economic opportunity and development • Transport industry employment and business opportunities	• Per passenger-mile or kilometer • Per trip • Per peak-period trip • Per dollar paid in fare or tax subsidy

Source: Litman (2005).

The evolution of transportation technologies and the influence of governmental policies on urban form are the subject of wide-ranging research efforts. While urban transportation improvements allow for economic growth and development within and among regions, transportation impact analysis is being confronted with the contentious nature of "economic-technological potential and environmental-social constraints."[81] Although it is recognized that transportation investments do have undesirable impacts on land use while providing a variety of benefits to firms and households, the nonuniform distribution of these benefits can be systematically biased toward particular social groups. Compared with the measurement of physical and technological impacts of urban transportation improvements, the measurement of social costs and benefits is somewhat subjective and quantitatively complex. Perhaps this is one reason the social impacts of transportation investments are so frequently overlooked.

NOTES

1. Ihlanfeldt and Sjoquist (1998).
2. Bryjak (2004).
3. Holzer (1991).
4. Gordon, Kumar, and Richardson (1989).
5. Source: U.S. Census (2001b).
6. This has been noted for some time. For example, "Most commuter-rail systems use a hub-and-spokes model, ideally suited for trips to and from a central business district" (Overton, 1994).
7. Kain (1968).
8. Wilson (1987).
9. Sanchez (2002).
10. Holzer, Ihlanfeldt, and Sjoquist (1994); Kain and Meyer (1970); Meyer and Gómez-Ibáñez (1981); Taylor and Ong (1995); Gómez-Ibáñez (1976).
11. Wachs and Taylor (1998); Ong and Blumenberg (1998).
12. Pucher and Renne (2003).
13. Murakami and Young (1997); Coulton, Leete, and Bania (1997); Meyer (1999).
14. Ong (1996); Blumenberg (2002); Raphael and Rice (2002).
15. Wachs and Taylor (1998).
16. Jackson (1985); Downs (1971).
17. Jackson (1985); Downs (1971).
18. Lee (1997).
19. powell and Graham (2002).
20. Bullard and Johnson (1997).
21. Lee (1997).
22. Stolz (2002).
23. Stolz (2002).
24. SAGE Council (2004).
25. The study by Kennedy and Leonard (2001) has more on the debate over the exact definition of "gentrification."
26. Sanchez (1998).
27. Hodge (1980); Laska and Spain (1980).
28. Brown v. Board of Education of Topeka, 347 U.S. 483 (1954).
29. Transportation Research Board (2002). This study estimated that 25 percent of trips were on school buses, and only 2 percent were by public transit.
30. American Public Transportation Association (n.d.). In cities with populations of 50,000 to 199,999, trips to or from school were 26 percent of all transit trips.
31. Transportation Research Board (2002), p. 17.
32. Transportation Research Board (2002), p. 16.
33. See the Los Angeles County Metropolitan Transportation Authority's Web site at www.mta.net/metro_transit/ fare_info/discount_passes_students .htm describing discounted fares for elementary, middle, and high school students (retrieved on January 19, 2005).
34. See the Metropolitan Transit Authority of Harris County, Texas, Web site at www.hou-metro.harris.tx.us/services/ fares01.asp describing reduced fares for middle and high school students (retrieved on January 18, 2005).
35. See the Washington Metropolitan Area Transit Authority Web site at www.wmata.com describing reduced fares for D.C. public school students (retrieved on January 19, 2005).
36. See Metropolitan Transportation Commission (2001), which describes the MTC's consideration of a proposal to provide free bus passes for low-income students as a means to improve student attendance.
37. Cabanatuan (2001).
38. Haley (2000); Girls Initiative Network. As a result of the efforts of Sisters in Action, Portland's transit agency serving the three-county area provides free bus rides to low-income high school students.
39. DARE Seeds of Change (2003).
40. Some states that do require charter school to provide transportation to students include Florida, Illinois, Kansas, Massachusetts, North Carolina, and New Jersey.
41. For more information about the segregative effect of charter schools, see Frankenberg and Lee (2003).

42. 107–110 Pub. Law § 1116.
43. The American Association of Community Colleges states that, "in urban areas, community college enrollments reflect the proportion of minorities in local populations" (American Association of Community Colleges, n.d.).
44. National Association of County and City Health Officials (2002).
45. Forkenbrock and Schweitzer (1999).
46. PM2.5 refers to particulate matter that is 2.5 micrometers or smaller in size.
47. Schulz et al. (2002).
48. Schulz et al. (2002).
49. U.S. Bureau of the Census (2001a).
50. Schulz et al. (2002).
51. Maantay (2001).
52. Frumkin (2002), citing Wernette and Nieves (1992).
53. Wjst et al. (1993); Weiland et al. (1994); Oosterlee et al. (1996); Mortimer et al. (2002).
54. Frumkin (2002); Centers for Disease Control (2002b).
55. American Lung Association (2000).
56. U.S. Environmental Protection Agency (2000).
57. Wjst et al. (1993); Weiland et al. (1994); Oosterlee et al. (1996); Mortimer et al. (2002).
58. Friedman et al. (2001); Lin et al. (2002).
59. These included "an integrated 24-hour-a-day public transportation system, the addition of 1,000 buses for park-and-ride services, closure of the downtown sector to private automobile travel, altered downtown delivery schedules." (Friedman et al. 2001).
60. Friedman et al. (2001).
61. Mortimer et al. (2002).
62. New York City Department of City Planning (2002).
63. New York City Department of City Planning (2002).
64. Perera et al. (2002).
65. National Association of County and City Health Officials (2002).
66. Perera et al. (2002).
67. Perera et al. (2002).
68. Centers for Disease Control and Prevention (n.d.).
69. Surface Transportation Policy Project (2002).
70. Surface Transportation Policy Project (2002).
71. Frumkin (2002), p. 117.
72. Frumkin (2002), p. 117; Surface Transportation Policy Project (2002), p. 13.
73. Data source: U.S. Bureau of the Census (2000).
74. Rivara (1999).
75. Frumkin (2002); see also Surface Transportation Policy Project (2002).
76. Bostock (2001).
77. For example, see Centers for Disease Control and Prevention (2002a), and Pucher and Renne (2003).
78. Centers for Disease Control and Prevention (2002a).
79. Surface Transportation Policy Project (2002).
80. Surface Transportation Policy Project (2002).
81. Nijkamp and Blaas (1994).

5

Transportation Policy and Equity in the United States

Nondiscrimination and achievement of environmental justice in relation to transportation actions funded by the federal government have been mandated by Title VI of the Civil Rights Act of 1964, the Federal-Aid Highway Act of 1970,[1] Executive Order No. 12898, U.S. Department of Transportation (USDOT) Order on Environmental Justice (DOT Order 5610.2), and the Federal Highway Administration's Order to Address Environmental Justice (6640.23). In addition, in the 1998 Federal Aviation Administration (FAA) Strategic Plan, a commitment was made to monitor FAA compliance with the DOT order on environmental justice. The identification and addressing of environmental justice is a requirement in all stages of federal processes and decision making to the greatest extent practicable and permitted by law, including transportation planning of alternatives and mitigation. This chapter identifies specific policies that have direct bearing on transportation equity and environmental justice concerns.

TITLE VI OF THE CIVIL RIGHTS ACT OF 1964

Title VI of the Civil Rights Act of 1964[2] prohibits discrimination on the basis of race, color, or national origin by recipients of federal financial assistance. It applies to all recipients of federal aid, such as state departments of transportation and metropolitan planning organizations (MPOs). Title VI also applies to all programs run by federal aid recipients, regardless of whether the specific program is federally funded.

Prohibited discrimination includes denial of benefits or services, provision of inferior benefits or services, segregation, and any other treatment of an individual or a group differently and adversely in the provision of benefits or services because of race, color, or national origin. The federal courts have defined these criteria to include limited English proficiency and accent. For example, a Title VI violation would occur if a state transportation agency decided to furnish replacement housing to whites but not to people of color being displaced because of a highway project.

In 2001, the U.S. Supreme Court in *Alexander v. Sandoval*[3] ended the ability of private individuals to bring a suit to enforce the Title VI regulations. Federal regulations under Title VI prohibit recipients of federal funds from conducting activities that have a less favorable effect or "disparate impact" on members of one racial or ethnic group than on another. Now individuals may bring lawsuits charging a violation of the Title VI statute only when they can prove that an action was taken intentionally to discriminate. They can no longer rely solely on statistical evidence to show that an action had a disparate impact on persons of a specific race, color, or national origin. Federal agencies, however, still can and must enforce the regulations. Individuals and groups can still file administrative complaints with federal agencies. These complaints are supposed to be investigated and findings made. Federal agencies may suspend or terminate funding to obtain compliance with Title VI or may seek equitable relief, such as an injunction. However, this is rarely done, and there are allegations that federal agencies are not sufficiently vigorous in their enforcement of the law.

The Supreme Court decision argues for the federal government to more rigorously enforce Title VI because individual lawsuits or lawsuits brought by advocacy groups are now severely limited. It is much harder to prove discrimination by intent rather than by disparate impact. Disparate impact is discrimination that results from methods of program administration or facially neutral practices that, though uniformly applied to all persons, nonetheless have the effect of disproportionately excluding members of a protected class; denying them an aid, benefit, or service; or providing them a lower level of service than others.

USDOT regulations require states to use a range of measures to ensure compliance with Title VI. States are required to have an adequately staffed civil rights unit, have procedures to address civil rights complaints, collect statistical data on protected populations, conduct annual reviews of programs, provide training for staff to explain Title VI obligations, and submit annual updates to the regional federal highway administration offices, among others.[4]

Through the issuance of the executive order on environmental justice and DOT guidance, the federal government clarified Title VI requirements as they relate to transportation issues. Specifically, the order requires all federal agencies to make achieving environmental justice part of their mission by identifying and avoiding "disproportionately high and adverse" effects on minority and low-income people. DOT's final guidance on implementing the order described the process for incorporating environmental justice principles into DOT programs, policies, and activities.

Furthermore, the Federal Highway Administration (FHWA) and Federal Transit Administration (FTA) issued internal guidance on "Implementing Title VI Requirements in Metropolitan and Statewide Planning."[5] This document focused primarily on public involvement and planning activities to be evaluated during an MPO certification process and the process for approving statewide transportation improvement programs and lists a series of questions to aid in verifying compliance with Title VI. Examples include:

- What strategies and efforts has the planning process developed for ensuring, demonstrating, and substantiating compliance with Title VI? What measures have been used to verify that the multimodal system access and mobility performance improvements included in the plan and transportation improvement program, and the underlying planning process, comply with Title VI?
- Does the public involvement process have an identified strategy for engaging minority and low-income populations in transportation decision making? What strategies, if any, have been implemented to reduce participation barriers for such populations? Has their effectiveness been evaluated? Has public involvement in the planning process been routinely evaluated as required by regulation? Have efforts been undertaken to improve performance, especially with regard to low-income and minority populations? Have organizations representing low-income and minority populations been consulted as part of this evaluation? Have their concerns been considered?

Although helpful for community organizations and federal aid recipients, the guidance failed to address the concerns most often raised by community groups regarding the accumulation of negative economic and environmental impacts caused by transportation projects and their location and the distribution of resources across metropolitan communities over time. The guidance called for processes to review potential Title VI or environmental justice issues, but it established no thresholds, expectations, or standards for these reviews.

THE DEPARTMENT OF TRANSPORTATION'S
ENFORCEMENT OF CIVIL RIGHTS

Although the federal government states that it is committed to the enforcement of Title VI, there appears to be little actual enforcement. For example, states receiving federal funds, in most cases, simply submit a single-page document assuring their compliance with Title VI requirements, including DOT regulations, without any accompanying evidence to support their assurance.

In addition, FHWA received fewer than 20 Title VI complaints in 2002 and initiated no Title VI investigations. In comparison, the Equal Employment Opportunity Commission (EEOC) received 29,910 race-based employment discrimination complaints and filed 246 lawsuits against employers in 2002. The U.S. Department of Education's Office for Civil Rights received 870 Title VI discrimination complaints based on race in 2000. We do not know why the volume of Title VI complaints to FHWA is so low, but possible factors include lack of information about how to file a complaint, perception that filing a complaint would not be effective, and lack of information about the agency's authority to enforce Title VI.

In August 2002, DOT's Director of Civil Rights issued a "White Paper on Civil Rights Operations at the U.S. Department of Transportation." In the paper, the director acknowledged that numerous studies had raised concerns regarding the authority of the agency's Civil Rights Office, the priority of the civil rights mission within the agency, the adequacy of resources and staffing, and the inability to establish clear measurements for performance and effectiveness. Regarding specific concerns raised in the document, the director commented that lack of resources prevented DOT from conducting audits of federal aid recipients, conducting pre-award reviews and full compliance reviews, monitoring federal aid recipients, and developing and implementing improved policies. Further, the director acknowledged that DOT is unable to provide sufficient technical assistance to regulated entities and the public, and its capacity to conduct internal training is limited.

In addition, the paper stated that independent reviewers have noted that collaboration among civil rights offices within DOT historically has been weak. The civil rights function is scattered widely in the agency, hampering coordination by administrative offices. An example of this lack of coordination can be found in the technical assistance and enforcement structure within FHWA and FTA. FHWA's Office of Civil Rights is responsible for Title VI compliance reviews, but the bulk of them are conducted by FHWA's divisional offices. There is one divisional office for each state, and each of them has, at most, one civil rights staff person and several planning staff. The FTA has its own civil rights staff and has offices at the regional level rather than the divisional level.

In the case of a recent civil rights complaint in Montgomery, Alabama, community members who filed the complaint with both FHWA and FTA traveled to Atlanta to meet with their regional FTA office. There they found not only that the regional staff were unaware of their complaint but also that their communications with the divisional FHWA staff had not been forwarded to their FTA regional counterparts. Because of these problems, some advocates have turned to environmental laws, community organizing techniques, and political pressure to seek protections for minority communities.

LEGISLATION AND EXECUTIVE ORDERS

National Environmental Policy Act of 1969 (NEPA)

The requirements of the National Environmental Policy Act of 1969 (NEPA) unquestionably apply to transportation decision-making processes.[6] In some instances, NEPA has given minority communities some protections because of the strong procedural requirements for public review and consideration of alternatives and mitigation involved at the transportation project stage. Specifically, NEPA requires (1) identification of the purpose and need for a proposed project or program; (2) an assessment of a project's or program's environmental effects "including human health, economic, and social effects" on minority and low-income communities and Indian tribes; (3) consideration of alternatives when significant impacts are expected; (4) identification of mitigation measures to eliminate or minimize significant impacts; and (5) a public process for review of need, impacts, alternatives, and mitigation options.

NEPA challenges to highway proposals increasingly highlight the lack of analyses examining cumulative environmental and social impacts in efforts to stop destructive transportation projects. Cumulative impacts on health and the environment result from the incremental impact of the proposed action when added to past, present, and reasonably foreseeable future actions, regardless of which agency or entity (federal or non-federal) or person undertakes such actions. Cumulative impacts result from actions that may be individually minor but are collectively significant over a period of time. At the plan level, it is important to focus on the combined effects of a series of actions occurring over a longer period of time (compared with individual actions at the project level). Some impacts may not be significant at the project level but may be quite appreciable when the combined effect of a series of actions is considered. MPOs and state transportation departments need to consider not only travel patterns encouraged and secondary land-use impacts but also the consequences for access and mobility, household expenditures for transportation, and urban congestion. However, groupings of unrelated projects from different infrastructure segments that have adverse effects on a community are usually not considered.

Laws and policies protecting people of color are often more difficult to advance than policies protecting the environment. For example, the Endangered Species Act (ESA)[7] effectively protects endangered species whose habitats are threatened with harm by transportation projects, but similarly strong laws are not in place to protect minority and low-income communities from inequitable transportation projects. Lawsuits under the ESA can effectively bring a project to a halt, while those under the civil rights statutes almost never can. For example, the Longhorn Pipeline project in Texas was held up for some time because it threatened an endangered salamander. It also threatened Mexican Americans, but their concerns were not sufficient enough under federal law to delay the project. See, for example, this excerpt from a fact sheet from the City of Austin, Texas:

> *Could endangered species be impacted?*
> Yes. Barton Springs Pool, the surrounding springs, and the aquifer are the only known habitat for the endangered Barton Springs Salamander. Barton Springs is the primary discharge point for water and contaminants entering the Barton Springs Segment of the Edwards Aquifer. Innumerable caves cover this segment of the Edwards Aquifer. Many of these provide habitat for cave-adapted species, classified as species of concern. In addition, explosions or fires resulting from accidents or spills could burn habitat for the endangered golden-cheeked warbler and black-capped vireo. Secondary impacts to these species may occur from stressed or denuded vegetation due to contaminant toxicity.[8]

No mention is made of people. In *Spiller v. White*,[9] on December 12, 2003, the U.S. Court of Appeals for the Fifth Circuit upheld a lower court's decision that federal agencies adequately complied with the law in determining that operation of the Longhorn gasoline pipeline would not significantly affect the quality of the human environment. Longhorn may therefore proceed with pipeline development and operation. The judge noted, "Congress has only authorized federal courts to ensure the agencies considered all the relevant factors and has not permitted this Court to decide whether the Court would let Longhorn shoot gasoline through 52-year-old pipe for 731 miles where failure would be disastrous for thousands of people for years to come," and ruled for the agencies and Longhorn. Thus, even "thousands of years" of potential adverse effects to people do not trump the rights of an endangered salamander. One can legitimately wonder if we have our priorities right.

Specific impacts on open spaces, plant and animal habitats, and other ecosystems tend to be easier to quantify than social and economic impacts such as decreased housing affordability, unemployment, weakened economic development, and weakened neighborhood cohesion.[10] NEPA requires an assessment of the impact of any planned transportation project on the environment and *community* before the project can begin.[11] Although some consideration has been given to quantifying or determining how to measure the impact on a community, little attention has been given to conducting these types of assessments.[12]

Current environmental justice efforts related to transportation are encouraging public involvement during the impact assessment phases of project development that can be crucial for residents of disproportionately impacted neighborhoods. While some policy makers are seeking to streamline the approval process for transportation projects, including the environmental impact assessment, assessing the impact on the community is a requirement that was never seriously implemented.

A major difference between environmental and civil rights law considerations is that environmental law considerations can stop a project, while civil rights law considerations typically do not take effect until after the project is under way. NEPA contains a requirement for mitigation; civil rights laws contain a requirement for remediation following a violation (discrimination) finding. Mitigation includes *avoiding* the impact by not taking or modifying an action; *minimizing, rectifying,* or *reducing* the impacts through redesign or operation of the project or policy; or *compensating* for irreversible impacts by providing substitute facilities, resources, or opportunities.[13] Individuals and groups are severely constrained in bringing federal civil rights suits; aggrieved individuals and groups are much less constrained under federal environmental law.

Executive Order No. 12898

On February 11, 1994, President Clinton issued Executive Order No. 12898, "Federal Actions to Address Environmental Justice in Minority Populations and Low-Income Populations."[14] The Environmental Justice (EJ) Executive Order requires federal agencies, to the greatest extent practicable and as permitted by law, to achieve environmental justice by identifying and addressing disproportionately high and adverse human health and environmental effects, including interrelated social and economic effects, of their programs, policies, and activities on minority and low-income populations. While the executive order was intended to improve the internal management of the executive branch and not to create legal rights by any party against the United States, federal agencies are required to implement its provisions "consistent with, and to the extent permitted by, existing law."[15] One of the laws directly implicated by EJ is Title VI of the Civil Rights Act of 1964, as amended. Title VI prohibits discrimination on the basis of race, color, and national origin by recipients of federal financial assistance. To implement the executive order, the U.S. Department of Transportation (DOT), on February 3, 1997, issued a Departmental Order on EJ.[16]

The EJ Executive Order instructed federal agencies to make decisions on projects and activities that have an impact on the environment so as to avoid disproportionately high and adverse effects on minority and low-income populations. This executive order recognized the growth of a new social movement, environmental justice or environmental racism, which has grown since the early 1980s. In regard to transportation, EJ advocates believe that "suburban sprawl, degradation of undeveloped lands, increased per capita energy consumption, flight of capital from urban centers, disaggregation of communities, and worsened air quality are largely a result of transportation policy decisions."[17] EJ advocates often believe that institutionalized decision making systematically results in choices that are adverse to the populations explicitly covered by EJ efforts.

In 1997, DOT published DOT Order 5610.2, its own EJ instructions, requiring programs, projects, and activities of DOT to avoid such impacts where possible. The DOT order makes use of concepts from Title VI of the Civil Rights Act of 1964, which prohibits discrimination on the basis of race, color, and national origin by recipients of federal financial assistance. Although the environmental justice executive order imposes duties only on federal agencies, Title VI applies to all federal financial aid recipients.

The 10 operating administrations of DOT must include EJ concepts in their planning, evaluation, and decision processes. Heavy emphasis is placed on early, serious, and accessible public participation. EJ also affects how organizations implement NEPA processes, adding much more emphasis to socioeconomic considerations.

Welfare Reform and Transport Mobility

Passage of the Personal Responsibility and Work Opportunity Reconciliation Act of 1996 (PRWORA) moved the existing welfare system—administered by the U.S. Department of Health and Human Services Department (DHHS)—from a cash-assistance program to one with a principal goal of transitioning participants from welfare to work. This act constituted a devolution of primary responsibility for welfare administration from the federal government to states and localities through block grant allocation of funds. Additional legislation supported this initiative and involved other federal agencies in achieving the goal of moving unemployed persons receiving public assistance to stable employment. The Balanced Budget Act of 1997 then established the Welfare to Work Program in the U.S. Department of Labor. Welfare reform legislation recognized several barriers to employment, among them being transportation mobility. The Transportation Equity Act for the 21st Century (TEA-21) recognized the role of the U.S. Department of Transportation (USDOT) in these efforts and committed resources to addressing the mobility needs of welfare recipients. The following discusses these three legislative measures, focusing on the transportation provisions of each measure and evaluation of the efforts to date.

Personal Responsibility and Work Opportunity Reconciliation Act of 1996 (DHHS). Effective October 1, 1996, the Aid to Families with Dependent Children (AFDC) and Job Opportunities and Basic Skill Training (JOBS) programs under the Social Security Act were replaced with a single, combined program. Block grant funding was provided to states by this program for fiscal years 1996 through 2002 with federally approved plans for Temporary Assistance for Needy Families (TANF) with a minor child. Once authorized, a state could use the block grants "in any manner reasonable calculated to accomplish TANF purposes; or in any manner . . . under the former AFDC and JOBS programs."[18] During the application process, state representatives were required to assess a recipient's skills, prior work experience, and employability to determine the level of support needed to achieve self-sufficiency. An individual responsibility plan was to be developed for each recipient that could include assistance for substance abuse treatment, child care, and medical care needs. The state could also use program funds for pre-pregnancy family planning services, home heating and cooling costs, other social service programs, funding development accounts for first home purchase and other qualified purchases, and for payments to job placement agencies. Both the authority and the flexibility to use these grant funds and those provided under the JOBS program allowed program funds for transportation purposes. However, the use of funds for transportation was not expressly provided for in the bill, and therefore each state differed in its respective policies about such provisions.

Specifics for Transit Mobility and Low-Income Wage Earners. The Welfare Reform Bill of 1996 sought to provide a variety of incentives for TANF recipients to achieve and maintain employment. The bill also increased the flexibility of states to develop programs that addressed the unique needs of their populations. Because a majority of welfare recipients do not own automobiles, many need an alternative form of transportation to get to and from work. The bill did not, however, specifically recognize or address the transportation needs of low-income wage earners.

Welfare to Work Program: Title IV, Part A of Social Security Act (DOL). Welfare to Work (WtW) funds were allowed to be used specifically for transportation services under "Support Services";[19] however, few details or guidance were given pertaining to these types of services. Further, other communications from the agency (Transmittal No. TANF-ACF-PA-00-2) indicated that WtW funds cannot be used for personal vehicle acquisition and cited part of the 20 C.F.R. § 645. There is no mention of this exclusion in the federal regulations, however. This has important implications for transportation mobility programs targeting auto ownership.

Evaluation of Efforts. In May 1998, the Government Accounting Office (GAO) (now Government Accountability Office) issued a report entitled, "Welfare Reform: Transportation's Role in Moving from Welfare to Work."[20] This report followed the 1996 adoption of the PRWORA and was issued during the deliberation on passage of TEA-21.[21] The purpose of the report was to (1) determine if current studies and research demonstrate the importance of transportation services in implementing welfare reform, (2) assess the preliminary results of FTA's current welfare-to-work programs and the Department of Housing and Urban Development's Bridges to Work program, and (3) determine how an Access to Jobs program would support welfare reform.[22]

The GAO report provided a profile of welfare recipients, showing that 75 percent of them live in either the central city or rural areas, with 25 percent living in the suburbs. Fifty percent of welfare recipients lived in central cities, compared with 30 percent of the total population. The majority of welfare recipients were single mothers, and approximately half have children under school age. In addition, nearly 75 percent of these females had a high school diploma or less education.

The lack of transportation mobility among welfare recipients was illustrated in the report by low rates of vehicle ownership, in some cases as low as 6 percent. In addition to low incomes, the low vehicle ownership rates may have been caused by previously established asset limitations in federal law of $1,000 per vehicle. This represented a significant challenge given that most states had overall resource limits of $3,000 for aid recipients (depending on such factors as household size, age of household members, and program participation). Approximately 26 states have since instituted rules that exempt the value of one or more vehicles from the resource limitation calculations. Some argue that asset limitations force welfare recipients to own older, poorly maintained vehicles, which appears to contradict other federal policy objectives such as the Clean Air Act for vehicle emissions and fuel efficiency standards.[23] With exemption of the value of the first vehicle, welfare recipients are no longer forced to sell their transportation in order to qualify for benefits.

The GAO report found that transit services inadequately met the travel needs of welfare recipients. The report found that 70 percent of such jobs (entry-level jobs are typically in the manufacturing, retailing, and wholesaling sectors) were located in the suburbs. Only 32 percent of these employers were within a quarter mile of a transit stop. Some of these locations were served by commuter rail, which was considered by many to be too expensive for low-income wage earners. The GAO report also found that entry-level jobs typically have nonpeak hour work shifts. Given that most welfare recipients are single mothers with children needing day care, the added travel requirements make transit significantly more time consuming compared with automobile travel. To meet these travel needs, more flexible approaches would need to be implemented, as will be discussed in a review of FTA's Job Access and Reverse Commute (JARC) program.

The GAO report also focused on evaluating other existing welfare reform programs. One demonstration program described was JOBLINKS. In Louisville, Kentucky, for instance, the program provided an express bus to an industrial park, reducing the commute from two hours to 45 minutes. In Fresno, California, the program provided transportation services to employment training centers in attempts to reduce the dropout rate. Of 269 participants, only 20 completed the program, and three had found jobs. These numbers were not particularly impressive on their own; furthermore, no baseline data were provided to indicate increases in program completion. The cost of the program was not provided, but speculation about the cost-benefit of such a program leads to questionable conclusions about its success.

Another program, HUD's Bridges to Work, attempted to address the perceived geographic mismatch of unemployed and underemployed workers with available jobs. One strategy was to provide better access to those jobs. The overall program goal was to place 3,000 participants in five cities in suburban jobs within four years. After two years, only 429 individuals had been placed in jobs. Some observers concluded that the reason for the low success rate was that the program accepted only job-ready applicants; however, the numbers of so-called "job-ready applicants" were not provided to support this conclusion.

The conclusions from the two demonstration projects, combined with the knowledge of welfare recipient profiles and existing transportation systems, led the GAO to make specific recommendations for implementation of the job access program. Principally, the GAO recommended that any program should be designed and implemented to include requirements for coordination among agencies and service providers. It was also recommended that "coordination"—as referenced in the authorizing legislation—be defined or have general guidelines provided to agencies making application. Considerable focus was placed on developing program objectives and specific criteria for project outcomes to ensure a means to measure the success of the program. The GAO noted that currently, under the Government Performance and Results Act of 1993, USDOT does not have a benchmark to measure the success of moving people to jobs—rather, such benchmarks focus on the "building and sustaining of transportation systems" but not on examining how they function to address the needs of society.

Transportation Equity Act of the 21st Century (TEA-21)

The FTA Access to Jobs program comprised two types of projects: job access and reverse commute. The job access projects were intended to provide new or expanded transportation services to help welfare recipients and eligible low-income individuals (those at or below 150 percent of the poverty line) get to jobs and other employment-related services (such as education, training, and child care). These projects could cover the capital or operating costs of equipment, facilities, and maintenance; promote transit use by workers with nontraditional schedules; support the use of transit vouchers; and support employer-provided transportation, including the transit pass benefit under the Internal Revenue Code of 1986 (section 132). Typically these services have included shuttles, vanpools, and additional buses to local scheduled service.

Reverse commute projects are those that transport individuals to suburban employment centers from urban, rural, and other suburban locations for all populations. Specifically, projects have included subsidies for additional reverse-commute bus, train, carpool, van routes, or service; subsidized van or bus purchases or leases by a nonprofit organization or public agency to shuttle employees from their residences to a suburban workplace; or anything to facilitate the provision of public transportation services to suburban employment opportunities.

While the Job Access and Reverse Commute (JARC) grants provided funding specifically for transportation projects, TANF and WtW also made funds available for the same purposes (providing mobility for low-income persons). The focus of the JARC grants appeared to be the strongest in the areas of mass public transportation funding. The requirement of coordination for JARC grants is a hallmark in transportation planning. By contrast, TANF and WtW programs do not require such extensive coordination. The JARC coordination requirement may serve to ensure that transportation service providers are in direct contact with persons with transportation mobility needs.

Evaluation of Efforts. In October 1999, the GAO published a report on transportation efforts in welfare reform. The report, entitled "Transportation Coordination: Benefits and Barriers Exist, and Planning Efforts

Progress Slowly,"[24] was commissioned to review (1) the benefits of and incentives for human services transportation coordination; (2) DHHS's and FTA's efforts to identify barriers to transportation coordination; and (3) DHHS's and FTA's efforts to enhance coordination through state and local transportation planning.

Addressing the first purpose, the GAO identified studies that concluded that coordination of transportation services resulted in cost savings. Specifically, the Community Transportation Association of America (CTAA) concluded that the average cost per passenger trip decreased from $7.92 to $4.06, and the average cost per vehicle-hour declined from $12.83 to $6.89 when services were coordinated.[25] CTAA also found that, in the experience of Medicaid transportation services coordination, issuance of monthly passes instead of per trip reimbursement may have substantial cost savings. Specifically, it was estimated that if just one percent of Medicaid recipients in metropolitan areas went to a monthly pass rather than individual tickets, savings of $215 million annually would result. The Flint, Michigan, school district provided students with passes on the Michigan Transit Authority instead of providing a separate school bus network, which lowered the average transportation cost per student from $660 to $264. The GAO also reported that coordination of transportation would improve clustering of passengers to use fewer one-way trips and to encourage sharing of equipment, personnel, and facilities. Reduced duplication of services and economies of scale were also anticipated. Such efforts were purported to improve overall regional mobility.

The report described a coordinating council between DHHS and USDOT (FTA's parent agency). The council struggled to agree on both planning guidelines for coordination and a strategic plan. The problems in reaching agreement were attributed to uncertainty regarding federal responsibilities for transportation (statutory, regulatory, and programmatic), fragmented accounting and reporting, uncertainty about using resources for other than program constituents, and prohibition against charging fares under the Older Americans Act. Other barriers identified included inadequate information technology (such as linking of Internet resource sites), the need for better data for project evaluation, and the challenges of coordinating between different levels of government.

The agency comments on this report spoke to the "devolution" initiative—the movement to reduce federal imposition into local issues. The imposition of the various legislation and programs is moving

USDOT, DHHS, the Department of Labor, and other agencies toward a multicentered federalism with shared responsibilities in meeting the needs of society. Rarely have transportation providers had to coordinate with social service providers (DHHS, Labor, and the like), and they have limited experience working with each other. Similarly, DHHS, under a system of providing checks to constituents or participants, has not had to concern itself with the issue of why individuals are unable to find and maintain employment. Problems arise around the ambiguity of agency goals as well as differences in principal missions and objectives. Traditionally, the USDOT has been a single-mission organization, while DHHS and Labor have had multiple objectives. These agencies also have generally different constituencies. These factors contribute to the problems surrounding coordination of services.

The GAO found that in 1999, 67 percent of the grantees were traditional transportation organizations. The nontraditional organizations that participated included human service agencies, employers, and metropolitan planning organization (MPO) agencies. Arguably, the last category of organizations—MPOs—were not new to applying for transportation grants and therefore were in a position to take a leadership role for coordination in metropolitan areas. Further, legislation requires coordination through MPOs in areas with population over 200,000. Most of the grants were to be used for expanding or providing links to existing transit and for information and education. Of the 181 grants awarded, 122 went to transit agencies, 13 went to community organizations, and the remainder was awarded to other government agencies. Half of the funding went to existing services, and the other half went to nontraditional services, including vans, shuttles, and demand-responsive systems. Other services included guaranteed rides home, vouchers, and traveler information systems targeted at low-income wage earners. Some of these services may also benefit all users of the transit system, beyond just low-income or unemployed persons.

Safe Accountable Flexible and Efficient Transportation Equity Act— A Legacy for Users (SAFETEA-LU)

In 2005, the U.S. Congress approved legislation renewing the nation's highway and public transportation laws. The bill, called the Safe Accountable Flexible and Efficient Transportation Equity Act—A Legacy for Users (SAFETEA-LU or HR 3), passed overwhelmingly, while being broadly criticized for including more than 6,000 pet projects and costing

$286 billion over six years. Scattered within the bill were several provisions that have implications for transportation equity and civil rights:

- Guarantees more than $700 million for the Job Access and Reverse Commute program by turning it into a formula grant program to the states. The bill also increases the federal share of projects to 80 percent, which will make it easier to get these projects funded. Unfortunately, Congress failed to close a loophole in the bill that could allow JARC funds to be used on projects not targeted at low-income residents, but that is something that can be organized around at the local, metropolitan, and state levels.
- Clears the way for local hiring agreements that could create job and training opportunities for low-income residents on more than $200 billion in federally aided highway projects.
- Requires public participation plans to be developed with the involvement of local residents in the metropolitan transportation planning process and requires greater financial transparency. The final bill also includes language requiring the use of visualization techniques and mandating that public involvement meetings be held at times convenient to local residents.
- Sets aside $1 million each year for transportation equity research demonstration programs to improve the quality and quantity of information available on the impact of transportation on low-income and minority communities.

In addition, the final bill included a new stand-alone New Freedom program designed to help people with disabilities to gain access to jobs otherwise out of their reach, and the bill increases funding for programs for elderly individuals and rural transportation providers. The bill also requires greater coordination among providers of public transportation and human service providers in the development of transportation programs and retains the Clean Fuel Bus Formula Program, which the administration had attempted to eliminate. The overall effect of these and other provisions will likely be minor in comparison with those in previous bills.

EQUITY AND THE COURTS

In the case of governmental services, the courts ultimately decide questions of distributional fairness, when these issues are brought to them under existing law. Municipal corporations are subject to legal rules

South Camden Citizens in Action v. New Jersey Department of Environmental Protection

An important recent federal court decision involving environmental justice concerned an African American and Hispanic community in Camden, New Jersey, that did not want a cement plant located in the community because of allegations of increased air pollution. The community wanted consideration by the State of New Jersey Department of Environmental Quality of the cumulative effects of all the present polluting projects and those planned in and around the minority community. The District of New Jersey Federal District Court ruled in favor of the community and granted a requested injunction against the cement plant.

Immediately after the U.S. Supreme Court eliminated an important legal avenue for civil rights plaintiffs in the case of *Alexander v. Sandoval*, the judge in the *Camden* case asked litigants to file briefs regarding its effect on their case. The judge kept the residents' case alive by invoking 42 U.S.C. § 1983, a federal law enacted after the Civil War to prevent states from revoking the federal rights of freed slaves, as adequate legal justification for their suit.

However, the *Camden* case, which artfully relied on Section 1983, instead of Title VI, to allow a private enforcement action, was set aside by the Court of Appeals. On December 17, 2001, it ruled that ruled that 42 U.S.C. § 1983 cannot be used to enforce a federal regulation "unless the interest already is implicit in the statute authorizing the regulation." In January 2002, the Third Circuit Court of Appeals denied the plaintiffs' request for a rehearing from the entire Third Circuit Court of Appeals. The State of New Jersey has since developed new environmental justice/equity consideration standards for proposed projects.

concerning the equitable distribution of public services. According to the equal protection clause in the Fourteenth Amendment of the U.S. Constitution, governmental services must be provided in a nondiscriminatory way throughout communities. The equal protection clause has been a way for the Supreme Court to rule unconstitutional many discriminatory state practices, including school segregation, malapportionment of state legislatures, and residency requirements for welfare recipients. Enforcement of the equal protection clause has also offered remedies for blatant discrepancies in governmental service allocation, such as lack of services in certain neighborhoods. The evaluation criterion of the court is of particular importance to planners. Planning policy that is legally viable will be durable and stand a better chance of discouraging or minimizing the service delivery inequities. The following discussion summarizes four court cases that illustrate the fundamental aspects of governmental service delivery equity.

Hawkins v. Town of Shaw[26] was the landmark case that elevated alleged municipal service inequities to the level of a constitutional equal protection issue. *Shaw* was a class-action suit filed on behalf of a group of African Americans in the Mississippi town of Shaw. The group claimed that town officials discriminated against them in their allocation of municipal services and that this discrimination was racially motivated. Initially, a U.S. District Court dismissed the complaint, but the plaintiffs appealed. Thus, the case was decided on appeal when the court reversed and remanded the district court's decision. *Shaw* is an ideal plaintiff's case in that inequalities of service along racial lines were blatant and statistically evident. The appellate court held that there were disparities in service provision based on the fact that nearly 98 percent of all homes fronting on unpaved streets in town were occupied by blacks and 97 percent of homes not served by sanitary sewers were in black neighborhoods. Furthermore, all new mercury vapor streetlights had been installed in white neighborhoods. Though the court decided in favor of the plaintiffs in *Shaw*, it made no attempt to formulate a measure for equity in municipal service delivery, and it did not set up any tests to resolve future legal disputes in the area. Nevertheless, as remedy for the perceived inequities, the court ordered the town of Shaw to submit a plan for the court's approval detailing how the town proposed to cure the results of a long history of discrimination. Unfortunately, most cases involving challenges to service equity are not blatant; rather, they have subtle and complex disparities to be found within large and complex urban systems.[27]

Beal v. Lindsay[28] required the application of the decision reached in *Hawkins v. Town of Shaw*. The action in *Lindsay* was brought by black and Puerto Rican residents of Crotona Park in New York City. They alleged that the city unconstitutionally discriminated against them by failing to maintain their park in a condition equivalent to that of other multicommunity parks in the Bronx. The court of appeals held that considerations of pleadings and other materials established that no remedy could be made to the plaintiffs because the city showed that it had provided an equal or greater input of services to the park but could not achieve the same results because of continued vandalism. The city supplied an affidavit by the Parks, Recreation and Cultural Affairs Administration detailing the facts that the municipal effort at Crotona Park was as good as or better than that at other Bronx parks. The city cited the fact that there were more personnel assigned to Crotona than to any other park and that the city had held meetings with community representatives to discuss how the situation could be improved. The city had set aside $75,000 to hire an architect or planner to work out a redevelopment plan, and $1.5 million would be allocated to this effort. Furthermore, the court found that the equal protection clause, while it does prohibit less state effort on behalf of minority racial groups, does not demand the attainment of equal results when extenuating circumstances such as vandalism prevail over the intended results. In the court's opinion, the city had met its constitutional obligations by providing equal input. Moreover, the court stated that *Hawkins* relied on "a substantial qualitative and quantitative inequity in the level and nature of services accorded 'white' and 'black' neighborhoods in Shaw" that was not present in *Lindsay*. Once again, however, the court did not venture to state how the qualitative and quantitative inequity should be measured for future litigation.[29]

The case of *Washington v. Davis*[30] had a significant impact on how the court viewed cases of racial discrimination. Unsuccessful black applicants to the police department claimed that a written personnel test was racially discriminatory. The plaintiffs provided evidence that passing rates for the personnel test were significantly different for whites and nonwhites, suggesting that applicants were not treated equally with respect to race. The court stated that, "Disproportionate impact is not irrelevant, but it is not the sole touchstone of an invidious racial discrimination forbidden by the constitution." This case shifted the requisite proof of discrimination from the evidence of disproportionate treatment to evidence of intent to discriminate. In the case of public service delivery, it can take extremely subjective measures to show purpose or intent in discriminatory practices, unless a strong historical or administrative record can be brought into question.

In *Ammons v. Dade City*,[31] the court's basis for discrimination in delivery of street paving, street resurfacing and maintenance, and stormwater drainage facilities relied on the concepts of "disparate impact" and "discriminatory intent." As in *Shaw*, the court found that there was significant statistical evidence for service disparity, considering service coverage and service expenditure levels in white and black residential neighborhoods. The court also found in *Ammons v. Dade City* that there was discriminatory intent. With multiple tests for intent, the findings were comprehensive and "covering practically every aspect of municipal conduct in Dade City throughout its history." Four factors established by the court for this purpose were (1) *discriminatory impact*, which was shown through the evidence of service level disparity; (2) *foreseeability*, which reflected the predictability of service deprivation due to current allocation processes; (3) *legislative and administrative history*, which was documentation of actions taken by the municipality that indicate a pattern of discrimination; and (4) *knowledge*, where the court felt that city officials had prior knowledge of the existing conditions. This case drew from the legal standards set by *Hawkins v. Shaw* and *Washington v. Davis*.

The case of *Ammons v. Dade City* provides a useful foundation for an equity-planning approach to governmental service delivery. Previous distributional analyses have concentrated on "discriminatory impact," providing evidence of service level disparities through quantitative analysis. However, very little analysis has been applied to examining the "foreseeability" of service allocation processes such as the capital improvement planning process. The standard of "legislative and administrative history" was used by the courts to establish the existence of a pattern of negligence toward providing similar levels of service to all households. It is likely that only in blatant cases will "prior knowledge" of service discrimination by governmental officials be documented. The concept of prior knowledge is useful for the evaluation of service delivery systems suspected of discriminatory practices. However, this type of investigation would not be part of a proactive equity-planning framework.

The fact that discrimination is illegal does not in itself ensure that all citizens will be treated equally. When appeals to local representatives by citizens contesting the fairness of service provision fail, challenges can often be pursued through the courts. Because this is the final source for redress, public service delivery policy should be structured so that it can avoid such challenges. With a dearth of case law to adequately define how the court will treat such challenges, it is important to consider the primary elements of the cases presented here. The court has used statistical data to decide cases of inequitable service distribution. However, little precedence regarding accepted quantitative methods exists.

It is possible that, if more communities employ indicators of equity for governmental service delivery, the courts will confront the viability of a range of indicators. More legal challenges will be needed for a consistent set of measures to emerge.

SUMMARY

In the current period of domination of the federal courts by conservatives, the trend is for contraction of governmentally protected civil rights. The U.S. Supreme Court has even overturned portions of federal laws strongly established by Congress. For example, the Americans with Disabilities Act has been diluted, especially in its definition of who is a person with a covered disability. While federal agencies are charged with enforcing the civil rights laws in regard to their funded programs, they are generally doing a poor job. As discussed elsewhere, the private right to file suit has been eviscerated by the Supreme Court. Federal agencies should make efforts to replace these private plaintiffs but have not. The prospects for new federal equity policy that would expand rights are practically nil. In September 2005's Hurricane Katrina, the nation saw the continuing vestiges of past illegal and legal segregation. Low-income African Americans were trapped in rising floodwaters and were de facto segregated in sports stadiums without food, water, restrooms, and public safety. While the federal government's public pronouncements sound as if something will be done in regard to this section of the nation's underclass, little has been forthcoming. Rather, waivers and privileges have been granted to employers and large companies to erase the few protections that did exist.

It has been said that the civil rights era is over, and it may be. On the other hand, the obvious separation of the races as seen in the aftermath of Hurricane Katrina may reawaken public consciousness, and the pendulum may swing back to increased public services. Regardless, the lingering effects of conservatives on the courts will be with us for at least a generation. It is hard to predict whether policy or law will solve the situation of increasing inequity in the United States. If change is to occur, it will probably be from community organizing, coalition building, and use of state law. As we have discussed, certain trends in transportation, such as increased use of economically regressive road and lane tolling, mirror the increased income and wage gap in the United States and thus exacerbate legal inequality with continued economic inequality.

NOTES

1. 23 U.S.C. § 109(h).
2. Title VI of the Civil Rights Act of 1964, 42 U.S.C. § 2000(d), *et seq.*
3. 532 U.S. 275, 121 S. Ct. 1511 (2001).
4. 23 C.F.R. Part 200, § 200.9.
5. U.S. Department of Transportation (1999).
6. See the U.S. Department of Transportation's Federal Highway Administration Web site. Transportation decision-making factors. Retrieved on March 6, 2005, from www.fhwa.dot .gov/environment/nepa/decision.htm.
7. Endangered Species Act of 1973, 16 U.S.C. § 1531.
8. *Austin City Connection* (2001).
9. 352 F.3d 235 (5th Cir. 2003).
10. Almanza and Alvarez (1995); Forkenbrock, Benshoff, and Weisbrod (2001).
11. National Environmental Policy Act, 42 U.S.C. §§ 4321–4347. Other laws and regulatory documents also require that the impact on a community be considered in transportation decision-making processes. See the FHWA's and FTA's environmental justice Web site. Retrieved on March 15, 2005, from www.fhwa.dot.gov/environment/ ejustice/facts/index.htm.
12. For example, see Brock et al. (1996).
13. 40 C.F.R. § 1508.20.
14. See Appendix III for the text of Exec. Order No. 12898.
15. 59 *Fed. Reg.* 7632–7633 §§ 6-608 and 6-609.
16. 62 *Fed. Reg.* 18377 (April 15, 1997).
17. Association of the Bar of the City of New York, Committees on Environmental Law and Civil Rights (February 13, 1996).
18. Pub. L. 104–193.
19. 20 C.F.R. § 645.220(f)(1).
20. GAO/RCED-98-161.
21. Pub. L. 105–178.
22. GAO/RCED-98-161, p. 1.
23. Dill (2001).
24. GAO/RCED-00-1.
25. CTAA (1998).
26. U.S. 437 F.2d 1286 (1971).
27. Lineberry (1974).
28. 468 F.2d 287 (1972).
29. Hagman (1980).
30. 426 U.S. 229, 48 L.Ed.2d 597 (1976).
31. 783 F.2d 982 (11th Cir. 1986).

CHAPTER

6

Extending Transportation Equity

Transportation equity is rooted in environmental racism and environmental justice and, over the last several years, has focused primarily on racial discrimination. The negative impacts identified include residential displacement, neighborhood disintegration, and environmental and health impacts resulting from new or expanded transportation infrastructure. More recent research has broadened the range of impacts to include employment accessibility, transportation service quality, wage inequality, transit fares, and safety issues. Yet, equity analyses have remained focused on race and class. Race and economic class are inextricably linked in the United States, despite many Americans thinking that racial tension is a thing of the past. Events arise, however, that expose an underclass whose situations are worsened by a lack of transportation equity. In fact, limited transportation mobility choice affects an underclass that reaches beyond race and class.

A 2003 report published by the Civil Rights Project at Harvard University sought to broaden the definition by which transportation equity is viewed by including discussion of gender, age, nationality, and English-language proficiency. Even so, the report relied upon a relatively narrow conception of transportation equity. By comparison, "social exclusion" in the United Kingdom focuses on constraints that prevent people from participating adequately in society, including education, employment, and public services and activities. Inadequate transport sometimes contributes to social exclusion, particularly for people who live in auto-mobile-dependent communities and are physically disabled, low income, or unable to own and drive a personal automobile. Because civil rights and social equity are not limited to race and class, neither should be the whole scope of transportation equity in the United States. In this chapter, we briefly discuss some aspects of transportation equity that move beyond the standard transportation equity framework. The following discussion will briefly consider indigenous peoples, language barriers, and racial profiling. In addition, issues of business and economic opportunity within the transportation industry are discussed from an equity perspective. Equity in transportation usually focuses only on transportation as a service and not as an industry. Chapter 7 will discuss age and physical disability as dimensions of equity that further extend the range of transportation equity.

NATIVE AMERICANS AND TRANSPORTATION EQUITY

Native Americans are a distinct example of an underserved population suffering from most, if not all, of the ill effects associated with transportation inequities. Indian tribes are nations within a nation in the United States. Their transportation needs are similar to the rest of the nation in terms of mobility and economics but have specific perspectives, often based on traveling long distances by road in rural areas. The relationship between tribes and the federal government is unique compared with that of other ethnic groups and the central government. By treaty, Indians have a government-to-government relationship. From its earliest days, the United States has recognized that Indian tribes possess attributes of sovereignty.[1] In addition, in early Indian treaties, the United States pledged to "protect" Indian tribes, thereby establishing one of the bases for the federal responsibility in government-to-government relations with Indian tribes.[2] These principles—the sovereign powers of Indian tribes to engage in self-government and the federal trust responsibility to the tribes—continue to guide the national policy toward Indian tribes. Pursuant to this national policy, Congress has enacted numerous statutes that affirm the authority of Indian tribes to engage in self-governance.[3]

Even with these sovereignty rights, which other racial and ethnic groups do not possess, tribes are not better off than other demographic groups. They often feel disadvantaged in transportation issues. Historically, railroad development has worked against them, for example, in helping to settle the Great Plains with Anglos. The impacts extend beyond the quality of transportation services, with some of the North Central tribes having serious concerns about transportation of nuclear waste across their lands. To help compensate for these disparities, distribute the benefits of transportation more widely, and help knit the country together, Congress has granted certain transportation benefits by statute.

Some may say that this is in fulfillment of promises committed to in treaties. One example is the U.S. Department of Transportation's (USDOT) Indian Reservation Roads (IRR) program of the Federal Lands Highways Program (FLHP). The IRR system provides access to and within Indian reservations, Indian trust land, restricted Indian land, and Alaskan Native villages. These roads link Native American housing, schools, emergency services, and places of employment. An adequate system of roads and bridges is a key element of economic development on tribal lands. More than two billion vehicle miles are traveled annually on the IRR system, although it is among the most rudimentary of any transportation network in the United States. More than 66 percent of the system is unimproved earth and gravel, and approximately 26 percent of IRR bridges are deficient. These conditions make it very difficult for residents of tribal communities to travel to hospitals, stores, schools, and employment centers.

The poor road quality also affects safety. The annual fatality rate on Indian reservation roads is more than four times the national average. TEA-21 clarified that funds under the IRR program shall be available to tribal governments from the Bureau of Indian Affairs (BIA) for direct contracting of transportation projects. TEA-21 also required the development of an IRR program funding formula and regulations through a negotiated rule-making procedure that reflects the unique government-to-government relationship between the Indian tribes and the United States. The Federal Highway Administration (FHWA) and the BIA, in consultation with tribal governments, have developed the "Indian Reservation Roads Program Transportation Planning Procedures and Guidelines" (TPPG). It has been widely distributed to the tribes as guidance on transportation planning. The TPPG clarifies policies related to funding issues and eligible activities and defines the relative transportation planning roles and responsibilities of the BIA and Indian tribal governments.

Indian Reservation Roads Bridge Program (IRRBP)

TEA-21 also directed the Secretary of Transportation, in cooperation with the Secretary of the Interior, to establish a nationwide priority program for improving or replacing deficient Indian reservation road bridges, using a set-aside of not less than $13 million of IRR funds per year. After soliciting comments on project selection and fund allocation procedures, through meetings with tribal representatives and a Federal Register notice, the FHWA developed guidance for the bridge program that was published as an interim final rule in July 1999. FHWA followed up with training sessions on the bridge program and has worked with the BIA and tribal governments to maximize the number of bridges participating in the IRRBP. To financial year 2002, $27.6 million was obligated for 51 bridge projects. Based on BIA plans, FHWA expected to obligate an additional $18.3 million for another 40 bridge projects.

Highway Safety in Indian Country

Motor vehicle deaths among Native Americans are substantially higher than for the rest of the nation's residents. In 2005, the Centers for Disease Control and Prevention reported that Native Americans die on highways at rates 1.7 to 2.0 times the national average.[4] Indian Health Service (IHS) statistics put the highway death rate for Indian country at 33 per 100,000, more than twice the rate reported for the rest of the nation. Depending on the region, motor vehicle deaths vary dramatically.[5] The Navajo area, encompassing the entire Navajo Nation, and the Aberdeen area, encompassing tribes in the Dakotas, Nebraska, and Iowa, have the highest rates, according to the IHS. The Billings area, covering Montana and Wyoming, and the Phoenix area, covering Arizona, Nevada, and Utah, follow closely. The high rate among Native Americans is attributed to several factors, including poor road conditions, low seat belt use, and alcohol. In particular, alcohol is twice as likely to be a factor in motor vehicle accidents for Indians as the general population, according to the IHS.[6]

Despite the disparity, the motor vehicle death rate in Indian country has decreased over the past two decades. In 1998, for example, it was 52.2 per 100,000 compared to 19.7 per 100,000 for the general population. Besides combating drunk driving, tribes have enacted mandatory seat belt laws. After the Navajo Nation enacted a seat belt law in 1998, the tribe saw seat belt use jump from 14 percent to 75 percent and the number of accidents drop. The costs associated with motor vehicle injuries also dropped by more than $10 million.[7]

Another benefit received by tribes, in distinction from other racial and ethnic groups, is Indian preference in employment. This occurs through the Indian Preference Act.[8] Applicants claiming Indian preference must submit verification of being Indian, as certified by tribe of affiliation or other acceptable documentation of Indian heritage.[9]

In *Morton v. Mancari*,[10] the Supreme Court upheld a Bureau of Indian Affairs hiring preference for certain members of federally recognized tribes as a "political rather than racial" classification. The Court specifically noted that the hiring preference at issue was "not directed toward a 'racial' group consisting of 'Indians'; instead, it applied only to members of 'federally recognized' tribes. This operated to exclude many individuals who are racially to be classified as 'Indians.'"[11] The Court held that this sort of "political rather than racial" preference would be upheld "[a]s long as the special treatment can be tied rationally to the fulfillment of Congress' unique obligation toward the Indians."[12]

In *Rice v. Cayetano*, for example, the Court recognized that "Congress may fulfill its treaty obligations and its responsibilities to the Indian tribes by enacting legislation dedicated to their circumstances and needs,"[13] but declined to address the substantial, unresolved question "whether Congress may treat the native Hawaiians as it does the Indian tribes," preferring instead to "stay far off that difficult terrain."[14] To the extent, however, that the programs reauthorized by S. 2711 could be viewed as authorizing the award of grants and other government benefits on the basis of racial or ethnic criteria, rather than tribal affiliation, the *Mancari* standard would not apply, and they would be subject to strict scrutiny under *Adarand Constructors, Inc. v. Pena*.[15]

Although Congress has broad powers over Indian affairs, pursuant to the Indian Commerce Clause of the Constitution, the Supreme Court, in *United States v. Sandoval*,[16] stated that this power extends only to "distinctly Indian communities." In modern parlance, "distinctly Indian communities" are federally recognized tribes.[17] Under the Supreme Court's decisions in *Mancari, Adarand,* and *Rice,* legislation providing special benefits to Indian individuals who do not have a clear and close affiliation with a federally recognized tribe likely would be regarded as a racial classification subject to strict constitutional scrutiny rather than as a political classification. It therefore would be necessary to show that any such use of race-based criteria to award government benefits is "narrowly tailored" to serve a "compelling" governmental interest.[18]

An example of tribal hiring preferences is the system known as Tribal Employment Rights Offices (TERO), which enforces tribal employment rights ordinances and which usually provides for Indian preference in any employment, contract, and subcontract conducted on or near a particular reservation. The purposes of the TERO Ordinances often include but are not necessarily limited to:

(a) To ensure that no covered employer discriminates against any tribal member or Indian in any aspect of employment, including but not limited to, hiring, promotion, demotion, transfer, change in work status, lay-offs, and termination from employment.

(b) To require that all covered employers give preference to qualified Indians in all aspects of employment, including but not limited to, hiring, promotion, demotion, transfer, changes in work status, lay-offs, and termination from employment.

(c) To require that all entities awarding contracts give preference to Certified Indian Preference Contractors for contract and subcontract work on the Reservation.

(d) To require all covered employers to utilize the TERO Hiring Hall in all hiring with respect to work to be performed on the Reservation.

(e) To require, in appropriate cases, that covered employers establish needed training programs intended to combat the effects of discrimination.

(f) To provide services to covered employers to assist them in meeting their requirements under this Ordinance, in locating qualified Indians to fill employment needs, establish needed training programs and meet federal requirements guarding against discrimination.

(g) To require all covered employers to contribute to the services provided by and the enforcement of this Ordinance by the fees established herein.[19]

Another protection granted by executive order of the president, rather than by treaty or statute, is Executive Order No. 13007, "Indian Sacred Sites" (see Appendix II). Executive orders only compel federal agencies to action and do not have the force of law. They can be ended or superseded by a new president. This executive order requires federal land managing agencies to accommodate access to and ceremonial use of Indian sacred sites by Indian religious practitioners and to avoid adversely affecting the physical integrity of such sacred sites. It also requires agencies to develop procedures for reasonable notification of proposed actions or land management policies that may restrict access to or ceremonial use of, or adversely affect, sacred sites.

Recognition of public participation, in the strong form of self-determination, is covered in Public Law 93-638—Indian Self-Determination and

Education Assistance Act, as amended. This is the response by Congress, in recognition of the unique obligation of the United States, to the strong expression of Indian peoples for self-determination, assuring maximum Indian participation in the direction of education as well as other federal services for Indian communities so as to render such programs and services more responsive to the needs and desires of Indian communities.

Indian transportation measures are of contemporary interest. For example, two tribal riders found their way into the $286.4 billion highway transportation bill that was signed into law on August 10, 2005. The first rider blocks the Environmental Protection Agency from recognizing tribal authority over tribal lands in Oklahoma without the state's consent. Tribes seeking "treatment as state" designations for water and air programs must sign a "cooperative agreement" with the state and must submit to a public hearing. The second rider also comes courtesy of members of Oklahoma's congressional delegation. It can be noted that Indians in Oklahoma sometimes have particular influence over elected officials because there are no reservations in Oklahoma—Indians there live "on the economy." The delegation changed an existing law to prevent the Shawnee tribe from acquiring trust lands just about anywhere in the state. The provision is aimed at blocking a casino in downtown Oklahoma City. The rider removes the mandatory aspect of the acquisition and forces the tribe to go through the two-part determination process for gaming, a move that requires state approval. Tribal officials have always said they planned to work with the state and local communities, but the process places an extremely high bar on the casino.

LANGUAGE BARRIERS

Like other obstacles to transportation accessibility, language barriers that are not addressed diminish social and economic opportunities, particularly for racial and ethnic minorities. Language barriers affect a person's ability to travel (such as by preventing a person from obtaining a driver's license) and prevent individuals from communicating their transportation needs to policy makers. How transportation policies are decided and who is able to influence those decisions have played important roles in creating and sustaining the inequities of transportation policies.

In particular, many Latinos and Asian Americans face language barriers. The 2000 census data show that only 1 percent of whites and 1 percent of African Americans speak English "not well or not at all," compared with 24 percent of Latinos and 17 percent of Asian Americans.

At the same time, Latinos and Asian Americans are the fastest-growing minority populations in the United States, suggesting that language barriers will continue to grow as a transportation accessibility issue.

Latinos account for 50 percent of all of those who speak English not well or not at all. Of those who speak English not well or not at all, 23 percent use public transportation to travel to work. These facts suggest that transportation agencies and those collecting transportation data would be able to serve and reach a significant portion of the population with language barriers by translating documents, announcements, and meeting proceedings into Spanish. Of course, every community has populations that differ in composition and may have significant non–Spanish-speaking populations with language barriers whose needs should also be addressed.

Collection of transportation data often fails to include individuals with limited ability to communicate in English. For example, the National Household Travel Survey, which is the only comprehensive survey of American travel behavior, was conducted only in English until 2001. The 2001 survey was offered in Spanish as well as English, but non-English speakers made up only 1.9 percent of the sample. In addition, the survey is conducted only on the telephone, so those who are less comfortable speaking English are more likely to decline to participate; responses from deaf persons are also unlikely to be included.

Figure 10. Multi-language Public Information

Source: Federal Interagency Working Group on Limited English Proficiency

Executive Order No. 13166, "Improving Access to Services for Persons with Limited English Proficiency," issued in August 2000, specifically addresses the need to improve access to federally funded programs and services for persons whose English abilities prevent them from effectively interacting with social service providers (see Appendix IV for EO 13166). The order reiterates the principles of nondiscrimination embodied in Title VI of the Civil Rights Act of 1964, which states that federally funded programs or services cannot discriminate based on national origin. Specifically, the order clarified to recipients of federal funds that "failing to provide meaningful access to individuals who are limited English proficient" may constitute national origin discrimination under Title VI. In addition, it required federal agencies to provide guidance to recipients of federal funds and create internal guidance for their own agencies to ensure compliance with the order and the 1964 Civil Rights Act.

In 2001, DOT issued "Guidance to Recipients of Special Language Services to Limited English Proficient (LEP) Beneficiaries." DOT's guidance emphasizes that recipients of federal funds "should take reasonable steps to ensure LEP persons are given adequate information, are able to understand that information, and are able to participate effectively in recipient programs or activities." It outlined the elements of an effective language assistance program. In particular, it suggested that recipients should "(1) conduct a thorough assessment of the language needs of the population and communities affected by the recipient, (2) develop and implement written language assistance plans, (3) ensure staff understand the recipient's language assistance policy and are capable of carrying it out, (4) provide necessary services to LEP persons, and (5) conduct regular oversight of their language assistance programs."[20]

This guidance suggests that data gathering for the transportation planning process must be done in a way that represents the service area and the people living there. Transportation planning agencies should assess the languages used, needs, and ability levels of the population, and adjust their data-gathering instruments and methods accordingly. These agencies must also allow meaningful access for those with limited English abilities to participate in the planning and data-collection processes.

Although no comprehensive survey has been conducted to determine how many transportation agencies have implemented strategies for overcoming language barriers, some agencies have taken steps to address the needs of those who are not proficient in English. For example, the New York City subway system has various multilingual maps and brochures as well as a language line that provides multilingual assistance for all transit-related matters every day from 6:00 a.m. to 9:00 p.m. The Washington, D.C., Metro system publishes its Metro guide in 10 languages in addition to English. Another example is the Minnesota Department of Transportation, which requires publishing notices in non-English newspapers, printing notices in languages other than English, and providing translators at public meetings as part of its "Public Involvement Procedures for Planning and Project Development." The Metropolitan Transportation Commission (MTC) for the San Francisco Bay Area has translated several documents, provided services, and provided translation services in languages other than English. Addressing language barriers in transportation planning is particularly important for public policy because leaving out large proportions of urban limited-English–speaking populations gives an inaccurate picture of service needs and concerns.

RACIAL PROFILING

Racial profiling includes the alleged practice by police officers of stopping African American and Hispanic drivers because of their color, using legitimate law enforcement goals as a pretext.[21] USDOT become involved in racial profiling, or "driving while black/brown" (DWB), because of efforts to encourage primary seat belt laws and because of airport security screening efforts. Primary seat belt laws permit police officers to stop and ticket drivers because they are not wearing seat belts. There is fear in some parts of the African American and Hispanic communities that such laws will permit more racial profiling under cover of law.[22] There are also allegations that airport security screeners select an unduly high percentage of air travelers of color and of Arab descent or appearance or Arabic accent for additional bag searches and screening at terminal security stations.[23] Bias-based traffic law enforcement, commonly referred to as "racial profiling," may involve differential treatment based solely on any number of personal attributes. This would, for example, include the stopping of motorists, the detention of a person, and/or the searching of a vehicle based solely on the individual's race, ethnic origin, gender, age, or income status. In other words, there is no legitimate cause to stop. Most law enforcement officers agree that this practice is unacceptable; yet some officers engage in this practice on a regular basis. The issue of considering race as a personal characteristic for a criminal offense that has been committed is not in question. The use of race, ethnicity, gender, age, or income status as a characteristic in general enforcement is illegal and undeniably discriminatory. Bias-based traffic enforcement is inconsistent with the most valued principles of policing. It is an indefensible police tactic that lurks behind the guise of enforcing the law.

To determine whether or not racial profiling exists requires, among other steps, collection of data in a systematic and objective way. Examples of how this can be done are discussed below, including essential elements of profiling data collection:

1. *Race/Ethnicity of Motorist.* It is critical to obtain information regarding the race/ethnicity of motorists stopped by police. Without this information, it is impossible to determine whether and to what extent people of color are stopped at a disproportionate rate.

2. *The Reason for the Stop.* People of color are often stopped for extremely minor traffic violations, such as burned-out license plate lights, overly worn tire tread, or failure to use the turn signal properly. These violations are often ignored when committed by white motorists, but law enforcement often uses these minor traffic violations as an excuse to stop, interrogate, and sometimes search people of color. Without information regarding the reason for the stop, it is impossible to know whether motorists of color are being singled out and stopped for minor violations that are ignored when committed by whites.

3. *Whether a Search Was Conducted.* Search data are absolutely essential. In some jurisdictions, people of color and whites may be stopped at similar rates, but people of color are searched at dramatically higher rates. If data are collected regarding only who is stopped, it may seem as if no discrimination is occurring, when in fact discrimination is rampant. In Maryland, for example, a study of traffic stops revealed that although African Americans composed only 17 percent of the drivers on the road, they accounted for nearly 75 percent of people who were stopped and searched. Racial profiling is partly an issue of who gets stopped, but it is also an issue of who gets searched and treated like a criminal once the stop has been made. Data on the race of motorists who are searched are equally important as data on the race of motorists who are stopped.

4. *Whether Drugs or Other Evidence of Illegal Activity Was Found.* It is not enough simply to learn that a search was conducted. Without information regarding whether drugs or other evidence of illegal activity was actually found during the search, it is impossible to rebut

the argument often made by law enforcement that it makes sense to target people of color because they are the ones most likely to be engaged in criminal activity. Studies of racial profiling have demonstrated that the "hit rate" for people of color and whites is nearly identical. Despite the widespread belief to the contrary, people of color are no more likely than whites to be carrying drugs in their cars. These data are necessary to eliminate racial stereotypes within and outside law enforcement regarding who the likely criminals are.

5. *Whether a Citation Was Issued or Arrest Was Made.* People of color regularly complain that they are stopped and questioned about who they are, where they are going, and what they are doing in a particular neighborhood and are sometimes searched and then released without a ticket or citation of any kind. The reason no citation is issued is because the supposed traffic violation was not the real reason for the stop. Indeed, the classic "DWB" stop is one in which the driver is stopped, questioned, and/or searched but no citation is issued. Assessing the extent of this practice is possible only if these data are collected.

USDOT and many other law enforcement jurisdictions believe in the efficacy of seat belt laws.[24] There are two types of safety belt laws: primary and secondary. A *primary* (standard) safety belt law allows law enforcement officers to stop a vehicle and issue a citation when the officer simply observes an unbelted driver or passenger. A *secondary* safety belt law means that a citation for not wearing a safety belt may be written only after the officer stops the vehicle or cites the offender for another infraction. Primary safety belt laws are much more effective in increasing safety belt use because people are more likely to buckle up when there is the perceived risk of receiving a citation for not doing so.[25]

In June 2002, the average safety belt use rate in states with primary enforcement laws was 11 percentage points higher than in states without primary enforcement laws.[26] A common fear among African Americans and Latinos is that these laws will be used as a pretext by law enforcement officers to stop them for "driving while black/brown."

How should transportation planners take these fears into consideration? There is debate as to their legitimacy, but perceptions of discrimination dominate the work of those in the civil rights law enforcement field. Certainly if one asks African American men about their experience while driving, many will relate stories of being pulled over, stopped, and questioned by police officers for no good reason or on a pretext, such as a tail light being out. As the racial profiling expert John Lamberth has noted, "This overwhelming evidence against the proposition that minorities are more likely to commit crimes that can be discerned during vehicle searches points out how counterproductive racial profiling is. That is, by concentrating on minorities, law enforcement ineffectively uses valuable time and resources by engaging in search activities that are likely to be unproductive."[27] Transportation planners already take into consideration subjective viewpoints, such as aesthetics and perceptions of safety and vulnerability. They can also take perceptions of discrimination into consideration. Putting people's minds at ease is one way to create a more egalitarian society. It has been hypothesized that white fear of African American men helped drive racism in the American South. Stanford professor George M. Fredrickson has stated, "Extreme racist propaganda, which represented black males as ravening beasts lusting after white women, served to rationalize the practice of lynching."[28] It seems reasonable that African American and other minorities' fears should be taken into consideration to create and sustain good relations between the races.

UNEQUAL ACCESS TO TRANSPORTATION CONSTRUCTION OPPORTUNITIES

While minorities often suffer the burdens of having large transportation construction projects placed in their neighborhoods, they do not usually reap the benefits of lucrative contracts or high-paying jobs in the construction industry. Policy makers generally contend that every $1 billion in federal infrastructure investment creates approximately 30,000 to 40,000 jobs in construction and related industries. For communities affected by these investments, the associated noise, dust, and inconvenience of the construction further intensify frustrations with transportation policies. Adding insult to injury, many communities have noted that too many of these jobs are filled by workers living in other neighborhoods and completely outside the area. Too little attention has been paid to who gets these jobs and whether any of those who live in the communities burdened by the transportation projects benefit by obtaining employment to construct the highways and transportation enhancements and associated infrastructure.

Local Minority and Low-Income Hiring Preferences

Federal law has acknowledged the value of allowing hiring preferences for individuals in certain low-income communities—local hiring preferences for workers on tribal reservations and in the Appalachian region of the country are or have been allowed—but these preferences overlook most of America's low-income communities, particularly in urban areas. TEA-21 allowed states to use a percentage of federal transportation funding to pay for supportive services to help women and minorities enter the transportation construction trades, but few states exercise this option.

In Los Angeles, a coalition of community groups, churches, and local elected leaders persuaded the Alameda Corridor Transportation Authority to incorporate a local hiring preference into the contract for a multibillion-dollar multimodal project. The project involved excavation of a 21-mile trench under numerous major and minor roads to lay a rail bed that now links the ports of Long Beach and Los Angeles to distribution centers in downtown Los Angeles. The project runs through a number of very poor and minority communities in South Central and East Los Angeles.

The contract required that 30 percent of all hours worked on the midcorridor portion of the project go to local residents. It also funded a pre-apprenticeship program, which provided stipends for 650 local residents. More than 700 pre-apprenticeship program graduates were placed in jobs in the construction industry; 188 received jobs on the project. Local residents performed 31 percent of all hours worked on the midcorridor section of the project, and 75 percent of them were minorities. Of that group, 190 were former welfare recipients, and 102 were women with children. The project finished on time and under budget.

The Alameda Corridor program succeeded only because a portion of the project was funded by a loan from DOT rather than a federally aided highway grant. The only portion of the project on which the Alameda Corridor Transportation Authority could require a local hiring preference was on the midcorridor portion; other portions of the project were excluded. Initially, the Alameda Corridor Transportation Authority would not agree to a local hiring preference unless DOT clarified that such a preference was legal. Grassroots groups successfully sought an opinion from DOT, which authorized the local hiring preference on the midcorridor portion of the project but concluded that Congress would need to create a new exemption to allow future local hiring preferences on federally aided highway projects.

The significance of hiring local residents to work in the transportation construction industry extends beyond a particular construction project. As the overrepresentation of Latinos in the construction industry suggests, these job opportunities provide the real possibility of sustained employment in a well-paying industry with the prospect for career growth. Given projected growth in the industry and the transferability of construction skills, strategies that ensure greater participation by minorities in local construction projects ultimately may create significant employment opportunities for minorities, particularly for low-income families with few other options.

Minorities' and Women's Employment in Transportation Construction

Minorities and women are either underrepresented in the construction industry or tend to be concentrated in the lowest-paying jobs. According to the U.S. Bureau of Labor Statistics, of the more than 6.25 million people employed in the construction industry, the percentages of minorities and women in the construction trades were: 2.5 percent women, 7 percent African Americans, and 17 percent Latinos/Hispanics.

By comparison, 2000 census data showed that women make up almost 51 percent of the U.S. population, African Americans approximately 12 percent, and Latinos/Hispanics 12.5 percent, indicating that women and African Americans are clearly underrepresented in the construction industry. While Latinos/Hispanics are overrepresented compared with their population in the United States, Latino construction workers are likely to be among the lowest-paid workers. Census data show that Latinos have lower incomes than non-Hispanic whites, and recent data from the Bureau of Labor Statistics reveal that the median weekly earning of Latinos is lower than that of all other racial groups.

Specific data on minority and female representation in the transportation construction trades, however, are currently unavailable. The agency responsible for tracking this information is the Federal Highway Administration (FHWA, which is part of DOT), and within FHWA this duty has been delegated to the Office of Civil Rights (OCR). States are required to submit annual reports to FHWA OCR based on data submitted to them by primary contractors about their workforces. Because of resource and staffing constraints, however, the FHWA OCR has not collected, compiled, or analyzed these data since 1995.

Given these data limitations, it is possible only to hypothesize about the economic benefit women and minorities receive from major federal investments in highway and transit construction. The majority of highway and street construction jobs are unionized positions and pay relatively well. According to the Bureau of Labor Statistics, the mean annual wage of managers in the transportation construction industry is more than $70,000; in construction and extraction, the mean annual wage is $35,000. Despite these good jobs, many low-income and minority community members look on investment in transportation construction with some skepticism because they often do not see women, minorities, or local residents holding jobs on construction projects in their communities. In addition to having the potential to increase employment opportunities for minorities, transportation policies can assist businesses owned by women and minorities. In 1998, when Congress was debating TEA-21, one of the most controversial elements of the proposal was DOT's Disadvantaged Business Enterprise (DBE) program, which was established by President Reagan in 1983.

The purpose of the program was to help small businesses owned and controlled by disadvantaged individuals, including minorities and women, by ensuring that they get a portion of the construction business generated by federal transportation funding. Although minorities represent more than 28 percent of the population, according to DOT, they own only 9 percent of all construction firms and received only about 5 percent of construction receipts. Women-owned construction firms receive only 48 cents of every dollar that they would be expected to receive based on their market availability. The purpose of the DBE program is to address these inequalities.

Since enactment of TEA-21, the DBE program has withstood various court challenges. In the most recent challenge, the current DBE program, which the federal government had refined from the original program, was found to meet constitutional scrutiny. In *Adarand Constructors, Inc. v. Slater*, the 10th Circuit Court found in 2000 that the program is narrowly tailored to meet a compelling state interest and therefore does not violate the equal protection clause of the Constitution. The decision discussed in great detail the government's evidence of discrimination impeding the ability of qualified minority businesses in construction subcontracting as well as discrimination against existing minority businesses impeding the ability of those firms to compete for contracts. For example, the government found that "the average loan to a black-owned construction firm is $49,000 less than the average loan to an equally matched nonminority construction firm." Prime contractors like to contract with subcontractors with whom they have long-standing relations, and as a result new minority businesses are frequently excluded from bidding for subcontracts in the absence of affirmative action requirements. In addition, minority construction subcontracting firms received 87 cents for every dollar that they would be expected to receive given their availability.

In 2001, a report by the U.S. General Accounting Office (GAO) examined DOT's DBE program. The report, in examining past court decisions, concluded that there was evidence of past discrimination that could justify the establishment of DBE participation goals for disadvantaged businesses. Similarly, the GAO found that there was insufficient information available to understand fully the economic impact of DBE programs. However, the GAO concluded that in the specific instances where DBE programs were eliminated in Minnesota and Louisiana, minority-owned businesses in the transportation construction industry suffered significant negative impacts—DBE participation, in both contracts and dollars awarded, fell precipitously.

According to DOT data, in fiscal year 2000 the DBE program helped to encourage more than $2 billion in investment to disadvantaged businesses, including minority- and women-owned businesses. The exact impact of this investment is impossible to determine due to current gaps in data. However, this is clearly a substantial sum of money that otherwise may not have been available to these small businesses. The DBE program remains vital to ensuring that disadvantaged businesses have access to transportation contracts.

SUMMARY

Although the impacts of transportation are widely distributed throughout American society, the benefits and disadvantages have uneven impacts on different social and economic groups. Some analysis has been devoted to differential impacts on the basis of race and class. But relatively little analysis has been done on adverse impacts on the basis of age, national origin, English proficiency, disability, and gender. More can be done, including data collection, soliciting public input and participation, making changes according to this input, and using transportation as a tool for increased social equity. Some attempts have been made to use transportation as a tool for change, in some cases with undesirable outcomes. Transcontinental trains helped doom Indian country. Freeways made white flight easier and segregated neighborhoods. Many good-paying construction jobs go to operating engineer union members who are mostly Anglo and male. The perspective needs to be broader and more inclusive. Park planners speak of "desire paths," the long curving routes people naturally take across a grassy area, avoiding the rough right angles planners love to build with cement. It is time that people in the transportation business examined the desire paths of underrepresented and traditionally discriminated-against groups and took those paths into serious consideration.

Chapter 7 discusses how age and physical disability have considerable equity implications. As with the issues discussed in this chapter, neither age nor physical disability has received substantial attention to date.

NOTES

1. Cherokee Nation v. Georgia, 30 U.S. (5 Pet.) 1, 17, (1831).
2. Seminole Nation v. United States, 316 U.S. 286, 296-97 (1942).
3. See, for example, Indian Self-Determination Act, 25 U.S.C. § 450; Indian Tribal Justice Support Act, 25 U.S.C. § 3601; and for those that seek to preserve Indian culture, see, for example, Native American Graves Protection and Repatriation Act, 25 U.S.C. § 3001. In the Native American Languages Act, 25 U.S.C. §§ 2901-2905, Congress combined the policies of self-governance and cultural preservation in a single piece of legislation. See also 25 U.S.C. § 2502(d).
4. Campos-Outcalt et al. (1999); American Academy of Pediatrics (2003).
5. Centers for Disease Control and Prevention (2003).
6. Roanhorse (2005).
7. Motor Vehicle Traffic Crash Fatality Counts and Injury Estimates for 2003, August 10, 2004.
8. 25 U.S.C. §§ 472-473.
9. "On Federal-Aid Highway Projects On and Near Indian Reservations" (DOT Notice N 4720.7).
10. 417 U.S.C. § 535 (1974).
11. Id. at 553 n.24; see also id. at 554 (emphasizing that "[t]he preference, as applied, is granted to Indians not as a discrete racial group, but, rather, as members of quasi-sovereign tribal entities"); Rice v. Cayetano, 528 U.S. 495, 519–520 (2000) (same).
12. *Mancari*, 417 U.S. at 555.
13. 528 U.S. at 519.
14. Id. at 518-19.
15. 515 U.S. 200, 235 (1995).
16. 231 U.S. 28, 46 (1913).
17. See 25 U.S.C. § 479a.
18. *Adarand*, 515 U.S. at 235.
19. Institute for Social and Economic Research (1995).
20. USDOT (2001).
21. See the very helpful and information Web site of Lamberth Consulting, www.lamberthconsulting.com.
22. See the American Civil Liberties Union Web site on racial profiling for an example of this dismay, including an online complaint form for victims, www.aclu.org/RacialEquality/RacialEqualitylist.cfm?c=133.
23. See, for example, Sikh Media Watch's Web site, which tallies such allegations and provides legal advice.
24. See, for example, the Web site of the National Highway Traffic Safety Administration, www.nhtsa.dot.gov/people/injury/airbags/Archive-04/PresBelt/fullreport.html.
25. National Safety Council (2002).
26. Safety belt use was 80 percent in primary law states versus 69 percent in states without primary enforcement, National Safety Council (2002).
27. Lamberth (n.d.).
28. Frederickson (2003).

7

Disability, Aging, and Transportation Equity

Transportation represents a major portion of consumer, business, and government expenditures. As discussed earlier, it gives people the opportunity to gain access to goods, services, and activities that provide benefits. It helps determine where people can live, shop, work, go to school, and recreate. It affects individuals' opportunities to gain access to education, employment, goods, services, and activities. For all these reasons, transportation has major impacts on equity.

As the population of the United States ages, there is an increase in the number of persons with disabilities. These trends present challenges for moving toward strategic goals of mobility and accessibility. As the population increases, there will be a higher demand for all modes of transportation, and the dimensions of travel (such as mode, time, routes, and destinations) will vary. An increase in the older population will increase the demand for elderly- and disabled-friendly fixed-route vehicles, paratransit, and other transit services that will provide opportunities for independent living and access to necessary goods and services.

Secretary of Transportation Norman Mineta has stated that accessibility is a civil right. Along these lines, DOT's Performance Plan under the Government Performance and Results Act states: "Transportation is vital in maintaining independence and mobility for people with disabilities, linking them to employment, health care, participation in the community, and for their overall quality of life."[1] Although the United

113

States possesses one of the safest and most extensive passenger transportation systems in the world, it is unable to provide optimal mobility
for selected and growing portions of the population. These segments
include the elderly, people with disabilities, and the poor. The number
of people with disabilities is estimated at about 54 million. Definitions of
disability vary widely, from those for civil rights programs to those for
benefits programs. One definition is as follows:

> A physical or mental condition that substantially impairs a major life
>   activity,
> Or a history of,
> Or being regarded as.[2]

The range of disabilities is immense in type and severity. However,
the federal courts have been narrowing the definition of disability covered by the law. In the United States, the number of people experiencing
transportation problems is growing, in part due to the graying of the
Anglo population. The number of people with disabilities is increasing
by about one million each year. In addition, the U.S. Census Bureau estimates that by 2025 more than 50 percent of the U.S. population will be
over 55 years of age. One thing is certain—with advances in medical
technology and the aging of "baby boomers," the percentage of the U.S.
population living with a disability will increase significantly over the
next 25 years. As the oldest of the post–World War II baby boomers turn
age 60 in 2006, the nation's age 65 and over population will increase
tremendously: nearly one in five persons will be 65 or older. Moreover,
with the aging of minorities, by 2030 nearly one in five elderly persons
will be a minority. The baby boom population is now poised and ready
to move into its sunset years.

However, it should be noted that there is a dichotomy in age trends
in the United States. The Latino population is younger and has larger
families than the Anglo population. Hispanics are more likely than non-
Hispanic whites to be under 18 years old. In 2000, 35.7 percent of Hispanics
were under 18 years of age, compared with 23.5 percent of non-Hispanic
whites. Relatively few Latinos were age 65 and older (5.3 percent) compared with non-Hispanic whites (14 percent). Hispanics also live in
family households that are larger than those of non-Hispanic whites. In
2000, 30.6 percent of family households in which a Hispanic person was
the householder consisted of five or more people. In contrast, only 11.8
percent of non-Hispanic white family households were this large.

Disability rates are also correlated with neighborhood poverty levels, although the relationship is not strong. In the most affluent neighborhoods, about 5 percent of children were classified as having one or more disabilities compared with 8 percent in the poorest communities.[3] However, as noted elsewhere, there is a strong correlation between poverty and minority status, thus linking health, disability, and poverty with race and ethnicity.

This chapter discusses the connection between disability and transportation equity. Given the relationship between aging and increasing disability levels, age as a transportation equity issue is also important to the discussion. While young persons suffer from low levels of personal mobility and access, it is assumed that their parents or adult guardians provide for their transportation needs. On the other hand, elderly persons can be at a greater disadvantage because they often have to meet their own travel needs without assistance. Those too old to drive must rely on alternative sources, which are often very expensive or nonexistent.

DISABILITY RIGHTS CAN BE DISTINGUISHED FROM OTHER CIVIL RIGHTS

Disability law has many affirmative requirements, as opposed to the "thou shalt nots" present in most other civil rights laws. There are several themes that emerge from concerns about disability rights, including participation and inclusion. "Nothing about us without us" is a slogan used by some of the more progressive disability rights advocates. It means that no plans or programs for people with disabilities should be made without consulting the people who have the disabilities. Those being planned for can provide valuable input based on their firsthand knowledge of their own needs and challenges. Along with participation, there is a strong emphasis on inclusion. People with disabilities want to be a real, functioning part of all aspects of society. They do not want to be kept locked away in institutions but want to be fully integrated into society. Many approaches involve the lowering or removing of barriers or obstacles wherever and whenever possible. This includes not only issues related to physical access but also access to information and opportunity. The disability advocacy community is committed to ensuring that advances of the past three decades are not eroded or waived even as these advances are under threat by a conservative federal judiciary.

PRINCIPLES OF TRANSPORTATION EQUITY
FOR PEOPLE WITH DISABILITIES

Transportation mobility is important because it widens the geographic horizon of our employment, housing, shopping, and recreation opportunities. Mobility also extends the trading area within which local goods and services are marketable. The following 10 principles increase the mobility of people with disabilities and/or expand their access to goods and services:

1. *Availability*: Transportation must be available if it is to be used to reduce immobility. For example, urban bus service can be enormously productive economically, and its curtailment, even in low-patronage, off-peak hours, can create added travel costs, income losses, and immobility that exceeds by many times the dollar savings to transit agencies from service reductions.[4]

2. *Equity*: Everyone should enjoy at least a basic level of access, even if it requires extra resources to accomplish this goal. People with disabilities should be served as effectively as people without disabilities to avoid physical and social isolation.

3. *Seamlessness*: Access should be an important criterion for transitions between transportation modes. For example, the Easter Seals Project ACTION has noted that many existing transit stations have direct connections to commercial, retail, and residential facilities, but the route among them is often not accessible. Project ACTION proposes that transportation agencies should include language in agreements they have with facilities that requires or encourages the provision of an accessible route from the direct connection point into the connected transit facility.

4. *Inclusiveness*: Technology, housing, transportation, and other aspects of community life should be designed to accommodate people with disabilities to ensure a more inclusive and productive society.

5. *Equivalence*: Service for people with disabilities should extend throughout the general service area and operate during the same hours as the system used by the general public. Contrary to some assumptions, people with disabilities are dispersed throughout the general population in geography and time, and their ultimate travel needs are not significantly different from those of the general population.

6. *Efficiency*: We should explore strategies that will ensure access and full participation in society for the greatest number of people at the

lowest and most rationally allocated cost. However, it should be noted that federal regulations prohibit charging more to people with disabilities, even if their transportation costs more.

7. *Safety*: Accessibility in and to transportation infrastructure should be safe for everyone, including people with disabilities. Changes being contemplated in transportation infrastructure may have consequences for disabled persons that are hard to anticipate without adequate attention paid to these specific needs. Safety concerns of the disabled are directly related to their disabilities. For example, the U.S. Access Board has noted that very preliminary and limited research suggests that roundabouts discourage pedestrian use and that they are a significant barrier to pedestrians with vision, mobility, and cognitive impairments. Modern roundabouts are traffic circles that are defined by two basic operational and design principles, "yield at entry" and "deflection for entering traffic." The principle of "yield at entry" requires that vehicles in the circulatory roadway have the right-of-way, and all entering vehicles on approaches have to wait for a gap in the circulating flow. The entry control is a yield sign. The principle of "deflection for entering traffic" dictates that no traffic stream gets a straight movement through the intersection. While this traffic pattern has been an asset to traffic planners in controlling and slowing the flow of traffic at intersections in lieu of having an intersection with a signal, the absence of stopped traffic presents a major problem for blind and visually impaired pedestrians when crossing. Pedestrians report that vehicles at roundabouts, right slip lanes, and other pedestrian crosswalks without signals often do not yield for pedestrians. Pedestrians with disabilities are particularly vulnerable in these situations. People who are blind or visually impaired are unable to make eye contact with drivers, making it impossible to "claim the intersection." Other vehicles often block a driver's view of people using wheelchairs. Pedestrians with slower-than-normal mobility may hesitate when entering the street. All of these situations may result in drivers misinterpreting the pedestrian's intention to cross.

Some safety issues for people with disabilities are not obvious. For example, in Oregon in 1999 it was found that many drivers hired to transport people with disabilities had criminal records. Background checks had not been done. To this end, the Department of Justice has published "Guidelines for Screening Persons Working with Children, the Elderly, and Individuals with Disabilities in Need of Support."[5]

Finally, the terrorist attacks of September 11, 2001, and Hurricanes Katrina and Rita in 2005 pointed out some of the special problems faced by people with disabilities in emergency situations. Transportation providers and infrastructure partners must see to it that the needs of people with disabilities are met in emergency situations. This will require emergency planning by working together with people with disabilities.

8. *Reliability*: Transportation should be reliable, and all transportation infrastructure users want the systems to be reliable. Yet, for people with disabilities, mechanical systems breakdowns may result in a complete denial of access. For example, out-of-service elevators and escalators in a transit system may be a mere inconvenience to non-disabled users but can create an inaccessible barrier to users with disabilities.

9. *Reality-Based*: Plans for use of transportation infrastructure elements in the United States should be cognizant of the realities of technology now but also be aware that technology improvements and changes are almost inevitable. New technology is not automatically accessible to people with disabilities. Early cell phones, for example, were less accessible than present ones. With fast adoption and change of technology, new equipment can become common before it is adequately evaluated for accessibility.

10. *Consultation*: People with disabilities should be thoroughly involved in the decision-making process for improved accessibility and mobility. Throughout each stage of planning and implementing actions for improved accessibility and mobility, disability advocacy organizations and knowledgeable resource individuals within the disability community should be active partners in creating a transportation network that is fully usable by people with varying types of disabilities.

Implementation of these principles will help ensure the inclusion of people with disabilities in all the benefits of society. Their use would also model a paradigm for transportation planning that would recognize and empower actual and potential customers and other users. It should be noted that a fully accessible transportation system is usable by everyone. Access is of two kinds: program and physical. Most discussions center on physical access, such as lifts, ramps, and curb cuts. But program access ensures all individuals equally effective entry to the services and

TABLE 4.   ACCESSIBLE TRANSPORTATION DESIGN PRINCIPLES

PRINCIPLE	DESCRIPTION
Equitable use	The designs are useful and marketable to people with diverse abilities.
Flexibility in use	Designs accommodate a wide range of individual preferences and abilities.
Simple and intuitive use	Uses of designs are easy to understand, regardless of the user's experience, knowledge, language skills, or current concentration level.
Perceptible information	The designs communicate necessary information effectively to the user regardless of ambient conditions or the user's sensory abilities.
Tolerance of error	The designs minimize hazards and the adverse consequences of accidental or unintended actions.
Low physical effort	The design can be used efficiently and comfortably and with a minimum of fatigue.
Size and space for approach to use	The design provides appropriate size and space for approaching, reaching, manipulating, and using, regardless of user's body size, posture, or mobility.

programs of a system. Program access means that a person with a disability receives the same benefits from a program or service as anyone else, without significant barriers or effort required to overcome them.

A different approach to accessibility for people with disabilities is universal design, the design of products and environments so they are usable by all people, to the greatest extent possible, without the need for adaptation or specialized design. Table 4 summarizes key design principles that are important for accessible transportation services.

STATUTES AND REGULATIONS

The federal government, as well as many of the states, has statutes and regulations that require nondiscrimination against people with disabilities and provide access to them. The following are some laws relevant to transportation and people with disabilities:

- Americans with Disabilities Act: Nondiscrimination against people with disabilities in transportation infrastructure and providers.
- Fair Housing Act: Requirements for accessibility in housing.

- Section 504 of the Rehabilitation Act of 1973 (federal financial assistance): Nondiscrimination against people with disabilities by recipients of federal financial assistance.
- Transportation Equity Act for the 21st Century (TEA-21): Provides flexibilities for state transportation funding on enhancements that lower barriers to people with disabilities. Extended the reach of the Air Carrier Access Act to foreign airlines operating in the United States. It also includes specific provisions for studying the lowering of barriers to people with disabilities, such as commercial over-the-road truck drivers who are insulin-controlled diabetics.
- New Freedom Initiative: The President's New Freedom Initiative is intended to provide additional tools to overcome existing barriers facing Americans with disabilities seeking integration into the workforce and full participation in society. (See also Executive Order No. 13217 "Community-Based Alternatives for Individuals with Disabilities" in Appendix V.)
- Section 508 of the Rehabilitation Act of 1973, as amended: Requires electronic information technology accessibility for software and hardware acquired by the federal government.
- Air Carrier Access Act (ACAA): Nondiscrimination against people with disabilities by commercial passenger airlines.
- Executive Order on Increasing Employment of Adults with Disabilities.
- Civil rights laws are not waived after a disaster. In fact, the Stafford Act, enforced by the Federal Emergency Management Agency, has specific civil rights provisions, including nondiscrimination on the basis of income. It is one of the very few federal statutes to cover this issue. Some state constitutions provide this protection also.

The most advanced framework has been by the federal government. As noted elsewhere, much of the funding for transportation in the U.S. comes from the federal government. Because many different federal agencies provide funds and have accessibility requirements, several agencies identified the need to coordinate efforts.

COORDINATION OF FEDERAL AGENCY EFFORTS ON HUMAN SERVICES ACCESS

As human services programs were established throughout the United States during the past 30 years, they recognized that access was important for the success of their programs. The programs were serving many families and individuals who did not have reliable transportation or any private transportation at all. Some alternative means of transportation was needed, either to transport the clients to programs or to bring the programs to clients. The easiest and quickest way to address this problem was to create a new transportation service. The net result was the proliferation of parallel transportation networks in many communities. As long as adequate funding was available, many of the individual programs operated effectively. Through the 1980s and 1990s, however, funding levels for many human services programs were reduced. In response, many agencies necessarily concentrated their resources on direct support of their clients, not on support programs like transportation. Some agencies reduced or eliminated transportation services without considering coordination with other agencies.[6]

The many different human services transportation providers created overlapping services, resulting in a high cost of offering transportation by providers other than public transit. Many human services agencies buy vans to transport clients and rarely coordinate with entities that provide related services, such as paratransit. Human services vans sometimes sit idly for extended periods of time while people with disabilities in the same community have difficulty gaining access to public transportation. Coordination efforts seek to eliminate inefficiencies such as these in current transportation systems by promoting initiatives such as agreements between urban and rural providers to pick up passengers in each other's areas when logical to do so.

Other obstacles to coordination (or decrease of overlap) include questions of liability for injury and potential user disinterest. Brownfields programs (those involving contaminated former industrial sites that are developed and reused to spur local economic development through federal, state, and local cooperation) have solved somewhat similar liability questions, so a model exists to study for human services transportation liability. Current nontransit human services transportation users might not want to give up their means of transportation, especially when those means are heavily subsidized, their cost is borne by third parties, and the service is individualized and door-to-door.

The benefits of successful coordinated transportation systems often include providing greater access to funding; creating a more cost-effective use of resources, including reduced duplication and overlap in human service agency transportation services; filling service gaps in a community or geographic area; serving additional individuals within existing budgets; and providing more centralized management of existing resources. The Department of Transportation (DOT) / Health and Human Services (HHS) Council has been in existence since 1986 and has been the subject of congressional and Government Accountability Office study. On USDOT's side, the Federal Transit Administration has led this effort. Legislation might be necessary to pare down the many types of grants for the same purpose, to require coordination on a local level, and to help ensure that cost savings will redound to the benefit of local people. There are also potential new partners in local areas and on the federal interagency level. These include public school district school bus fleets and fleets of vehicles belonging to faith-based organizations. In involving the latter, the White House and HHS Faith-Based and Community Initiatives Offices might have a role. Possible federal partners include the Departments of Education, Housing and Urban Development, and Labor.

DOT and HHS are both interested in, and take responsibility for, assisting transportation services for persons who are disadvantaged in terms of their ability to obtain and use their own transportation. Such persons may include the elderly, persons with disabilities or with low or limited incomes, the young, and others without access to private automobiles. Many of these persons need specialized transportation to gain access to the human service programs funded by HHS. The Council, jointly staffed by DOT and HHS, was first established in 1986. Its goals include increasing the cost-effectiveness of resources used for specialized and human service transportation and increasing access to these services.

Pooling existing resources is one of the least developed areas with potential for significant improvement in accessibility in transportation. Fleets of vehicles of varying accessibility stand unused for much of the day and week. These include school buses, church vans and buses, Administration on Aging–funded vans, and Medicaid-funded vehicles. Legislative changes to make restrictions on use more flexible and creation of liability and insurance safe harbors may be necessary to make such pooling of resources financially and legally practical.

OTHER TRANSPORTATION BARRIERS CONFRONTING PEOPLE WITH DISABILITIES

There is a broad range of approaches to transportation barriers for persons with disabilities. Many deal directly with providing alternative types of service that can give increased access. Other approaches

Planning and Mainstreaming

Accessibility is often considered a separate issue or an afterthought to program or project. However, it is essential that it be incorporated into the first phases of programming, planning, designing, operating, and constructing pedestrian facilities. To make this happen, accessibility needs to be institutionalized throughout all functions that affect the usability of the pedestrian system.

Accessibility should not be an "added feature." Problems are created when there is a lack of planning for accessibility in the initial stages of planning and project development. Inadequate funding, poor design, and lack of right-of-way are examples of problems that stem from adding pedestrian facilities at the last minute. The result many deny a substantial percent of the population with the mobility services that the non-disabled population takes for granted.

Many organizations are not aware of disability prevalence statistics, or possibly the figures do not have sufficient impact because the population with disabilities is not mainstreamed into the general pedestrian transportation system. The connection between the lack of pedestrian service and the lack of pedestrians is often a misunderstood connection within transportation agencies. Making these changes and creating awareness can be difficult within bureaucracies.

address physical barriers proactively to meet accessibility needs or to retrofit situations that were otherwise poorly suited for access by seniors or disabled persons.

Paratransit

Government investment in paratransit has provided many of the transportation options available to the disabled and seniors. Paratransit can include a variety of smaller, often flexibly scheduled and routed, non-profit transportation services using low-capacity vehicles, such as vans, to operate within normal urban transit corridors or rural areas. These vehicles are usually run by public transit services at substantially greater expense than fixed-route buses and generally carry those who would be served with difficulty, if at all, by standard mass transit. Paratransit or shared-ride services address many of the barriers preventing the use of public transportation by older individuals. Although paratransit fills an important transportation gap for many parts of the population, it has been heavily subsidized by governmental funding rather than from its own revenues.

Curb Cuts

People with disabilities often say that their first priority in making transportation infrastructure accessible is building and maintaining curb cuts in America's cities, towns, and suburbs. Curb cuts, also called curb ramps, are the sloping transitions between sidewalks and streets and roads. These allow people with mobility impairments to move independently from sidewalk to street as part of an accessible route. Although curb cuts have been in essence required in entities that receive federal financial assistance since 1973, hundreds of thousands, and perhaps millions, of curb cuts have not been built. Many cuts are not properly maintained or were not built properly. Curbs cuts cost approximately from $500 to $2,600 each when retrofitted to existing sidewalks, curbs, and streets, with a commonly quoted cost of $1,200 each. Curb cuts provide benefits to many other users, such as families pushing baby strollers, people pulling home grocery carts, and children on bicycles and roller blades. However, at least one group of people with disabilities has expressed reservations about curb cuts—some blind advocacy groups say that sharp, angled, distinctions between sidewalks and streets are easier for the blind to locate by feel. USDOT generally has jurisdiction over curb cuts because curbs run along the edges of streets and roads, and curbs are often rebuilt when a road is fixed.

Transportation facilities should include features that will allow people of all abilities to use them. The federal-aid highway program can work hand in hand with the Americans with Disabilities Act (ADA), which requires that many pedestrian facilities be accessible for people with disabilities. Accessibility design is fundamental to the walking environment, because all pedestrians with or without disabilities benefit from accessible design. It is a safety issue for the more than 54 million people in this country who have some form of disability. FTA believes that many bus stops are inaccessible because of a lack of curb cuts and because of inaccessible sidewalks. A Transportation Cooperative Research Program report stated:

> Making new stops conform to ADA physical dimension requirements is relatively easy. . . . Modification of existing stops is more difficult, especially if the stops are at sites with limited easement or not subject to the transit agency's control, such as shopping malls, on state rights-of-way, or suburban

subdivisions. . . . The ADA . . . involves accessibility from the point of origin to the final destination . . . to get to the bus stop, individuals with limited mobility or vision need a path that is free of obstacles, as well as a final destination that is accessible. A barrier-free bus stop or shelter is of little value if the final destination is not accessible . . . an accessible vehicle is clearly a critical link in the barrier-free trip.[7]

Rural Issues

Despite more than 20 years of federal involvement in supporting rural transit programs, nearly 1,300 rural counties in the United States have no public transportation.[8] Forty percent of all rural residents live in an area with no form of public transportation, and another 28 percent live in areas with very low levels of service provision.[9] Nearly 80 percent of rural counties have no public bus service, compared with 2 percent of metro counties.[10] One in every 14 households in rural America has no vehicle, and nearly 57 percent of the rural poor do not own a car. Overall, 96 percent of public assistance recipients have no personal automobile.

Lack of transportation is one of the most frequently cited problems facing the approximately 13.2 million people with disabilities living in rural areas. Despite the significance of the problem, few models for delivering transportation to people with disabilities in rural areas have been reported. Accessible rural public transportation systems are rare and costly to operate because of low usage and long distances traveled.

William C. Field, Director of the Breaking New Ground program at Purdue University, has made the following recommendations about providing rural accessible transportation:

- Reserve some accessible transportation system investments for rural areas.
- Increase resources to rural disability organizations, such as rural independent living centers, to provide transportation services in more isolated areas. These resources would strengthen these organizations and result in leveraging of local resources.
- Encourage the faith community in rural communities to step in and provide transportation services at least to their members and extended families. There are rural churches with fleets of three to 10 buses that sit idle for most of the week.
- Use the USDA AgrAbility Program to increase public awareness about rural transportation issues.[11]

Over-the-Road Buses

Some of the most active disability advocacy groups feel strongly that over-the-road buses (OTRBs) should be fully accessible to people with mobility impairments. These are large intercity buses that typically carry luggage and packages under the passenger area. Currently very few such buses are accessible. They provide one of the few kinds of public transportation in rural areas and are used largely by low-income people. Many disabled people are also low-income because of the very high unemployment rate among people with disabilities.

USDOT issued regulations under the ADA in 1998, requiring the phased-in accessibility of over-the-road buses. This rule was highly controversial. Long sought by members of the disability community and strongly opposed by the OTRB industry, the rule was issued more than five years after the ADA's statutory deadline. It contained information collection requirements to respond both to disability community concerns that bus companies would not provide the required accessible buses and service and to industry concerns that the cost of accessibility would have few benefits as measured by increases in ridership by persons with disabilities. Over-the-road bus companies said they feared adverse economic impacts on their profitability if they had to make their buses accessible.

The USDOT regulation required large, fixed-route over-the-road bus services like Greyhound, whose service is the backbone of the intercity bus system, to make sure that all new buses they obtain are accessible, with wheelchair lifts and tie-downs that allow passengers to ride in their own wheelchairs. The rule requires fleets to be completely accessible by 2012. Most smaller fixed-route companies also will acquire accessible new buses, although they do not have a deadline for fleet accessibility. Companies may provide equivalent service in lieu of obtaining accessible buses. Charter and tour companies will have to provide service in an accessible bus on 48-hour advance notice. Fixed-route companies must also provide this kind of service on an interim basis until their fleets are completely accessible. The rule makes carriers accountable for providing this advance-notice service by requiring them to compensate passengers when they fail to provide the required service on time. Small carriers that provide mostly charter or tour service and also provide a small amount of fixed-route service can meet all requirements through 48-hour advance-reservation service.

DOT estimates that the cost of compliance will be $22 to $30 million annually and that new passenger traffic will reduce the cost to an estimated net cost of $15 to $26 million per year. The Transportation Equity Act for the 21st Century (TEA-21) authorized an average of $4.86 million in federal assistance from fiscal 1999 to 2003 to over-the-road bus companies to help pay for accessible costs.

Car Ownership

There is a strong correlation among not owning a car, poverty, and the infirmities associated with aging. Not owning a car is most prevalent among the poor, including the elderly poor, the working poor, and the unemployed. Physical disabilities associated with aging are another significant correlate of not owning a car. Physical disabilities that require wheelchair use are widely recognized as a powerful correlate of mobility disadvantage, but this population is much smaller than the number of people who do not own a car because of poverty or aging. Not owning a car is also strongly correlated with urban location. Lack of car ownership is most isolating for those who live alone in suburban communities. Not owning a car seems to be least isolating for those with a large friendship circle and least immobilizing for those who live in urban settings suited to walking and the use of public transportation. The mobility available to those who do not own cars hinges on the ability of others to provide transportation when and where it is needed. These "others" include transit agencies, taxi companies, paratransit providers, family, friends, coworkers, neighbors, schools, churches, senior centers, and social service agencies.

The Community Transportation Association of America (CTAA) reports that there are more than 100 million low-income and older Americans and people with disabilities at risk of being unable to provide or afford their own transportation and who are likely to be dependent on others for their mobility. The President's New Freedom Initiative of 2001 was proposed to help address these problems.

Job Access Placement and Transportation

Not every job is a good job. If the cost of providing transportation to remote locations exceeds the weekly pay of the returning worker, after a subsidy is exhausted, then the person will not be able to keep the position. If transportation needs to be provided, the job developer and agencies must consult and work with the transit operator to ensure that the needed service is available and affordable to the worker before they complete the job placement.

FTA has addressed some of these issues through its Job Access and Reverse Commute program (JARC) and through expanding efforts to work with the Department of Labor on issues relating to the role of local One-Stop Career Center Systems in addressing individuals' transportation needs as they relate to employment. JARC was established to respond to the opportunity issues in transportation. This Transportation Equity Act for the 21st Century (TEA-21) initiative had two major goals: (1) to provide transportation services in urban, suburban, and rural areas to assist welfare recipients and low-income individuals with access to employment opportunities; and (2) to increase collaboration among the transportation providers, human service agencies, employers, metropolitan planning organizations, states, and affected communities and individuals (see the discussion of JARC in Chapter 5).

Availability of Oxygen on Commercial Flights

FAA regulations prohibit passengers from bringing their own oxygen on board for use during flight. Passengers can check empty oxygen cylinders as baggage for retrieval at their destinations, but only carriers can provide medical oxygen for passenger use in flight. A few do not provide it at all, citing training and other costs. Most do provide it, at an additional charge that deters some oxygen users from traveling. The disability community would like USDOT to require all carriers to provide it, at no or nominal charge, through an amendment to the Air Carrier Access Act (ACAA) regulations. For a number of years disability advocates have asked the department to issue a regulation requiring air carriers to provide oxygen to passengers needing it, but there remain a number of accessibility issues still unresolved:

- Accessible terminal transportation systems;
- Boarding chair standards;
- Substitute transportation for persons unable to board small aircraft;
- Accessible lavatories on narrow-body aircraft;
- Open captioning for in-flight movies and videos;
- Teletypewriter service on aircraft.

Trip Planning

According to Easter Seals Project ACTION, trip planning is the most critical segment of travel for people with disabilities. Here, they must use the telephone or Internet, maps, advice of others familiar with the transportation system's barriers and problems, and other aids to assess the feasibility of the trip. Ascertaining feasibility requires anticipating the barriers that the trip will present and mentally overcoming them beforehand. Only when feasibility is firmly established can travelers with disabilities begin a trip with substantial likelihood of successfully completing it. Easter Seals's Project Action, a grantee of the Federal Transit Administration, has initiatives dealing with trip planning for people with disabilities.

Heavy-Rail Vehicles

According to USDOT,

> the percentage of transit vehicles providing accessible service under the ADA varied dramatically by type of transit, but was generally higher in 1997 than in 1993. About 68 percent of buses were ADA accessible in 1997, up from 53 percent in 1993. Only 29 percent of commuter rail vehicles were accessible in 1997, but this was higher than the 18 percent in 1993. A relatively large percentage of heavy-rail vehicles were ADA accessible, 78 percent in 1997, but there has been no improvement since 1994.[12]

In fact, there has been a reported slight decline in accessibility of heavy-rail vehicles since 1994. There are reports that this decline may be an artifact of statistical reporting. Note that these statistics apply to public transit vehicles and not Amtrak. The Federal Railroad Administration (FRA) does not appear to have statistics available on the number and percent of accessible Amtrak passenger cars. At current rates of improvement in accessibility, all commuter rail vehicles will not be accessible until about 2015. Another difficulty is platform-to-car gaps.

There are some definitional issues regarding heavy-rail vehicles. Some are public transit vehicles, under the jurisdiction of FTA, discussed elsewhere in this document. Others are Amtrak passenger railroad cars, under the jurisdiction of the FRA, which has jurisdiction over the ADA compliance of Amtrak. FRA is developing new compliance review initiatives for monitoring the accessibility of Amtrak rolling stock and facilities.

Call Boxes

Emergency call boxes along highways are not always accessible to people with disabilities. Advocates believe that the Federal Highway Administration and other appropriate state and local agencies should ensure that these call boxes are accessible and that traffic signals and poles show flashing lights when emergency vehicles are approaching. However, it should be noted that call boxes are not necessarily under the jurisdiction of the FHWA. Individual entities that control call boxes are moving to make them accessible, including installing TTY-type interfaces. But cell phones and intelligent transportation systems (including proprietary "On-Star" type car-and-dispatcher systems) are superseding call boxes for obtaining emergency assistance.

Speed Bumps and Humps

There is concern among some segments of the disability community, especially among those with back pain and with spine, hip, and muscle problems, that speed bumps in roads affect them adversely. For example, the Commission on Disability of the City of Berkeley, California, testified before the City of Berkeley Transportation Commission and has received input from citizens concerning the problems that speed bumps cause for the disabled community. For some people with disabilities, the pain and injury that can result from driving or riding over speed bumps makes these "traffic calming devices" into virtual barricades. For others, the unpredictable outcome of going over bumps results in a deterrent to travel. When speed bumps are located in the only clear path (sometimes the side of the roadway), they can also be an obstacle for those using wheelchairs. Those who believe strongly in this subject state that speed bumps are designed to cause discomfort for the average driver and that what is uncomfortable for a healthy person can be extremely painful and possibly injurious to certain fragile, disabled individuals.

USDOT and local jurisdictions have been in the position of encouraging use of speed bumps and humps for safety and traffic-calming reasons. More research and legal analysis may be needed to determine if that enthusiasm is producing situations that unnecessarily adversely affect people with disabilities.

SUMMARY

The isolation experienced by disabled and older persons in regard to transportation is not unlike that experienced by low-income racial minorities. While current wisdom declares that the elderly have disproportionate political influence because of their entitlement programs, high rate of voting, numbers, and effective lobbying groups like AARP, their isolation grows. One could attribute this in part to the fragmentation of American society generally.[13] Putnam warns that our stock of social capital—the very fabric of our connections with each other—has plummeted, impoverishing our lives and communities. We should be sympathetic to transportation inequities experienced by people with disabilities and the elderly because we may become members of the first group and hope to become members of the second.

Many of the changes necessary to make transportation accessible and available to these two groups have been required in one form or another since 1976, with the Section 504 of the Rehabilitation Act of 1973 regulations, or since 1991, when the Americans with Disabilities Act took effect. The average design life of a civic structure in America is 40 years. Much of that design life has passed already. Many necessary changes could have been made and their cost amortized over decades. Viewing cost in this way, over the long term, will help reduce objections to necessary changes.

The concept of such investment in the future may be foreign. In some respects, Americans are like perpetual teenagers, thinking that we will never become old or disabled. In these two areas, no particular empathy is required to see the need for change toward greater equity. Why, then, does it either not happen or happen very slowly? Are the growing inequities in American society in areas such as income gaps reflected in the way we treat people with disabilities and the elderly? Are we culturally allergic to showing respect for our elders? A major theme of this book is to encourage civility and empathy through pointing out disparities and how they can be fixed. We hope readers will promulgate these themes and help create the public will necessary to make the changes real, before we become the victims of isolation ourselves.

NOTES

1. USDOT (2002).
2. Americans with Disabilities Act (1990).
3. Mather and Rivers (2006).
4. See Crain & Associates with Ricardo Byrd and Omniversed International (1999).
5. National Criminal Justice Reference Service (1998).
6. Community Transportation Association of America (n.d.).
7. Transportation Research Board (1996).
8. Community Transportation Association of America (n.d.).
9. CTAA (1998).
10. U.S. Federal Highway Administration (1995).
11. Journal of Mine Act (2002).
12. Bureau of Transportation Statistics (1999).
13. See, for example, Putnam (2000).

CHAPTER

8

Conclusions

In this book we have attempted to present and clarify aspects of transportation equity to highlight linkages with civil rights, environmental justice, and social equity concerns. The discussion first focused on personal transport in the metropolitan context, for which there are substantial data available. We consider demographic trends to be very influential on the persistence of transportation inequities into the future. These demographic trends are a function of both historic and current forms of discriminatory policies that have, among other things, resulted in racial segregation and concentrated poverty. We recognize that transportation mobility is only one factor affecting social and economic opportunity for individuals, workers, and households. But, as we also argue, transportation mobility and accessibility affect the locations of employment and housing opportunities. This means that mobility and accessibility are in fact crucial and interrelated to social and economic outcomes. The ability to travel is synonymous with the ability to participate.

Distributional equity is an inherent component of transportation equity. The question of equity or fairness is derived from circumstances where the costs and benefits of certain goods are not provided throughout society in a way that satisfies all needs. In most cases, and true in the case of transport services, demand outpaces supply. We see this in cases where economic competition and pricing dictate not only how much transport can be consumed but also the quality of the good provided. We have argued that costs and benefits of transportation (private and public) are not equitably distributed and that resulting imbalances have long-lasting social implications—some of which reinforce past inequities and pave the way for future inequities.

Our discussion of federal policies provides the backdrop for which civil rights are incorporated into the transportation planning process. The objective of certain federal requirements is to increase awareness of civil rights considerations at early stages of planning and investment as well as provide mitigation, monitoring, and enforcement mechanisms. While current policies and regulations are not perfect, they in fact represent improved processes in comparison to historic practices. Through issuance of executive orders and guidance, federally sponsored research on topics of environmental justice (such as Transit Cooperative Research Program and National Cooperative Highway Research Program reports), academic and foundation-sponsored research, and concerns about civil rights in transportation continue to be evaluated. Many advocates would argue that they are not sufficiently evaluated and that political changes control how much they are enforced. These efforts are needed over time to ensure that continued progress will be made to overcome institutional barriers to social justice.

The substantially adverse and disproportionate effects of Hurricane Katrina on African Americans in August 2005 demonstrated to many advocates that what they call "institutional racism" as one such barrier continues to exist in the United States. Institutional racism includes underlying systems and policies that keep people of color and white unequal. There are certain areas of local policy where racism becomes prominent and visible, including policing, zoning, housing, and transportation. Governmental policies and programs can either promote equality, tolerance, and justice or (consciously or not) promote division and inequality and engender the belief that specific racial and ethnic groups are second-class citizens.

Chapter 6, "Extending Transportation Equity," and Chapter 7, "Disability, Aging, and Transportation Equity," expand how equity is considered in transportation planning. We highlight some areas of civil rights that have received little previous attention or are just beginning to emerge as civil rights issues. For example, while racial profiling is not new for African Americans, the profiling of Middle Eastern, Islamic, and Arab American persons in airport security checkpoints is common in the wake of the September 11 attacks. In addition, changing demographics is also increasing the needs for non–English language information for travelers, especially on public transportation. Nearly all public transportation systems in the United States receive funding from the federal government, with concomitant requirements to address issues of illegal service delivery discrimination based on "race, color, or national origin." A 2005 report by the GAO reported that the number of persons in the United States who do not speak English well grew by 65 percent from 1990 to 2000, and many of these rely on public transit as their primary means of mobility.[1] The discussion on disability and age represents two particularly pressing dimensions of transportation equity, given the trends in our aging population.

Each chapter also represents a distillation of civil rights–related topics. We expect that as these perspectives evolve and civil rights and transportation experiences accumulate, transportation equity as an area of public concern and academic research will also evolve. One of our objectives was to chronicle the current state of affairs and thinking on transportation equity. Other sources have provided valuable case study examples without providing the context that we attempt here. We have attempted to stay away from the tone of outrage common in advocacy writing on the subject. Nevertheless, some of the current vestiges of past illegal segregation are outrageous.

We recognize that "research" comes in varied forms, depending on the source and objectives of research activity. Academics in the areas of planning and transportation have attempted to provide both anecdotal and empirical evidence about disparate impacts of transportation-related policies. Taken as a whole, these research efforts provide a broad and seemingly incoherent approach to social and economic equity. This is understandable, given that there is no consensus on what "transportation equity" does or should encompass. This is also evidenced by the separate yet overlapping research interests represented by the Transportation Research Board (TRB) Committees on Social and Economic Factors, the Committee on Environmental Justice, and the Joint Subcommittee on Community Impact Assessment. There is also a substantial amount of research on transportation equity–related research that occurs outside of TRB spheres, much of which has been referred to throughout this book. While we do not advocate for all of these activities to occur under one large tent, we do hope that they are directed toward the common goal of expanding social and economic opportunity for all persons.

A strictly academic approach, as is commonly found in TRB and its parent, the National Academy of Sciences, however, has its drawbacks. For example, epidemiologists and other scientists require a much higher level of proof than civil rights law enforcers, who in turn require a higher level of proof (preponderance of the evidence) than advocates, who routinely rely on anecdotes. We are presented with an epistemological problem of how we know what we know. How can groups communicate across these chasms? Since our research is history, observation, and action oriented, we can advocate for recognizing that problems in transportation equity exist, as lived by people on the ground; recognizing and empowering those affected people by seeking them out and listening to them; developing commonalities of discourse, so that we share a language; increasing the sensitivity of experts; and providing models for what an equitable transportation system would look like.

One area of planning with increasing potential to implement transportation equity principles is metropolitan planning organizations (MPOs). While state DOTs control the majority of overall transportation planning decisions, MPOs play an important role in shaping urban transportation policies that affect the major concentrations of population within states that also include significant numbers of minorities and low-income individuals. Both of these organizations can play an increasingly important role in promoting social equity through the broad view of social inclusion. Some argue that a regional approach better addresses questions of spatial equity related to transportation networks and land use. To be effective, this requires balancing the roles of state, regional, and local agencies through a coordination, listening, and action mechanism that does not currently exist.

It is in the best interest of MPOs to proactively address issues of fairness in decision making, planning, and representation, especially as they relate to allocating transportation funds. Many MPOs already have policies guided by either Title VI of the Civil Rights Act or Executive Order No. 12898, with several of them outlining specific strategies for public participation as key elements to guide planning. In addition, MPOs can protect themselves against legal challenges such as those faced by the Southeast Michigan Council of Governments (SEMCOG), where constituents challenged the representativeness of voting board members and were dissatisfied with expenditure levels for transit compared with highways in the Detroit metropolitan region. Successful challenges may either be the impetus to improve MPO processes or, if ignored, could undermine MPO effectiveness.

The concept of MPOs, as federally mandated regional institutions, is different than the fair housing paradigm. Transportation by definition involves movement from one place to another. Housing is regarded as static. In 1966, the White House Conference on Civil Rights developed four housing goals that went further than merely removing barriers to free selection of housing. The goals were affirmative action to achieve open markets, dispersion of moderate- and low-cost housing throughout metropolitan areas, development of racially inclusive new towns and suburbs, and revitalization of the existing ghettos. As we have noted, transportation, education, and housing are joined together in perpetuating racial separation in America. Education, like housing, is segmented by governmental jurisdiction. For this reason, its success is viewed by advocates and analysts as insufficient. Transportation planning, because it crosses government jurisdictions in the form of MPOs, should be more successful in reducing barriers between people of different racial and ethnic groups. But the Anglo–dominated governance structure of MPOs seems to work at keeping transportation as a social barrier. We do not conclude that this is due to institutional racism, which it appears caused some of the problems following Hurricane Katrina. In part, because transportation equity is discussed so little, it helps to explore discussion of housing and education equity as proxy measures. Discussion of equity in a regional context also helps to substitute for the lack of transportation equity discussion and analysis.

Jurisdictional issues help keep inequities in place. School integration, which had its heyday between 1966 and 2000, always stopped at the borders of school districts. There are more than 15,000 school districts in the United States. In all states but two, school board members are elected. This example of grassroots democracy has kept school districts racially distinct. Generally, older cities have poor schools, and suburbs have better schools, measured in terms of achievement. As we have discussed, the ability to get to and from the suburbs depends on transportation infrastructure. The freeway system, government housing policies, and suburban developers kept them separate. Have any of the 1966 goals been achieved? An argument can be made that they have not.

Metropolitan planning organizations were supposed to address regional transportation needs. Their primary goals did not include transportation equity. Even so, there are no similar housing and education regional entities. There were some voluntary efforts to permit black students from inner cities to attend public schools in the suburbs. Scott A. Bollens stated:

> While there are a growing number of regional policies that indirectly address equity issues, such policies are likely not to be sufficient without the local

formulation of a regional equity plan based on the shared benefits of combined and cooperative action. Without such an explicit agenda, regional policies to boost economic competitiveness may be biased toward development-related objectives that will not improve and may even worsen the problems of the metropolitan poor . . . regional equity policies are coming in through the back door, more as a product of intergovernmental directives or broader quality-of-life issues than through the concerted or deliberate efforts of political coalitions or community-based organizations. Instead of advancing an explicit metropolitan equity agenda, most regional entities serve as channels for implementation of state and federal housing, transportation, and growth management programs. Rarely do regional bodies independently pursue policies specifically aimed at reducing social and economic disparities. Rather, when such policies exist, they enter by way of the back door.[2]

While Bollens's premise, that there are a "growing number of regional policies that indirectly address equity issues," may be wrong, his conclusion is well taken. This theme of progress "through the back door" is a unifying one for this book. How does this backdoor progress take place? One way is through advocacy. But advocates need to become better at using the political system, building coalitions, and making legal challenges. We also propose use of social marketing as a tool for changing attitudes and behaviors.

TERRORISM AND NATURAL DISASTERS

Recent events, including the terrorist attacks of September 11 and the devastating hurricanes in the Gulf Coast region during 2005, have highlighted the importance of planning and, in the case of Hurricane Katrina, the importance of transportation mobility in response to such events. Anticipating terrorist-related attacks involves significant planning around safety and security throughout national and local transportation systems. Particularly susceptible are public transportation facilities where large numbers of people are concentrated either in stations or on transit vehicles. There are a number of lessons that have become apparent following Hurricane Katrina. Many resonate with other themes developed in this book.

The case of New Orleans and Hurricane Katrina represents the chronic neglect of warnings about inevitable disaster and, in this case, the lack of attention devoted to clearly foreseen risks and the planning to deal with them. Particular examples include the lack of foresight in evacuation planning for people in New Orleans who did not own cars or who could not afford gas. One could argue that this was a completely unique set of circumstances; however, some South Florida cities that have extensive experience with disasters ranging from fire to hurricanes actually monitor car ownership statistics and have emergency plans that feature sending public transportation to neighborhoods with low car-ownership rates.[3] The information from public transportation route planning (which often takes into account mobility levels) could be easily used to identify the locations of residents likely to need assistance during evacuations. Related to these planning efforts should be the coordination and use of existing infrastructure, such as fleets of school buses. This would result in the consequent need for legal liability safe harbors that are common barriers to interagency sharing of resources.

A variety of other issues could also be used to inform future planning efforts, many with political implications, thus requiring a larger dialogue and potentially significant changes to governance or bureaucratic structures. These include but are not limited to:

1. *Jurisdictional boundaries as obstacles to cooperation.* This is reflected in "my county, your city, your state, your federal government" approaches to regional problems. In a social equity context, the obstacles to racial integration presented by school district boundaries are well-known problems. In a transportation context, metropolitan planning organizations are supposed to cross jurisdictional boundaries. In a disaster-planning context, infrastructure acquired by jurisdictions, such as electronic communications devices, are not necessarily compatible. But disasters, terrorist events, mobility issues, and equity issues naturally cross artificial governmental lines. While the historical desire for freedom and democracy in the United States has resulted in decentralized governance and a tension between center and periphery in public administration, demographic issues and opportunities flow differently. They proceed along class and economic lines. Rules of nondiscrimination, both legally prohibitive and those not set out in law but covered in the public interest, can restrict the freedom to act on stereotypes and prejudices. People should not have to be coerced into cooperating with one another. But sometimes our very social contract has to be examined and put into force to require creative cooperation and mutual assistance across jurisdictional boundaries. Such boundaries, especially when reinforced by and matching racial and national origin demographic divides, can

be implemented through malicious compliance, following a rule in the worst possible way. In the case of New Orleans, such malicious compliance let poor African Americans become isolated and suffer.

2. *Long-term planning mistakes.* One obvious example is locating water pumps below sea level in New Orleans. Others include the lack of proper land-use controls, pricing, and disincentives. In the case of New Orleans, a deep-seated antigovernment and antiplanning culture paralyzed reasonable controls along the Gulf Coast. Properties with multiple flood insurance program losses account for 25 percent of the government's flood insurance losses but represent only 2 percent of its insured properties. Another example is a lack of cumulative impact assessment when new infrastructure is proposed. Cumulative impact is the impact on the environment that results from the incremental impact of an action when added to other past, present, and reasonably foreseeable future actions regardless of what agency (federal or nonfederal) or person undertakes such other actions. Cumulative impacts can result from individually minor but collectively significant actions taking place over a period of time.[4]

3. *Institutional racism.* We arrive at this conclusion only reluctantly after resisting it for many years and only after observing New Orleans after Katrina. Surveys also continue to reveal that many nonblack Americans express high levels of social distance (the degree to which people desire close or remote social relations with members of other groups) from African Americans. Institutional racism is the concept that underlying systems and policies keep people of color and whites unequal. There are certain areas of local policy where racism becomes prominent and visible, including policing, zoning, and housing. Municipal and other government policies and programs can either promote equality, tolerance, and justice or (consciously or not) promote division and inequality and engender the belief that specific racial and ethnic groups are second-class citizens.

4. *The misapprehension of risk, failures in communicating risk, and using this misapprehension for political purposes.* This can be a function of a lack of transparency and ineffective public involvement processes. Underlying this is also corruption, which undercuts good potential results of public social policy. Risk is the hazard level combined with the likelihood of the hazard leading to an accident and the hazard exposure or duration. Risk is also described as the probability of a mishap times the likely severity of a mishap. Emotions also play a

role, in that hazard can be determined by technical assessment and outrage by emotional assessment.

Risk communication includes activities to ensure that messages and strategies designed to prevent exposure, adverse human health effects, and diminished quality of life are effectively communicated to the public. As part of a broader prevention strategy, risk communication supports education efforts by promoting public awareness, increasing knowledge, and motivating individuals to take action to reduce their exposure to hazards. Risk communication includes the exchange of information and opinions concerning risk and risk-related factors among risk assessors, risk managers, consumers, and other interested parties.

The goals of risk communication include the following:

- To improve the effectiveness and efficiency of the risk analysis process.
- To promote consistency and transparency in arriving at and implementing risk management decisions.
- To promote awareness and understanding of the specific issues of the risk analysis process.
- To strengthen the working relationships and mutual respect among risk assessment and management participants.
- To exchange information among interested parties to risk analysis and management.
- To foster public trust and confidence in risk analysis and management.

5. *The dangers of inflexibility*. Territorialism can be one aspect of inflexibility; however, in terms of transportation planning this can mean too much reliance on a particular mode of service. One example might be the current enthusiasm and large amount of investment in light-rail systems. These investments can be detrimental to other transportation investments (such as bus service), leading to less resilience, robustness, and redundancy in transportation infrastructure.

It would be unfair to characterize the Katrina response experience as completely negative. There were certain aspects that were deemed successful and applicable to future disaster planning and emergency response:

The success of the military model in the example of the Coast Guard. The Coast Guard responded fully and well. It is worth noting that the Guard views itself as a humanistic military service. Its staff enjoys saving lives. As a national service, it normally crosses jurisdictional boundaries. As a military service, it has a chain of command and institutional values against discrimination. The Coast Guard plans for disasters and implements its plan. It places a high value on professionalism and service. Difficult circumstances do not faze the Guard. This is a great contrast to the New Orleans Police Department, where a substantial number and percent of officers went missing or broke down under the stress of Hurricane Katrina. The NOLA PD was attuned to a different mission. Other governmental services appear to have been "fair-weather" ones that functioned satisfactorily under good conditions but failed under stress. It is worth further study to determine why the Coast Guard model succeeded where other models failed.

The success of private enterprise improvisation, as exemplified by the Wal-Mart rolling warehouse trucks. During the aftermath of Hurricane Katrina, private businesspeople stepped forward to help. Wal-Mart redirected trucks with supplies to the Gulf Coast. Costco provided parking lots. Local gasoline distributors provided fuel and met up with the Wal-Mart trucks at the Costcos. Much of this cooperation and innovation came about through informal relationships among businesspeople. These informal relationships—or networking, as it is referred to in business literature—are especially critical in some parts of the United States. The downside of informal relationships from an equity perspective is that they can manifest in-groups that can work to the disadvantage of marginalized demographic or social groups. Luckily, in New Orleans, they did not.

The success of a voluntary organization, in the example of the Salvation Army. The Red Cross has come under criticism for how it functioned in Hurricane Katrina, with alleged lax controls and direction. The Salvation Army is more like the Coast Guard example discussed above—with a clear humanistic mission, a tight chain of command, and a history of functioning wholesomely in disasters and expecting no recompense. The Red Cross has a structure in fiscal tension, since it charges for some of its services and expects to be compensated. It also functions heavily with volunteers, rather than professionals, and has difficulty scaling up to a major disaster.

The success of informal human networks, as when a local sheriff called his brother at Costco, who called a friend at a trucking company, and so on down the line. See the discussion above of informal business networks. Some networks that should have functioned better were churches. Unfortunately, fleets of church buses did not function. More research needs to be done on the failures of the African American church structure to serve members in terms of evacuation and sustenance.

It should be noted that natural-disaster *mitigation* is not the same as disaster *prevention*. It will be interesting to see if Hurricane Katrina finally teaches us that such "natural" disasters are often cautionary tales—about our failure to address the mix of long-term environmental, economic, social, and political circumstances that accentuate our vulnerability to these events. Improved techniques are needed to better identify hazardous areas and how to create incentives and livelihood opportunities elsewhere for the poor and endangered communities living there, and then implement those incentives. Addressing specific disaster threats only when they occur also often fails to address other pressures that increase vulnerability to disasters—such as a lack of livelihood opportunities that drive the poor to settle in hazard-prone areas. As seen from the Hurricane Katrina experience, a lack of physical mobility freezes people in place geographically, socially, and economically.

Developing the city, the suburbs, and the exurbs can go beyond their capacity to absorb the human demands placed on the environment. The environment places demands on humans, and humans change the environment. For example, in the Gulf, natural wetlands that used to absorb the shock of hurricanes have been destroyed. We have discussed environmental issues relatively little in this book, because that is not our topic. Nevertheless, though our topic is humans in motion, it cannot be forgotten that they are in motion across the environment, that the environment is the substrate.

Attitudes about disasters pose significant challenges. Disaster preparedness can create a false sense of control, at times raising expectations without increasing local capacity to address root causes of vulnerability. Politics invariably enters into the picture as bigger, politically contentious issues that drive vulnerability are not addressed—such as the costs of relocating people to more safe areas, if they have the willingness to be relocated. In New Orleans, there has historically been an intense sense of place and a general unwillingness to relocate. While we write of transportation as people in motion, people staying where they are both are the product of culture and create culture. Culture must be recognized, as when we write of the need for cultural competence and sensitivity among those who interact with different demographic groups.

We must link research and concrete interventions in disaster mitigation to underlying vulnerabilities, including the health burden and transportation capabilities or potentialities of populations at risk. Disasters cause tremendous health and transportation burdens, either directly on populations or indirectly on the capacity of health services to address primary health care needs and transportation infrastructure carrying capacity. Disaster-risk analysis should be part of routine epidemiological analysis and systematic control and prevention, rather than merely treated as an emergency medicine or humanitarian matters. Note, however, the problem with standards of proof used by epidemiologists. Epidemiologists are scientists who insist on a scientific standard of proof—similar to the criminal justice standard of "beyond a reasonable doubt." If we wait for epidemiologists to bless causation of adverse effects on humans, we will find few such findings.

We need to understand and analyze the underlying trends that affect vulnerability. Addressing vulnerability includes examining historical and emerging data, trends, and development options that affect the ability of natural and human-made systems to absorb the effects of recurrent disasters. Examining these data, understanding their interactions, and designing strategies that take into account these relationships are early steps to examining disasters in the context of their interrelated causes, vulnerabilities, and impacts.

We should promote dialogue, community empowerment, and political will to increase adaptive capacity to respond to disasters through purposeful and unified action. The will to action must reach a critical mass and, when disaster strikes, become movement. There are dangerous political and civil rights implications in involuntary movement, such as forced evacuation. Must people be allowed to suffer in place? Is that their right in a democracy? Policy makers might invest in long-term plans that reduce or mitigate threats, generate a timely warning system to reduce potential costs when a disaster strikes, and plan short-term relief responses while working at longer-term rehabilitation. But these efforts will have a greater impact when implemented across sectors and at national, regional, and local scales, with the sensitivities discussed. Disasters and terrorism happen. When they do, the nature of our social contract is such that they should not be allowed to adversely affect one group much more than another. Basic humanitarianism dictates rescue without regard to race or ethnicity. Why then should the preparations for disaster be predicated on any other basis?

GETTING INVOLVED

The transportation planning and project design process can feel daunting to most community residents. Information on projects, including documentation of the planning process, may not be readily available. The technical language used in the transportation planning process may deter some community residents, even those with a background in community planning, from being able to speak with confidence in public meetings and forums. In many instances, it may not always be clear how a community resident can participate in the transportation planning process, either because the decision-making process itself lacks clarity or because opportunities for public participation may be poorly advertised or designed.

Despite these barriers to public participation, residents who are concerned with transportation equity have a range of options available to them to engage in the transportation planning process. The most obvious avenues include, but are not limited to, participating in formal public participation processes developed by transportation planning and implementing agencies or participating in the work of existing grass-roots organizations pursuing reforms in these same agencies. Community residents may also consider forming their own ad hoc efforts to push for reforms in transportation agencies, but such strategies are best saved for a different book.

Advocacy

The last two decades have seen the emergence of a vibrant and diverse infrastructure around transportation equity advocacy at the local, regional, and national levels. Transportation is a nexus issue that crosses a wide range of stakeholder groups. These stakeholders include but are not limited to civil rights, environmental, women's, disability rights, construction, labor, pro-business, and smart-growth advocates. At times, this wide range of stakeholder interests has been able to work in coalitions to achieve broader objectives in transportation policy, but for the most part these various constituencies work in parallel, occasionally at cross-purposes, for their own specific reform agendas.

Although at times the community of national advocacy organizations engaged in transportation equity issues may feel rather removed from the day-to-day concerns of community residents, there is an important and effective infrastructure in place at the national level actively monitoring the U.S. Congress and federal agencies involved in the transportation planning and project delivery process. This section includes a partial listing of these organizations and the roles that they play in national transportation advocacy.

The Surface Transportation Policy Project (STPP) is a national coalition that comes the closest among national organizations to representing the wide range of stakeholders interested in reforming the nation's transportation system. Stakeholders represented on the STPP steering committee include social justice advocacy organizations, passenger rail advocates, bicycle and pedestrian advocates, public transportation advocates, and environmentalists. STPP, and the coalition it represents, was instrumental in advocating for the Intermodal Surface Transportation Efficiency Act in 1991, which marked an important shift in how Congress approached transportation policy in the United States.

Other advocacy groups include the Transportation Equity Network, the Center for Community Change, the Gamaliel Foundation, and Smart Growth America, which focus on issues ranging from transportation equity to regional equity and community development. In addition, Environmental Defense is one of the more established national environmental organizations and is an important player in national transportation policy. As an organization, Environmental Defense has used both national and grassroots lobbying and litigation to advance its reform strategy.

Among disability rights organizations, the Paralyzed Veterans of America, the Association of Programs for Rural Independent Living, ADAPT, and the National Council on Independent Living have played important advocacy roles. Among civil rights organizations, the Lawyers Committee on Civil Rights Under Law, the National Urban League, and the Leadership Conference on Civil Rights have played an important part. The Community Transportation Association of America (CTAA) has played an important role in representing rural interests in the public transportation debate, as have organizations representing Native American tribes, like the National Congress of American Indians and the Tribal Transportation Association.

Building Partnerships

Transportation is an issue that engages a wide range of interest groups that do not typically work together. As an issue campaign, transportation can create new opportunities for collaboration, but such collaborations among unfamiliar constituencies can sometimes focus attention on existing tensions among these communities.

A coalition is a collective body of organizations that have drawn together around a common cause or objective. Coalitions typically form out of clear and specific self-interest. For these reasons, it is not necessary or even preferable for coalitions to last for very long periods of time. In an ideal situation, a coalition may form among a diverse set of organizations until the coalition has achieved its common set of objectives. At that time, the coalition will dissolve, but the relationships among the organizations will have been strengthened as a result of their collaborative work, and they will be better prepared to collaborate on future common objectives or crises.

In some instances, coalitions may turn into permanent organizations. Such coalitions can be difficult to sustain, and the work of sustaining them may take on a life of its own and stretch the resources of its member organizations. For each member organization, membership in a coalition is frequently evaluated in order to determine whether the benefits— stronger political clout, access to additional resources or expertise, opportunities to reach out to new constituencies—are balanced against the drain on staff and resources coalitions can create.

Partnerships between Low-Income and Environmental Organizations. At both the local and national levels, external observers often remark that there do not seem to be solid long-term coalitions among organizations representing low-income and minority constituencies and organizations in the traditional environmental advocacy community. In fact, this is generally an accurate observation. There are numerous reasons for this disconnectedness, despite the common interests shared by these constituencies around reforming the nation's transportation planning and project design processes.

All organizations tend to be shaped by their leadership, their membership, and their issue priorities. At the risk of making generalizations, the organizations in the environmental advocacy community tend to focus their attention on social change strategies grounded in specialized expertise, for example use of litigation, media, and policy analysis. Environmental organizations, especially established institutions, tend to represent a higher-income, whiter constituency and have greater access to financial resources than organizations grounded in low-income communities. Environmental organizations also tend to have a more highly educated constituency and are more likely to be drawn into regional or national political matters, including electoral activities and partisan politics. Environmental organizations tend to have more access to policy makers, and, in the field of transportation, environmental advocacy groups have an established presence in negotiating compromises with respect to the impact transportation projects may have on air quality, water quality, wildlife protection, and the protection of other natural resources. Finally, and perhaps most significantly, race plays a significant factor in dividing the environmental activists who focus their attention primarily on natural resources and activists of color who place greater emphasis on the impact of environmental and transportation decisions on minority communities. Some environmental organizations concentrate particularly on animals and trees, rather than on people. An entire powerful statute, the Endangered Species Act, provides much greater protections for rare animals than the civil rights laws provide for endangered people.

An important example of this tension is reflected in the ongoing struggle of the environmental justice movement. Proponents of environmental justice have sought for decades to bring attention to the impact of environmental racism on minority and low-income communities. Dr. Robert Bullard of the Environmental Justice Resource Center at Clark Atlanta University, along with a wide range of allies, has developed a compelling case for how federal, state, and local transportation decision-making

---

TriMet's Diversity and Transit Equity Department: Creating a Model for the Nation

The Tri-County Metropolitan Transportation District of Oregon (TriMet) is a municipal corporation that provides public transportation for the three counties in the Portland metropolitan area. The district covers roughly 575 square miles of urban, suburban, and rural areas and serves a population of about 1.3 million. Nationally, TriMet is known as a leader in bus and light-rail service, carrying more people than any other U.S. transit system its size.

With 44 miles of light-rail track and 93 bus lines, the district's residents and visitors boarded a bus or light-rail car nearly 96 million times in FY2005.

Like most transit agencies, TriMet has worked to build a broad ridership base, focusing on ways to get people out of their cars and into alternative modes. The majority of TriMet's riders (70 percent) are "choice" riders, meaning they either have a car or have consciously decided to forgo one and use transit instead. Nearly one-quarter (21 percent) of TriMet riders are considered "transit dependent," either because they don't have a car available or don't drive. While TriMet has received national accolades in many areas, there is a less well-known element that has fortified its position as a leader within mass transit, specifically on behalf of the carless population.

Need for TriMet's Diversity and Transit Equity Department

In 1998, TriMet Board of Directors appointed Fred Hansen as general manager. In his first day on the job, Hansen directed the agency to make diversity a priority in its strategic objectives. That commitment was put to the test almost immediately. At the time, TriMet was looking to build its next light-rail project through an area with the most diverse population and one of the highest poverty rates in the City of Portland. Many people of color along the proposed alignment were skeptical of TriMet's commitment to addressing the community's needs or sharing the economic benefits of the work. They soon found out that Hansen was ready to meet the challenge.

Central to Hansen's goals for TriMet's Interstate MAX light rail system was involvement of communities of color in making TriMet's disadvantaged business enterprise program (DBE) a national model. Emphasis was placed on providing more opportunities for minority-and women-owned firms and workers, especially those that living in the local community along the new alignment. To that end, Hansen recruited local staff and directed the agency to carry out his vision to create more opportunities for local disadvantaged businesses. TriMet did not employ set-asides or goals in light of the U.S. Supreme Court's decision in *Adarand v. Peña*, but rather set an aspirational goal of 16 percent. Its efforts resulted in 19 percent, or $35 million, of contract dollars going to local DBE firms, which included $8.1 million going to firms in the area surrounding the light-rail project.

Boosting apprenticeships and workforce inclusion of people of color and women on the project was also central to TriMet's goals, and TriMet exceeded its objectives. Women made up 10 percent of the project workforce, and racial minorities 23 percent. The agency also exceeded its apprenticeship goal to bring new workers into the construction: 17 percent of project hours were performed by apprentices. Apprentices provided 18.45 percent of total project hours, with people of color and women apprentices providing 7.72 percent of the total hours.

As the light-rail project began winding down, Hansen was interested in expanding the successes of Interstate MAX to the entire agency. He knew that by proactively incorporating transit equity principles into the planning process, the agency would include underrepresented populations in its decision-making processes and serve all of its customers. In fall 2002, Hansen created a Diversity and Transit Equity Department within TriMet.

processes have disadvantaged minority and low-income communities. Unfortunately, the broader environmental community has rarely placed a race-based analysis at the center of its own discussion around environmental protection. Advocates for environmental justice, as a result, have argued forcefully that the environmental advocacy community lacks a critical mass of people of color in positions of leadership who could help frame the relationship between race and environment.

Grassroots organizations grounded in low-income and minority communities, as compared with environmental advocacy organizations, tend to be grounded in particular communities (either based in geography or in identity, for example African American). They tend to have access to fewer financial resources and as a result have been unable to build the same kind of advocacy infrastructure available to environmental groups, for example, policy expertise, media resources, and access to legal assistance. Because their constituents tend to have less educational and economic opportunities, their members tend to have a different relationship to power. Their communities may lack basic services and be suffering from long-term issues of neglect. As a result, their membership may have a much more desperate relationship to issues that may determine the ability of their members to get and keep jobs, feed their families, make medical appointments, and the like. These organizations also spend a great deal of time focused on empowerment-oriented activities, including educational programs and direct citizen involvement. If these organizations are also committed to community organizing, a social change strategy that differs significantly from legal or policy advocacy strategies, they may be more willing to use tactics that heighten public tension between local residents and policy makers than established environmental organizations are comfortable using.

In working with coalitions of environmental, environmental justice, and transportation equity organizations, it is important to tend to these tensions in a proactive and transparent manner:

- *Be clear about the self-interest of the coalition's members.* This will often require being explicit—internally and sometimes externally—about the role of race and poverty in how and why issues are selected and discussed.
- *Be specific about the policy goals of the coalition.* The more specific the policy demands, the clearer various constituencies will be about why they are committed to the work of the overall coalition.

- *Acknowledge the disparity in resources and the range of assets that all organizations can bring to the coalition.* In the case of transportation equity, environmental organizations may bring to the coalition legal and regulatory expertise. Low-income groups may bring greater authenticity and urgency to an issue campaign, as well as real people.
- *Demand transparency from all coalition partners.* Environmental organizations often enjoy access to policy makers that may not be readily available to low-income constituencies. Any discussions with potential allies or adversaries should be done in a transparent manner within the coalition. Otherwise, coalition partners may quickly lose trust in each other.
- *Take the time to build relationships.* Within a coalition, it will often be the case that some groups are staff directed while others are more democratic in their internal decision-making process. This is often a major difference between environmental advocacy organizations and grassroots organizing groups. It will take time to build an effective level of buy-in from the membership of a grassroots organization, and environmental advocacy groups need to take some responsibility for ensuring that this happens.

Partnerships with Faith-Based Institutions. Similar principles apply to building relationships with faith-based institutions. The biggest mistake made by environmental organizations and antipoverty organizations is to assume that faith-based institutions, even openly progressive ones, share their self-interest. More often than not, environmental or antipoverty groups approach a church, synagogue, or mosque asking that institution to lend its name to a particular issue campaign without fully understanding the internal concerns or decision-making processes within that institution. A church that has an active peace and justice program is not necessarily one that fully understands the relationship among transportation, race, and poverty. And even if it does, faith-based institutions are generally cautious about being used by any organization, particularly secular groups, that may have what appears to be a very narrow set of issue priorities.

This is also true among faith-based institutions. As a case in point, a coalition of churches in the central city and inner-ring suburbs of Detroit that was engaged in a campaign to increase funding for public transportation as an antipoverty strategy knew from the beginning that churches further out in the suburbs might not share their same self-interest. The organization, called MOSES (Michigan Organizing Strategy to Enable Strength), began a process of one-on-one conversations with pastors and church leaders in a number of suburban churches in the larger metropolitan area that lasted several months. At the end of that process, MOSES found that a number of the members of these churches experienced the issue of transportation equity very differently—families in suburban churches were experiencing financial pressure because the lack of viable public transportation options meant they had to purchase more and more vehicles. They were also concerned about the safety of their children who were driving longer and longer distances to get to jobs, school, and other recreational and worship opportunities. It was only after these conversations had happened that MOSES was prepared to develop a framework that these suburban churches could fully buy into and support.

THE FUTURE OF TRANSPORTATION: WHERE DOES EQUITY FIT?

As more efforts are directed at integrating emerging technologies with transportation (such as Intelligent Transportation Systems [ITS], the use of electronic devices and methods in transportation infrastructure), effects will vary among traditionally discriminated-against groups. For example, people with disabilities may benefit from "smart" tools, such as "seeing" devices for the blind. But groups on the rough side of the Digital Divide (the gap in use of the Internet and computers) may suffer through lack of access to information and services available only through high-speed Internet connections and up-to-date computers. In addition, safety and communications innovations typically appear first in expensive cars, which lower-income people cannot afford. As discussed elsewhere in this book, there is a high correlation between minority and disability status and low income. Thus, low-income people will continue to be less safe and have fewer conveniences in transportation than higher-income people.

Because governmental investment is often a zero-sum game in these days of tight budgets, will lower-income people be disadvantaged if substantial investments are made in ITS? For example, in California the question has been raised as to whether the state should invest hundreds of millions of dollars to build the wireless communication backbone that makes ITS possible. By one estimate, it would take $100 million to wire the Bay Area.

Telecommuting is becoming more common, though not as fast as some thought it would. Telecommuting, or working at home for an entity located outside the home, can have major benefits for people with severe disabilities that make travel difficult for them. However, for minorities, the benefits are unknown. If white-collar jobs are those best suited for telecommuting, then some minority groups are less likely to benefit because of the types of job they disproportionately occupy. They will then continue to suffer the burden and cost of driving to work and taking public transportation. According to the Reason Foundation, a Libertarian think tank, "People working from home now outnumber mass transit commuters in 27 of the nation's 50 largest metropolitan areas."[5] If this trend continues, will investments in public transit look even less attractive than they do now? Will governments and corporations want to invest more in high-tech infrastructure, thus continuing to create a disadvantage for lower-income groups?

Telecommuting is also an example of convergence. Convergence is a coming together of two or more distinct entities or phenomena. Convergence is increasingly prevalent in the information technology world; in this context, the term refers to the combination of two or more different technologies in a single device. Taking pictures with a cell phone and surfing the web on a television are two of the most common examples of this trend. President Dwight D. Eisenhower stated, "Together, the united forces of our communication and transportation systems are dynamic elements in the very name we bear—United States. Without them we would be a mere alliance of many separate parts."[6] How this trend will affect low-income people and traditionally discriminated-against groups is a significant social equity concern.

FINAL THOUGHTS

Transportation mobility and access will continue to be critical to how cities, regions, and nations grow and prosper. Advances in technology have created new opportunities for communications and movement of information, but people and goods will still need to move from place to place. Mobility and access represent social and economic opportunity. Historically, the ability to travel long distances created opportunities through discoveries of new lands and resources. Transport for trade provided economic development as well as cultural exchange.

Lack of mobility and access can have the reverse effect. We have provided many examples where limited access and mobility have negatively affected particular social and economic classes. With sufficient planning these impacts can be reduced. The challenge is to maintain equity as a priority in planning.

We are not pessimistic about the future. Civil rights, social justice, environmental justice, transportation equity, and other related perspectives have been gaining momentum within planning processes. Improved planning decisions at the local, regional, state, and federal levels will play a part in building fair and equitable communities.

NOTES

1. U.S. General Accountability Office (2005).
2. Bollens (2003).
3. Raphael and Berube (2006).
4. 40 C.F.R. § 1508.7.
5. Moore (2005).
6. Dwight D. Eisenhower (1955).

I

Transportation Equity Terminology

Access

The ability of people to obtain desired goods, services and activities (Bureau of Transportation Statistics, U.S. Department of Transportation, 1997). Access is affected by the quality of mobility (movement of people and goods), substitutes for personal mobility (such as electronic communications and delivery services), land-use patterns, socioeconomics, demographics, historical usage, and other factors. For example, access for nondrivers can be improved not only by providing better transit service (a mobility strategy), but also by ensuring that they can find suitable housing within convenient walking distance of services such as stores and medical facilities, and that they are able to use the Internet and other communication technologies to obtain information and order goods and services.

Accessibility

The measure of the capacity of a location to be reached from different locations. It is a key element in transportation in general, since it is a direct expression of mobility in terms of people, freight, and information. Well-developed and efficient transportation systems offer high levels of accessibility while less-developed ones have lower levels of accessibility. Therefore, the capacity and the structure of transport infrastructure is a key element in the determination of accessibility. All places are not equal because some are more accessible than others, which implies inequalities. The idea of accessibility consequently relies on four core concepts:

- *Location*, where the relativity of places is estimated in relation to transport infrastructures, because they offer the means to support movement.

- *Distance*, which is derived from the connectivity between locations. Connectivity can exist only when there is a possibility to link two locations through transportation. It expresses the friction of space (or deterrence), and the location that has the least friction relative to others is likely to be the most accessible. Commonly, distance is expressed in units such as in kilometers or in time, but variables such as cost or energy spent can also be used. Accessibility is a good indicator of the underlying spatial structure because it takes into consideration location as well as the inequality conferred by distance.
- *Barriers*, especially physical ones as used in discussions of disability, in terms of inaccessibility.
- *Legal and conceptual obstacles*, such as institutional racism and inability to travel. Discrimination is a special type of intergroup friction, which can manifest as isolation, the ultimate lack of accessibility.

Adarand

U.S. Supreme Court case in which preferential presumptions on the basis of race and ethnicity in the awarding of federal government contracts were limited. Such preferences are subject to strict scrutiny under the equal protection component of the Due Process Clause of the Fifth Amendment to the U.S. Constitution. *See Adarand Constructors, Inc. v. Peña*, 515 U.S. 200 (1995); *Rothe Development Corp. v. Department of Defense*, 262 F.3d 1306, 1318-22 (Fed. Cir. 2001). Consequently, the provision's authorization of racial preferences can be sustained only if (1) they are enacted to achieve a compelling government interest; (2) they are narrowly tailored to further that interest; (3) there is a defined and quantified need based on historical and present lack of access to public goods; (4) less discriminatory means have been tried and failed; and (5) the preferences have some end point in time.

Adverse effects

Totality of significant individual and cumulative human health and environmental effects, including interrelated social and economic effects, which may include, but are not limited to, bodily impairment, infirmity, illness, or death; air, noise, and water pollution and soil contamination; destruction or disruption of man-made or natural resources; destruction or diminution of aesthetic values; destruction or disruption of community cohesion or a community's economic vitality; destruction or disruption of the availability of public and private facilities and services; vibration; adverse employment effects; displacement of persons, businesses, farms, or nonprofit organizations; increased traffic congestion, isolation, exclusion, or separation of minority or low-income individuals within a given community or from the broader community; and the denial of, reduction in, or significant delay in the receipt or benefits of an entity's programs, policies, or activities.

Affirmative action
The first time the phrase officially appeared was in an executive order by President John F. Kennedy on March 6, 1961. Affirmative action programs are adopted by institutions in the United States to promote equality, usually in employment, and usually directed to benefit a group of people who have historically been discriminated against. Affirmative action is sometimes thought to be inconsistent with the general principle of color-blind decision making by government. But this is a recognized exception to the rule—an inconsistency grounded on the unique conditions of the American history of past discrimination. Affirmative action can be distinguished from nondiscrimination and from reparations. In its famous *Bakke* decision, the Supreme Court struck down the affirmative action plan of the medical school of the University of California at Davis, which required a fixed quota of minority admissions. Five of the justices ruled, however, that a university could nonetheless take race into consideration as one of a number of factors. In 1988, in the *Croson* case, it declared unconstitutional a Richmond, Virginia, ordinance that gave preference to minority-owned firms in awarding municipal construction contracts. In the 1996 *Hopwood* case, the U.S. Court of Appeals for the Fifth Circuit applied these Supreme Court decisions to universities. It struck down the University of Texas law school's affirmative action plan and declared that race-sensitive admissions polices could not be used to seek racial diversity. The Supreme Court has ruled over many decades that classifications according to race are inherently "suspect" and must therefore be subject to a strict scrutiny that imposes the following three tests: Race-sensitive admissions plans must serve a compelling governmental interest, entities must not be able to pursue that goal adequately without them, and they must be narrowly tailored to achieve that goal. Identifying all uses of race as suspicious, and subjecting them to a strict scrutiny, allows judges to determine illegitimate uses of race. "Absent searching judicial inquiry into the justification for such race-based measures," Justice O'Connor said, "there is simply no way of determining what classifications are 'benign' or 'remedial' and what classifications are in fact motivated by illegitimate notions of racial inferiority or simple racial politics." In 2004 in the University of Michigan student admissions cases, use of diversity as one factor was permitted.

Antidiscrimination
The United States condemns the different treatment of otherwise similarly situated individuals on the basis of race, color, sex, national origin, disability, religion, and other protected characteristics. Some jurisdictions also prohibit discrimination on the basis of sexual orientation, and fair housing laws prohibit discrimination on the basis of family and marital status. Some antidiscrimination laws, such as Title VII of the Civil Rights Act of 1964 and other older civil rights enactments, contain prohibitions on actions by institutions, while other

laws, such as the Americans with Disabilities Act of 1990 (ADA) and the Family and Medical Leave Act of 1993 (FMLA), contain positive requirements for barrier lowering, as well as prohibitions. Antidiscrimination focuses on equality of treatment, as distinct from accommodation to a condition like disability or religion, which focuses on effectiveness of access. Antidiscrimination is a law enforcement effort, as opposed to hortatory laws, which are not self-enforcing. Antidiscrimination is usually enforced through investigating complaints of discrimination made to a neutral governmental body.

Barrier effect

The way that roads and traffic can reduce pedestrian and bicycle mobility. It is sometimes recognized as a problem when a new highway is constructed across a neighborhood (and therefore "solved" by building a pedestrian overpass), but often ignored by traffic engineers in North America. It is less common to acknowledge that incremental increases in vehicle traffic volumes and speeds can be detrimental to non-motorized travel. These costs are often paid by traditionally disadvantaged populations without access to motor vehicles, including people of color, children, the poor, the elderly, and people with disabilities.

Brownfields

Abandoned, idle, or underused industrial and commercial facilities where expansion or redevelopment is complicated by real or perceived environmental contamination from their past use. Toxic contamination can be very expensive for a present owner to clean up, and there is substantial legal liability involved. Brownfields grants can remove this roadblock to reuse by determining actual cleanup needs, assessing costs, and identifying financing. Creation of legal safe harbors is another solution. EPA's Brownfields Initiative is designed to empower states, local governments, and other stakeholders in economic redevelopment to work together to assess, clean up, and sustainably reuse brownfields. Important links exist between transportation and brownfields. Because of their valuable commonly central locations, the revitalization of brownfields can reduce trip lengths, make more efficient use of existing infrastructure, support transit systems, and make walking and biking viable mode choices. The U.S. Environmental Protection Agency considers infill brownfields redevelopment to be a transportation control measure.

Community benefits agreement

A potentially powerful equitable development strategy providing community members the means to ensure that public investments result in defined public benefits tailored to community needs.

Community impact assessment

An iterative process of understanding potential impacts of proposed transportation activities on affected communities and their subpopulations throughout transportation decision making. Assessments focus on issues that affect the community and the quality of life of its people. Issues of usual concern include safety; mobility/access; community cohesion; displacement of people, businesses, and farms; adverse employment effects; tax and property value losses; noise; access to public facilities and services; aesthetic values; destruction or disruption of man-made and natural resources; disruption of desirable community growth; and nondiscrimination. As mitigation is proposed, anticipated impacts of that mitigation on the community and its subpopulations must also be considered. Transportation planners must consider both the benefits and burdens of their decisions. Detailed documentation of activities, data, findings, decisions, and commitments are critical for continuity.

Community needs assessment

A process in which a community's needs, demographics, resources, and priorities for comprehensive services are systematically determined. Results are used to determine the segments of the community in greatest need and to guide program design and service delivery.

Contract bundling

An attempt by federal agencies to make contracting for goods and services more efficient and easier to administer by grouping smaller contracts into a "bundle," thereby creating fewer, larger contracts. Small and disadvantaged businesses object to this bundling because it means they have fewer opportunities to bid on federal contracts. Such loss of opportunity may be unintentionally (or intentionally) discriminatory. Offices of Small and Disadvantaged Business Utilization or OSDBUs (see elsewhere in this section) are supposed to work with the Small Business Administration to (1) identify proposed solicitations that involve bundling, (2) facilitate small business participation as prime contractors, and (3) facilitate small business participation as subcontractors and suppliers where participation by small business concerns as prime contractors is unlikely.

Cultural competence

Understanding of the cultural, ethnicity, disability, religious, gender, and gender preference factors that impact both providing and receiving social services. This includes the impact of culture/ethnicity on development, sociocultural identity, and values and beliefs. It is also a set of interpersonal skills that allows individuals to increase their understanding and appreciation of cultural differences and similarities within, among and between groups. It requires a willingness and ability to draw on community-based values, traditions, and customs, and to work with knowledgeable persons of and from the community in developing focused interventions, communications, and other supports (Orlandi, 1992). A set of cultural behaviors and attitudes integrated into the practice methods of a system, agency, or its professionals, that enables them to work effectively in cross-cultural situations. Cultural competency is achieved by translating and integrating knowledge about individuals and groups of people into specific practices and policies applied in appropriate cultural settings.

Cultural diversity

Considering race, ethnicity, language, nationality, sexual orientation, migration experience, disability, age, gender, economic considerations, educational status, and other factors. Factors that may be considered include the following:

- Role of family;
- Community values;
- Gender roles, especially the role of women in traditional societies;
- Attitudes toward death, especially respecting different communities' rituals;
- Migration experiences, especially if the victims are refugees who have experienced previous oppression and hardship;
- Religion and religious beliefs and support systems;
- Education and employment: groups with less education and income are more likely to suffer crime and have less access to legal remedies;
- Language: whether the victim can communicate effectively with service providers, and if interpreters should be used; and;
- Degree of assimilation into the dominant culture (Ohio Coalition, 1991; "Cross-Cultural Service Delivery," 1992; Ogawa, 1990).

Cumulative effects (cumulative impacts)

Impacts on health and the environment which result from the incremental impact of a proposed governmental or private industry action when added to other past, present, and reasonably foreseeable future actions, regardless of which agency or entity (federal or nonfederal) or person undertakes such actions. Cumulative impacts result from actions that may be individually minor but are collectively significant while taking place over a period of time. At the plan level, it is important to focus on the combined effects of a series of actions occurring over a longer period of time (compared to individual actions at the project level). The National Environmental Policy Act (NEPA) at 40 C.F.R. § 1508.7 speaks to them.

Cumulative risk assessment (CRA)

Evaluating and measuring risks to estimate differential health risks from environmental exposures within populations. Identifying populations at increased risk from environmental exposures is the first step toward mitigating such risks as required by the fair treatment mandate of environmental justice. CRA methods remain under development except for a limited application in pesticide regulations. CRA adds a health dimension to pollutant concentrations to produce a more comprehensive understanding of environmental inequities that can inform decision making. It is a viable tool to identify high-risk areas and to guide surveillance, research, mitigation, law enforcement, and interventions.

Economically disadvantaged individuals

Socially disadvantaged individuals whose ability to compete in the free enterprise system has been impaired due to diminished capital, funding, credit, insurance, bonding, or access opportunities, as compared with others in the same or similar line of business in a competitive market area who are not socially disadvantaged.

Economic costs of highways due to public health impacts

The U.S. Department of Transportation has estimated the national aggregate health costs of criteria air pollutants from highways at $40 to $68 billion per year (Table 9, Addendum to the 1997 Federal Highway Cost Allocation Study Final Report, U.S. Department of Transportation, Federal Highway Administration [May 2000]).

Economic development

The entire array of activities, some conducted by government and some by the private sector, often in partnership with government, that are intended to expand the economy of a designated area to increase the number and quality of jobs available to the population of that area, and to improve the tax base.

Economic opportunity structure

Industrial composition, the location of jobs, and the overall demand for labor. The deterioration of employment for inner-city residents has been linked to each characteristic. For example, the decline in the manufacturing sector in general and its relocation out of cities to industrial parks and overseas are often mentioned as important determinants of inner-city unemployment. Minority employment, and especially youth employment, is very sensitive to the overall demand for labor.

Equal Employment Opportunity Commission (EEOC)

The federal agency responsible for enforcing the Equal Pay Act of 1963, Title VII of the Civil Rights Act of 1964, the Age Discrimination in Employment Act of 1967 as amended (ADEA), the Americans with Disabilities Act (ADA) of 1990, the Civil Rights Act of 1991, and other federal laws that prohibit employment discrimination. The EEOC carries out its work at headquarters and in numerous field and district offices throughout the U.S. It investigates complaints, litigates, and issues policy guidance. The EEOC's guidance does not have the force of law. Controlling law is determined not by the commission but by the courts.

Section 8(a) program

A business development initiative designed to help small and disadvantaged businesses overcome social and economic disadvantage and transition them into the economic mainstream by extending preferential federal contracting benefits and opportunities. *See* 15 U.S.C. § 637. Under Small Business Administration regulations, members of certain racial and ethnic groups (such as blacks, Hispanics, and Asian-Americans/Pacific Islanders) are presumed to be socially disadvantaged and thus are granted preferential treatment in the awarding of government contracts under that program. *See* 13 C.F.R. § 124.103(b)(1). This aspect of the section 8(a) program, and comparable provisions of individual agency programs patterned after that program, have been repeatedly challenged on constitutional equal protection grounds in extensive litigation. *See, e.g., Adarand Constructors, Inc. v. Peña*, 515 U.S. 200 (1995); *Rothe Development Corp. v. U.S. Dept. of Defense*, 262 F.3d 1306 (Fed. Cir. 2001); *Dynalantic Corp. v. U.S. Dept. of Defense*, 115 F.3d 1012 (D.C. Cir. 1997). The 8(a) program gets its name from Section 8(a) of the Small Business Act. The businesses are assisted through a combination of management and technical assistance and increased access to federal contracting opportunities. While being certified as 8(a) does not guarantee a firm a government contract, it greatly enhances the participant's chances either through noncompetitive award or by winning a bid. The program runs for a maximum of nine years for each business. During this time, participants must complete an initial four-year development phase and gradually wean themselves away from dependence on special 8(a) contracting opportunities.

Electronic tolling

Collecting fees for road use, outside conventional highway toll plazas. Also called highway speed tolling, open road tolling, express tolling. One newsletter uses the term "electronic toll express" and the acronym ETX. A form of electronic tolling is dynamic tolling, which changes the toll based on road use demands according to time of day.

Empowerment Zones/Enterprise Communities (EZ/EC)

These areas, designated by the U.S. Departments of Housing and Urban Development (HUD) and Agriculture (USDA), are eligible for preferences and flexibility in many federal grant programs. EZ/ECs are chosen competitively based on community poverty characteristics and local strategic planning processes.

Environmental assessment (EA)

A concise public document that analyzes the environmental impacts of a proposed governmental action. If an agency determines that the proposed action will not have a significant impact on the human environment, the agency issues a Finding of No Significant Impact (FONSI). In this case, there is no need to prepare an Environmental Impact Statement (EIS). However, if a potentially significant impact is found, the agency must issue a Notice of Intent (NOI) and complete an EIS before deciding to undertake the proposed action. Environmental assessments are prepared for actions that are not exclusions and do not clearly require the preparation of an EIS. The EA should not contain long descriptions, detailed information, or analyses (40 C.F.R. § 1508.9).

Environmental impact statement (EIS)
A detailed, written statement required by Section 102(2)(C) of NEPA (National Environmental Policy Act of 1969 [42 U.S.C. § 4321 *et seq.*]). The statement must be prepared when the proposed action may significantly affect the quality of the human environment. The EIS must include explicit discussion of alternatives to the proposed action. The formal process begins when the sponsoring agencies publishes a Notice of Intent (NOI) to prepare an EIS in the Federal Register. After a scoping process, the proposing agency prepares and issues a Draft Environmental Impact Statement, and files it with the Environmental Protection Agency (EPA). EPA then prepares a notice in the Federal Register that informs the public of the public comment period. At the close of the comment period, the agency reviews and considers the comments, and makes changes as appropriate. The Final Environmental Impact Statement (FEIS) is then issued with an EPA notice in Federal Register. The FEIS is then used by the agency is selecting the action that it will pursue (which may be different from the preferred alternative in the EIS), and this decision is documented in a Record of Decision.

Environmental indicators
Measures of environmental quality that can be used to assess status and trends in the environment's ability to support human and ecological health (i.e., health impacts, number of species at risk of extinction, percentage of population served by drinking water systems). An indicators report will also include program performance indicators, which are measures of whether programs are meeting their intended goals (i.e., number of children tested for blood lead levels, number of inspections conducted).

Environmental justice
Ensuring that the effects of transportation planning and projects are appropriately and fairly spread throughout the communities of all the people who live in and visit an area. It is important to make sure that minorities and those in poverty do not bear the brunt of the negative externalities associated with transportation projects while making sure they receive their fair share of the benefits.

Environmental justice complaint
An administrative complaint filed by a member of the public, a group of people, or their representatives against a recipient of federal financial assistance, a transportation provider, or a transportation-related entity, alleging discrimination or adverse environmental effects against a specified minority or low-income community or population group because of a project or activity funded or carried out by a governmental agency.

Equality
Commensurateness or fairness looked at from an active or passive perspective. The active perspective, for example, looks at equality between different modes of

traffic and different groups of people. The passive perspective is concerned with the fact that a mode of traffic has negative impacts on people who do not use it.

Equal opportunity
A level playing field in institutions or the economy. Conducting all personnel activities to assure equal access in all phases of the employment process. Basing employment decisions solely on the individual merit and fitness of applicants and employees related to specific jobs without regard to race, color, religion, sex, age, national origin, disability, or marital status, or other characteristics not related to merit.

Equity
Derived from a concept of social justice. It represents a belief that there are some things that people should have; that there are basic needs that should be fulfilled; that burdens and rewards should not be spread too divergently across the community; and that policy should be directed with impartiality, fairness, and justice towards these ends. It is generally agreed that equity implies a need for fairness (not necessarily equality) in the distribution of gains and losses, and the entitlement of everyone to an acceptable quality and standard of living.

Equity impact statement
An entity's official statement that considers the distribution of the opportunities to participate in decisions and the outcomes of those decisions (in terms of mobility, economic, environmental, and health effects) that different strata (spatial, temporal, modal, generational, gender, racial, cultural, and income) of the population receive.

Equity-justified
Making the case for public support for transportation services, such as transit, on grounds of fairness of service to people, usually traditionally discriminated-against classes or others who might otherwise miss out on the use of the service. About half of transit subsidies are equity-justified, meaning that they are intended to provide basic mobility for nondrivers, and so result in service in lower-density areas and during off-peak hours, which can be costly and inefficient.

Equity planning movement
A response of planners to what was seen as the racial crisis in America's cities, including segregation and poverty. This is the modern version of what was once the most important social equity movement in the field, advocacy planning. Other related strains of thought are postmodernism and social mobilization. Conscious equity planning can be a corrective to the mistakes that urban planners have made in the past in wiping out stable minority communities through urban renewal.

Ethnicity

A common heritage shared by a particular group (Zenner, 1996) based on tracing heritage to a particular country or region. Heritage includes similar history, language, rituals, and preferences for music and foods.

Ethnic fractionalization

A way of looking at diversity. Ethnic groups can be defined according to the old five Census categories (White; Black; American Indian–Eskimo–Aleutian; Asian–Pacific Islander; and Other). There are also measures of cultural diversity based on language, lifestyle, and attitudes.

Exit-ramp economy

Expansive, low-density, and auto-dependent growth. Locating office, commercial retail, and high-tech business campuses along suburban freeways miles from the urban core. Residents and businesses in these conglomerations have found that they produce traffic congestion, dead nights, overcrowded schools, disappearing open space, and diminished quality of life.

Expulsive zoning

Using minority neighborhoods as dumping grounds for Locally Unwanted Land Use (known in planning by the acronym LULU or commonly as NIMBY: "not in my backyard"). Examples of such uses are landfills, transfer stations, and concentrations of group homes for people with chemical dependencies. Localities often accomplish such exclusion by granting variances, conditional use permits, and spot zonings in residentially zoned low-income minority neighborhoods. These actions effectively "expel" residential use and residents from an area and lower the property values of the remaining residences. In many cities, stable residential minority neighborhoods are also externally controlled by the fact that they were zoned commercial or industrial years ago. When they attempt to seek residential "downzoning" to maintain stability they are rebuffed. Zoning also controls aspects of the accessibility and availability of child care, elder care, and other services needed to maintain neighborhood livability.

Exurban

Many Americans have been moving to rural homes within the commuting range of urban areas. The low-density, rural housing these homebuyers seek is known as exurban development. A major link of exurban areas with cities and suburbs is employment and the mobility that comes with freeways.

Fair housing

The ability of persons of similar incomes to have the same options in housing choice without regard to race, color, religion, gender, national origin, or familial or disability status. People should have the choice to live where they want and can afford to live without the fear or threat of discrimination. Because housing choice is so important to individual and community well-being, government officials, business leaders, and private citizens sometimes promote fair housing as a benefit to everyone. The choice of residence influences accessibility to services such as health care, banking, education, and employment. Fair housing is protected by federal and many state laws.

Fair Housing Act

A federal statute that prohibits discrimination because of race, color, religion, sex, national origin, disability, and familial status in most housing-related transactions. It makes it unlawful to indicate any preference or limitation on these bases when advertising the sale or rental of a dwelling. The act also prohibits harassment of anyone exercising a fair housing right and retaliation against an individual because he or she has assisted, or participated in any manner, in a fair housing investigation. It covers housing in the public and private sectors. It is enforced by the U.S. Department of Housing and Urban Development, and by numerous state agencies.

Fairness

A concept that cannot be reduced to a single measure and that is related to equity, equality, and nondiscrimination. In terms of transportation, it touches on a range of issues, including distribution of costs and benefits, environmental justice, economically regressive efforts of tolling, taking a group's views into consideration, extending into the present the vestiges of past illegal and legal discrimination, and respect for social and cultural values. Even at a young age, people often have an intense sense of what is fair, and become angry if they perceive that they are not treated fairly.

Gentrification

Whiter, higher-income people moving into predominantly minority and lower-income neighborhoods, fixing up houses, and driving minorities and lower-income people out because of rising housing prices. New businesses that cater to the new population often follow. Sometimes this is followed by improved community services, which the minority community had not been able to achieve because of lack of political power. Sometimes longtime, low-income community members—primarily people of color—can be protected and the neighborhood culture preserved. While there are still versions of traditional urban renewal at work in some communities, the overall picture is a mix of large- and small-scale private development, regional economic forces, and efforts to contain sprawl within urban growth boundaries. Some American cities now are witnessing both public and private investment flows back into the urban core. Disenchantment with suburban traffic congestion and long commutes, renewed investment in downtowns, and the vibrant cultural life and architectural heritage of urban centers have created new demand for downtown living. Lured by the possibility of generating increased tax revenues, public leaders aggressively advance policies to encourage commercial and residential investments in low-income neighborhoods. Historically, the gentrification process starts first with disinvestment, often fueled by white flight. Decades of economic disinvestment of central cities (and more recently, of older suburban communities) isolated many low-income and communities of color from economic opportunities. The decline of these areas was fueled by federal, state, and local policies that drew resources out of the cities to the sprawling fringes of metropolitan regions; major shifts in industrial production and technology that led to the abandonment of industrial infrastructure and toxic land in urban core communities; practices of private investors and financial institutions that denied capital needs; and race factors that both "pushed" and "pulled," ranging from white flight when school integration was mandated to the gains of the civil rights movement that afforded middle-class mobility for communities of color, leaving greater concentration of poverty in the disinvested communities.

Geographic Information System (GIS)
A computer hardware and software system designed to collect, manipulate, analyze, and display spatial and location-based data for solving complex resource, environmental, and social problems. The analysis combines relational databases with spatial interpretation and outputs, often in form of maps.

Government-to-government relations
The relationship between the United States and federally recognized Indian tribes, as reaffirmed in the president's memorandum on "Government to Government Relations with Native American Tribal Governments" (April 29, 1994). The memorandum directs federal agencies to operate "within a government-to-government relationship with federally recognized tribal governments." It also directs agencies to consult with tribes prior to making decisions that affect tribal governments and to ensure that all components in the agency are aware of the requirements of the memorandum. In addition, Executive Order No. 13175, "Consultation and Coordination with Indian Tribal Governments," directs federal agencies to consult with tribal governments about issues that "significantly or uniquely affect their communities." These are due to the unique legal relationships that exist between the federal government and Indian tribal governments, as reflected in the Constitution of the United States, treaties, federal statutes, executive orders, and numerous court decisions. As domestic dependant nations, Indian tribes exercise inherent sovereign powers over their members and territory. The federal government has a federal trust relationship with Indian tribes, and this historic relationship requires the federal government to adhere to certain fiduciary standards in its dealings with Indian tribes.

Greenbelt

A series of connected open space that follow natural features such as ravines, creeks, or streams. A greenbelt is usually a combination of natural vegetation and landscaped or regularly maintained areas. Ideally, it provides pedestrian, bicycle, and wildlife connections to other open spaces in a larger open space system or to destinations such as schools, libraries, and neighborhood commercial areas. Perimeter roads along one or both sides of a greenbelt are encouraged for several reasons:

1. They provide access as they parallel a greenbelt;
2. They permit public observation of activities within a greenbelt, making it a safer place;
3. A greenbelt provides a driver with an aesthetic contrast to the built environment.

Greenbelt width requirements are intended to promote a sense of openness and avoid a sense of enclosure. The concept had its origins in England in the 1920s; was implemented in Greenbelt, Maryland, in the 1930s; and today is often reduced to a single row of trees.

Healthy community

A community that embraces the belief that health is more than merely an absence of disease; a healthy community includes elements that enable people to maintain a high quality of life and productivity. For example:

1. A healthy community offers access to health care services that focus on both treatment and prevention for all members of the community.
2. A healthy community is safe.
3. A healthy community has roads, schools, playgrounds, and other services to meet the needs of the people in that community.
4. A healthy community has a healthy and safe environment (*Healthy People in Healthy Communities*. U.S. DHHS, February 2001).

Hispanic

The terms "Hispanic" and "Latino" are used interchangeably in many documents and refer collectively to Mexicans, Puerto Ricans, Cubans, Central and South Americans, Dominicans, and others of Spanish and Latin American descent. Latinos may be of any race; therefore, unless denoted as "non-Hispanic," persons of Hispanic origin may be included in both the "Black" and "White" racial categories of the U.S census. Data on Latinos in the United States do not include the 2.8 million residents of Puerto Rico. The current usage of the term "Hispanic" is driven by Directive 15 of the Office of Management and Budget. This directive was issued in 1978 to increase the availability of data on persons of Hispanic origin and to encourage uniform collection and reporting of data on different racial and ethnic groups by federal agencies. The directive defined as "Hispanic" a person of Mexican, Puerto Rican, Cuban, Central or South American, or other Spanish culture or origin. "Latino" may be a more historically and geopolitically accurate term to describe and identify populations of Caribbean and Latin American origin living in the United States. The term emphasizes the origins and history of those who are indigenous to Latin America, not to Spain. There is much controversy in the affected communities as to the preferred term of reference.

Lack of hope
Many people who are socially excluded feel little hope for the future, especially if barriers such as disability or health problems, lack of transportation, low skills, discrimination, or a lack of local jobs limit the opportunities to work or participate in society in other ways. This feeling may be exacerbated by fear that the prospects for their children may be no better. Increasing wage gaps, lack of access to higher education, and conservative federal court decisions that undercut civil rights gains can make lack of hope a realistic reaction to one's environment.

Human environment
The physical, social, and economic components, conditions, and factors that interactively determine the state, condition, and quality of living conditions, employment, and health of those affected directly or indirectly by a proposed institutional project (Outer Continental Shelf Lands Act, 43 U.S.C. § 1331).

Human rights
Principles recognized as applying universally to all human beings. A human right is a claim each person has, by virtue of being human, to those conditions and resources that are fundamental to life and dignity. They do not need to be specifically granted, nor can they be taken away. They exist for each person, regardless of the attitudes or laws that govern a society. Human rights encompass an array of political, social, economic, and cultural rights. In most nation-states the Universal Declaration of Human Rights and its successor, the International Covenant on Social, Economic and Cultural Rights, are formally accepted. However, human rights are not necessarily respected.

Human services transportation
Transportation related to the provision of human or social services. Includes transportation for the elderly and people with disabilities when the transportation is provided by an arrangement other than the public service available to all. Transportation for clients of a specific agency that is usually limited to a specific trip purpose. These trips are often provided under contract to a human service agency and may be provided exclusively or rideshared with other human service agencies or general public service.

Inclusion

To be given the opportunity to participate in all activities available in a community. People are either included or excluded. Discussion of inclusion typically addresses issues related to diversity, community building, and the consequence of exclusion. Inclusion, used with respect to individuals with disabilities, means the acceptance and encouragement of the presence and participation of such individuals in social, educational, work, and community activities. Inclusion enables individuals with disabilities to:

1. have friendships and relationships with individuals and families of their own choice;
2. live in homes close to community resources, with regular contact with individuals without disabilities in their communities;
3. enjoy full access to and active participation in the same community activities and types of employment as individuals without disabilities; and
4. take full advantage of their integration into the same community resources as individuals without disabilities, living, learning, working, and enjoying life in regular contact with individuals without disabilities.

Inclusionary zoning (IZ)

Through land-use regulation, requiring developers of housing projects that have more than a set number of units to offer a certain percent of the units to low- and moderate-income households. The developer can build the housing or contribute to a fund to develop it elsewhere. This tool has particular relevance in gentrifying communities, where high-income and luxury apartment developments can overrun the existing low- and moderate-income housing stock. Inclusionary zoning (IZ) is increasingly used as a policy tool for creating affordable housing by setting aside affordable units in new or rehabilitated housing developments. In the process, IZ also promotes the creation of mixed-income communities.

Indian tribe

An Indian tribe, band, nation, or other organized group or community, including a Native Village, Regional Corporation, or Village Corporation, as those terms are defined in section 3 of the Alaska Native Claims Settlement Act (43 U.S.C. § 1602), which is recognized as eligible for the special programs and services provided by the United States to Indians because of their status as Indians and which the Secretary of the Interior acknowledges to exist as an Indian tribe pursuant to the Federally Recognized Indian Tribe List Act of 1994, 25 U.S.C. § 479a (November 6, 2000, Executive Order).

Infrastructure

The physical underpinnings of society, including, but not limited to, roads, bridges, transit, waste systems, public housing, sidewalks, utility installations, parks, public buildings, and communications networks. "Infrastructure" is resources required for an activity and the underlying foundation or basic framework, especially the basic installations and facilities on which the continuance and growth of a community or state depends. When we think of infrastructure we think of built infrastructure such as roads, electric power lines, and water systems as well as social infrastructure such as schools, hospitals, and libraries. Major cities require a vast array of supporting infrastructures including energy, water, sewers, and transport. Among the most important urban infrastructures are the following:

- Public utilities, including power, telecommunications, piped water supply, sewage, waste collection and disposal, and piped gas.
- Public works, including public transit, roads, and transport terminals (ports, rail stations, airports).

Infrastructures can be publicly or privately owned. Public infrastructures have the advantage of being available to a larger share of the population at a low cost, but are expensive for the government to maintain. Private infrastructures are servicing only a limited share of the population, at the choice of the infrastructure company, but can be financially profitable.

Indigence
The concern that some members of other protected categories are additionally oppressed by impoverishment as a consequence of power inequality. One example is the exclusion of abortion from Medicaid funding.

Indirect effects
Effects caused by the proposed action and are later in time or farther removed in distance, but are still reasonably foreseeable. Indirect effects may include growth-inducing effects and other effects related to induced changes in the pattern of land use, population density or growth rate, and related effects on air and water and other natural systems, including ecosystems (40 C.F.R. § 1508.8).

Institutional Racism
An indirect and largely invisible process—the usually long-standing, unintentional, or intentional barriers and procedures that disadvantage members of ethnic and racial minority groups. (Excerpt from A. J. Price [1997] *Human Resource Management in a Business Context*.) The network of institutional structures, policies, and practices that create advantages and benefits for white people, and discrimination, oppression, and disadvantages for people from targeted racial groups. The advantages created for white people are often invisible to them, or are considered "rights" available to everyone as opposed to "privileges" awarded to only some individuals and groups. Institutional racism generally encompasses the collective effect of practices and behaviors that prevent

a targeted group from fully realizing the benefits of their own efforts or from sharing in publicly supported opportunities and activities. Murray and Clark (1990), writing in the *American School Board Journal*, identified eight patterns of racism that constitute institutionalized racism in schools:

1. Hostile, insensitive acts
2. Harsher sanctions against particular ethnic groups
3. Bias in attention: public praise, help, encouragement
4. Bias in selection of curriculum
5. Unequal instruction: allowed misbehavior, unchallenging work
6. Bias in attitudes: favoritism, "You're not like other . . . "
7. Failure to hire people of color
8. Denial of racist actions

These concepts can be extended to many other aspects of social infrastructure.

Integration
The bringing of people of different racial or ethnic groups into unrestricted and equal association. Contrast segregation. In U.S. history, it has been the goal of the civil rights movement to break down the barriers of discrimination and segregation separating African Americans from the rest of American society. Desegregation is sometimes seen as a direct action against segregation; that is, it signifies the act of removing legal barriers to the equal treatment of black citizens as guaranteed by the Constitution. The movement toward desegregation, breaking down the nation's Jim Crow system, became increasingly popular in the decade after World War II. Integration, on the other hand, Professor Oscar Handlin maintains, implies several things not yet necessarily accepted in all areas of American society. In one sense it refers to the "leveling of all barriers to association other than those based on ability, taste, and personal preference"; in other words, providing equal opportunity. But in another sense integration calls for the random distribution of a minority throughout society. Here, according to Handlin, the emphasis is on racial balance in areas of occupation, education, residency, and the like.

Intergenerational equity
The success of cities of the future will largely depend upon the legacy on current cities on resources and the environment. National capital assets passed on to the next generation must be at least equal value.

Interstate system
That system of highways which connects the principal metropolitan areas, cities, and industrial centers of the United States. The interstate system also connects at suitable border points with routes of continental importance in Canada and Mexico. The routes of the interstate system are selected by joint action of

the state highway department of each state and the adjoining states, subject to the approval of the U.S. Secretary of Transportation.

Jim Crow laws

Jim Crow was the name of a minstrel routine (actually called "Jump Jim Crow") begun by the father of the American minstrel show, Thomas Dartmouth Rice. Minstrel shows were variety shows that entertained, using distorted images of black life. By the 1890s, the term Jim Crow came to describe laws that sanctioned subordination and segregation of black people in the South. The first Jim Crow or segregation law was passed in Louisiana. A black man named Homer Plessy sued when he was jailed for sitting in a railroad car designated for whites. The case, *Plessy v. Ferguson* (1896), was eventually heard by the Supreme Court. The decision of the court held that since Plessy was "a colored man and be so assigned, he has been deprived of no property, since he is not lawfully entitled to the reputation of a white man." The Court stated that the 14th Amendment "could not have been intended to abolish distinctions based upon color, or to enforce social as distinguished from political equality." This decision legally established the idea of "separate but equal," and led to the passing and enforcing of Jim Crow laws. People were fired from jobs, jailed, and killed for breaking these laws.

Jitney

Unaffiliated group passenger cars or vans operating on fixed routes in cities (sometimes with minor deviations) as demand warrants without fixed schedules or fixed stops. They are permitted in only about three U.S. cities, where local laws often prohibit such private entrepreneurs. The rates are lower than for taxis. Passengers are picked up anywhere along the route (*flag stops*). Because there are no schedules, headways are usually five to 10 minutes so passengers have only brief waiting periods. Jitney service is sometimes used in the United States to provide seasonal, tourist, or park and ride service. It is a more common public transportation mode in other countries where private entrepreneurs are often the providers of service.

Job Access and Reverse Commute Program (JARC)

This federal transportation program is intended to respond to opportunity issues in transportation. Under the Transportation Equity Act for the 21st Century, it has two major goals: (1) to provide transportation services in urban, suburban, and rural areas to assist welfare recipients and low-income individuals in accessing employment opportunities; and (2) to increase collaboration among the transportation providers, human service agencies, employers, MPOs, states, and affected communities and individuals. One of the criteria for project selection is the degree to which collaborative and consensus-based planning and decision-making processes have been used, with particular evaluation of participation by nontraditional grassroots organizations. Many of the projects are focused on expanding early morning, night owl, and weekend services. JARC was intended to provide funding on a competitive basis to communities trying to address gaps in transportation services to low-income people who are trying to work. It aims to establish a regional approach to job access challenges through the establishment of an Area-Wide Job Access and Reverse Commute Transportation Plan to facilitate regionwide collaboration among transportation and human service providers to connect welfare recipients and low-income individuals to employment activities. For more information, see www.fta.dot .gov.

Journey solutions

An initiative in the United Kingdom to ease trips. One of the first initiatives of the project is PLU.S.BU.S., a joint ticketing scheme for buses and trains throughout the country. Part of PLU.S.BU.S. is providing good quality information about the local bus system at participating rail stations. Other ways Journey Solutions seeks to make public transport attractive is by improving the connection between modes such as the coordination of schedules, securing passage between transport stops, and making all necessary travel information available before the trip begins. Planned improvements include encouraging public transport services to and from airports, and better integration of services in rural areas.

Justice

Treating people justly and fairly under the law, promoting just or fair social institutions, fighting injustice, giving people their due, distributing benefits and burdens equally, distributing benefits and burdens according to need, distributing benefits and burdens according to a fair procedure that protects basic rights.

Key stations

The 685 key public transit rail stations nationwide at 33 transit properties. Criteria for identifying key stations include the number of passenger boardings; whether or not the station is a transfer station, a major interchange point, or an end station; and whether the station serves major activity centers. FTA employees take in situ measurements, record specific accessibility features at stations, and simultaneously provide technical assistance. Assessments ensure that stations certified as ADA compliant remain in actual compliance with current standards. Key stations have higher standards for disability accessibility than other stations.

Land use controls (LUCs)

The legal mechanisms that protect public health and the environment from contamination at brownfields and other sites. LUCs can be used to help spur brownfields cleanup and redevelopment by streamlining the cleanup process and allowing residual contamination to remain onsite while limiting the types of activities that can occur there.

Lead

According to the Centers for Disease Control and Prevention, about one in 11 children in America has high levels of lead in his or her blood. The long-term effects of lead in a child can be severe, including learning disabilities, decreased growth, hyperactivity, impaired hearing, and even brain damage. Even children who appear healthy may have high levels of lead; that is why testing of children's blood levels is important. However, the federal government's goal is for primary prevention—that is, to reduce lead hazards before children are poisoned. Effects of lead on adults include reproductive problems, high blood pressure, digestive problems, nerve disorders, and memory and concentration problems. Before lead was banned from gasoline in the United States, much lead was put into the atmosphere. Although lead has long since been removed from paint, some environmental justice advocates believe that lead is still present in the soil near freeways and roads, where many people of color and low-income people live. It is thought that children ingest lead by chewing on window sills in old houses that were painted long ago. Lead paint can often be encapsulated by painting over it with acrylic paint.

Light rail

Generally applies to electric passenger rail transportation capable of operating short train sets and that uses exclusive, but not usually grade-separated, rights-of-way. Contrast with heavy rail. Light rail travels at an average point-to-point speed of 17 mph or so. Light rail is the modern version of the streetcar or trolley. It uses electrically powered cars with steel wheels on tracks in the street and often runs in a special lane but can also operate in mixed traffic. Generally speaking, light-rail vehicles are larger and faster than streetcars. Because light rail and streetcars travel mostly on the streets, they are cheaper and quicker to build than a subway. Under the federal New Starts program, many cities invested in light rail, which is sometimes only lightly used. There are special problems with making light rail accessible to people with disabilities. It has a cute, nostalgic feel to it, the transportation equivalent of megafauna in environmental wildlife preservers.

Linguistically diverse

Including and accommodating differences of language or communication systems.

Linguistically isolated households

A linguistically isolated household is one in which no person aged 14 or over speaks English at least "very well." That is, no person aged 14 or over speaks only English at home, or speaks another language at home and speaks English "very well." A linguistically isolated person is any person living in a linguistically isolated household. All the members of a linguistically isolated household are tabulated as linguistically isolated, including members under 14 years old who may speak only English.

Linguistic competence

The capacity of an organization and its personnel to effectively communicate with persons of limited English proficiency, those who are illiterate or have low literacy skills, and individuals with disabilities. This may include, but is not limited to, bilingual/bicultural staff and other organizational capacity such as telecommunication systems, sign or foreign language interpretation services, alternative formats, and translation of legally binding documents (e.g., consent forms, confidentiality and patient rights statements, release of information), signage and health education materials. The organization must have policy, structures, practices, procedures, and dedicated resources to support this capacity (Goode & Jones, 8/00).

Linked trip

A trip from the point of origin to the final destination, regardless of the number of modes or vehicles used. (*See also "Trip chaining"*)

Literacy

Ability to read, or demonstrate functional competence in a learned skill, such as basic mathematics or financial information. Expectations about how much formal education people need tend to increase with each generation (Resnick & Resnick, 1977). Estimates of literacy, or more accurately of "English literacy," indicate that a large number of adults lack some or many literacy skills that are considered necessary to function in contemporary U.S. society. Many policy makers regard data from literacy surveys as barometers of national well-being, as indicators of the country's economic preparedness for competition in a global economy, or as gauges of how well schools are equipping students with skills assumed to necessary for full social, economic, and political participation. In 1982, for example, the English Language Proficiency Survey (ELPS) estimated the number of those nonliterate in English to be between 17 and 21 million; approximately 7 million of that group were from homes where languages other than English were spoken (National Institute of Education, 1986; National Clearinghouse for ESL Literacy Education, 1991). The 1992 National Adult Literacy Survey (NALS) showed that 40 to 44 million adults could perform literacy tasks in English at only the lowest level of a five-point scale on each of three types of tasks. Ninety million—about half of the entire U.S. adult population—could perform tasks only up to the second level (Kirsch, Jungeblut, Jenkins, & Kolstad, 1993). Again, nonnative English speakers, especially those born outside the United States, were disproportionately represented at the lowest levels of ability. There has been considerable debate over how literacy should be defined (*see* Macias, 1990; Mikulecky, 1990). Surveys often overemphasize oral English ability, thereby equating speaking English with being literate in English. Although English is unquestionably the dominant language in the United States, it is unrealistic to assume that it can meet all the needs of those who speak other languages. There are three patterns of literacy among language minority groups in the United States: (1) native language literacy; (2) second language literacy (usually in English), which implies no native language literacy; and (3) biliteracy, literacy in two languages (typically in one's native language and in English). Nonliteracy (i.e., no literacy in any language) is also a possibility.

Livable Communities Initiative (LCI)

Created by the Federal Transit Administration to promote transit as the means to strengthen the link between transportation and communities. The LCI was intended to provide an alternative to low-density sprawl development patterns served primarily by automobiles with higher density, mixed use development reinforced with travel demand and parking management policies (U.S. Dept. of Transportation, 1996a and 1996b). The LCI was designed to promote and support transit-oriented design (TOD) or neotraditional urban design (Beimborn et al., 1991; Rabinowitz et al., 1991). The objectives of the LCI were to (1) strengthen the link between transit and community planning including supportive land-use policies and urban design; (2) stimulate active and diverse participation by the community in the decision-making process; (3) increase access to employment, education, and other community facilities and services; and (4) leverage resources from other federal, state, and local programs. Livable communities should ensure the long-term health of ecosystems and humans, economic vitality, and community well-being. Examples of projects include, but are not limited to, community redevelopment and revitalization, integrated community planning, green business practices, integrating smart growth principles into planning, mitigating the impacts of sprawl, community education and capacity building, and waste reduction and materials reuse.

Live Near Your Work (LNYW)

A cost-effective public/private home purchase initiative designed to encourage people to live closer to their places of work. This reduces the environmental and fiscal costs associated with long-distance commuting, while at the same time increasing investment and home ownership opportunity.

Local bus service

A term used to describe a route along which many stops are made, allowing flexibility in where passengers may board and depart. It is typically used in contrast to express bus, a bus that makes a limited number of stops and is targeted more at long distance riders. Local bus service is important in rural areas unless feeder or connector service is available to bring people to the station.

Local hiring strategies

Plans that require developers and governmental entities which benefit from public money to reserve a percentage of jobs for local residents. This ensures that un- or under-employed residents in economically isolated communities benefit from economic development and reinvestment happening in their community, and promotes balance within a region's employment opportunities. There are legal obstacles to local hiring preferences, including FHWA regulations. In a New Jersey case, the U.S. Supreme Court ruled that such local ordinances might be unconstitutional, and established a three-part test to evaluate the constitutionality of future ordinances:

- The jurisdiction must document "substantial reason" for preferential treatment;
- It must be shown that nonresidents "constitute a particular source of evil," or can be held partly responsible for the documented problem; and
- The suggested remedy must not sweep unnecessarily broadly, but be narrowly tailored to address the problem.

Location Efficient Mortgage (LEM)

An innovative mortgage product being offered in a number of American cities to low- and moderate-income borrowers who are interested in living in urban areas served by public transportation systems. The LEM recognizes that when families rely on public transit rather than automobiles for their travel needs they spend less on transportation. The LEM acknowledges that families save money when they "live locally." Those who shop, work, recreate, socialize, learn, and participate in the resources of their local community need to travel outside the area less because their more densely populated, urban area is pedestrian friendly and amenity-accessible. The LEM's computer software and mapping system can calculate such a family's annual and monthly transportation-related and population density-related savings under a variety of situations and conditions. If a borrower chooses a LEM, a portion of this savings would be integrated into the calculation of borrowing capacity as part of the customary mortgage application process. This procedure would create significant "stretch" in borrowing capacity. Households typically save a couple of thousand dollars a year in transportation costs, plus $500 in reduced residential parking costs. Using a complex formula that includes availability of public transportation and the number of stores within walking distance, the program assumes that families save money on transportation costs in certain neighborhoods. The idea was originally created by three nonprofit organizations interested in environmental and transportation issues: the Center for Neighborhood Technology, the National Resources Defense Council, and the Surface

Transportation Policy Project. Working with national mortgage lender Fannie Mae, the groups have found banks willing to try the idea.

Long-range transportation plan

The following is what a comprehensive long-range transportation plan should include, but it may not be applicable to all entities:

- An evaluation of a full range of modal choices and connections between modes to effectively and economically meet short- and long-term transportation needs.
- Trip generation studies including determination of traffic generators due to land use. These studies determine current and future levels of service of existing and proposed transportation facilities. This information is used to identify needed improvements to existing facilities and construction of new facilities.
- Social and economic development planning to identify transportation improvements and needs to accommodate existing and proposed land use in a safe, economical way, such as housing developments, school bus routes, public fire trails, health care, employment centers, educational facilities, and gaming facilities.
- Safety planning and analysis to identify portions of a transportation system that pose high risks to the user, such as high-accident locations, narrow bridges, and poor sight distance.
- A review of the existing and proposed transportation system to identify the relationships between the transportation system and the environment. This means balancing the needs of the user with the protection of the environment.
- Cultural preservation planning to identify those issues of importance to the community, and developing a plan that is sensitive to community preservation.
- Scenic byways and tourism plans that identify demands for improvements to existing transportation facilities and the development of new facilities to accommodate the influx of tourism as a result of a national park, scenic landscape, historic places, and/or buildings.
- Energy conservation considerations to promote the efficiency of existing and proposed transportation facilities.
- A prioritized list of short-term transportation needs. The Long-Range Transportation Plan is not necessarily a list of projects.
- Analysis of funding alternatives to achieve plan recommendations.

Low income

USDOT's planning regulations (23 C.F.R. § 450) require metropolitan planning organizations (MPOs) and states to "seek out and consider the needs of those traditionally underserved by existing transportation systems, including, but not limited to, low-income and minority households." As required by NEPA and 23 U.S.C. § 109(h), impacts on all communities, including low-income communities, must be routinely identified and addressed. The FHWA Order defines "low income" as "a person whose household income is at or below the Department of Health and Human Services poverty guidelines." The U.S. Department of Health and Human Services (HHS) poverty guidelines are used as eligibility criteria for a number of federal programs. However, a state or locality may adopt a higher threshold for low-income status, as long as the higher threshold is not selectively implemented and is inclusive of all persons at or below the HHS poverty guidelines. The most current HHS poverty guidelines may be found at http://aspe.os.dhhs.gov/poverty/.

Major disaster

Any natural catastrophe (including hurricane, tornado, storm, high water, wind driven water, tidal wave, tsunami, earthquake, volcanic eruption, landslide, mudslide, snowstorm, and drought), or, regardless of cause, fire, flood, or explosion, in any part of the United States, which in the determination of the president causes damage of sufficient severity and magnitude to warrant major disaster assistance to supplement the efforts and available resources of states, local governments, and disaster relief organizations in alleviating the damage, loss, hardship, or suffering.

Major Investment Study (MIS)

A study done on major transportation improvement projects such as fixed guideway transit projects and controlled access highways that would involve the use of federal funds. The study includes factors that would justify a proposed project, such as its cost effectiveness and overall effectiveness, and evaluates various modes of travel to solve a transportation problem.

Mapping

Transforms spatial data into a visual, usually two-dimensional, form, enabling users to observe, conceptualize, validate, and communicate the information.

Marginalized groups

Groups characterized by their physical or mental disabilities (persons living with HIV or AIDS), ethnic origin (African tribes, First Nations of the Amazon), race (blacks and Indians in South Africa), social status (lower castes in India), sexual orientation, beliefs, political affiliation, that put them at a disadvantage to a majority or predominant group. From the concept of "living at the margins of society." A group can also be marginalized by not having its views considered by a group in political, social, or economic control of a society.

Market-oriented approaches

Approaches to social change that use economic incentives. These include fees; penalties; subsidies; marketable permits or offsets; changes in liability or property rights (including policies that alter the incentives of insurers and insured parties); safe harbors; accelerated tax depreciation; and required bonds, insurance, or warranties.

Mass transportation

Transportation together with other people by bus, rail, or other conveyance, either publicly or privately owned. Mass transportation is available to the public and provides general or special service (but not including school, charter, or sightseeing service) on a regular basis.

Mass transportation system

A system that provides transportation by bus, rail, or other conveyance, through regular and continuing general or special transportation to the public, but not including school bus, charter, or sightseeing transportation. Mass transportation systems may be multimodal (e.g., using both bus and rail modes).

Meaningful involvement

Involvement of affected people in governmental decisions, so that (1) potentially affected community residents have an appropriate opportunity to participate in decisions about a proposed activity that may affect their environment and/or health; (2) the public's contribution can influence the regulatory agency's decision; (3) the concerns of all participants involved will be considered in the decision-making process; and (4) the decision makers seek out and facilitate the involvement of those potentially affected.

Means test element

The assessment of a minimum level of income, calculated by taking the circumstances of the claimant and any dependants into account. The income of the claimant and any partner they may have is then compared with the notional minimum, and where it is relatively low, the claimant is eligible to receive support. Means-tested eligibility standards are used in Medicaid, food stamps, Supplementary Security Income (SSI), federal public housing assistance (Section 8), school lunch program, and Low Income Home Energy Assistance Program (LIHEAP).

Medicaid transit passes

The local or state Medicaid office (or an agency appointed or subcontracted by them) contracts with the local transit authority to purchase monthly transit passes. These transit passes are then distributed to Medicaid clients who are able to use public transportation for medical travel needs.

Melting pot

The "melting pot" American ideal of unity is often expressed as "E Pluribus Unum" (out of many, one), suggesting that immigrants assimilate into American culture and lose their distinctiveness. Not currently a popular theory. Although the phrase "melting pot" has been used to describe the creation of a new American culture, it has more accurately described efforts to require conformity to Anglo-American culture and behavior.

Metropolitan Capacity Building (MCB) Program
The Federal Highway Administration (FHWA) and Federal Transit Authority (FTA), in a collaborative effort with the American Association of State Highway and Transportation Officials (AASHTO), the American Public Transportation Association (APTA), the Association of Metropolitan Planning Organizations (AMPO), and the National Association of Regional Councils (NARC), launched this program to strengthen metropolitan planning organizations (MPOs). The program targets not only transportation professionals but also the elected officials who make transportation decisions. Collecting, synthesizing, and disseminating examples of successful innovations by states, MPOs, and transit operators, the initiative provides multiple mechanisms for getting critical information to decision makers. It is intended to help spread real innovation in decision making by publicizing new techniques and strategies developed by state and local officials. This initiative has supported peer exchanges focusing on transportation modeling and fiscal constraint.

Metropolitan planning organization (MPO)
The forum for cooperative surface transportation planning and decision making for metropolitan planning areas pursuant to 23 U.S.C. § 134 and 49 U.S.C. § 5303. An MPO is required in each urbanized area having a population of over 50,000. There are currently approximately 340 MPOs in the United States. These MPOs, in cooperation with states, transit operators, local municipalities, counties, and other key transportation entities in the metropolitan area, carry out the surface transportation planning process, but do not usually concern themselves with airports. The work of MPOs involves public involvement, analysis of travel trends and forecasts, assessment of community and environmental impacts, and financial planning to ensure that programs are financially feasible. Many are also councils of government (COGs) or regional planning agencies or both. Responding to urban interests, the 1962 Federal Highway Act called for a "continuing, cooperative, coordinated" planning process carried out by representatives of local governments in metropolitan areas of over 50,000 population. One important new responsibility was given to MPOs under the Clean Air Act Amendments of 1977 and was continued under the 1990 amendments. In nonattainment areas, MPOs have responsibility for planning for transportation control measures and analysis of the conformity of transportation plans, programs, and projects to the state implementation plan. The basic framework remained intact: a relatively weak regional institution representing the interests of local agencies and often dominated by the DOT.

Metropolitan Statistical Area (MSA)
MSA is a relatively freestanding metropolitan area (MA) typically surrounded by non-metropolitan counties.

Metropolitan Transportation Plan (MTP)

Formerly known as the Long-Range Transportation Plan. The official 20-year planning document that identifies existing and future transportation deficiencies and multimodal needs, as well as network improvements needed to meet mobility requirements over the planning period. In Clean Air Act nonattainment areas, this plan must also address how the region's transportation system will improve air quality. To receive federal funding, transportation projects must be included in the MTP and programmed in the Transportation Improvement Program (TIP). The MTP is developed by the metropolitan planning organization through its established planning process.

Microenterprise

Programs that help self-employed entrepreneurs obtain very small loans for small business enterprises to begin the process of growing out of poverty. Without microenterprise programs administered by the Agency for International Development and many nongovernmental organizations, poor entrepreneurs abroad would not be able to borrow the small amount of money needed to get their repair shops, sewing shops, or similar businesses off the ground. Experience has shown that these small loans are repaid, and, in the process, these small-scale enterprises generate income and jobs for poor families.

Microloans

In their modern form, microloans were pioneered by Muhammad Yunus, the Nobel Peace Prize–winning economist who founded the Grameen Bank to provide a source of credit for poor people in his native Bangladesh. Today more than 1,000 microfinance organizations offer microloans to 5 million clients from poor rural communities or urban slums in Africa, Asia, and Latin America—primarily to women to enable them to expand small businesses. Microloans are typically unsecured loans of between $150 and $500—an amount that can be as much as 100 percent of the recipient's annual income. Risk screening and peer pressure for repayment is typically accomplished by having would-be borrowers form groups within a community that are jointly responsible for loan repayment. So successful are microloans at increasing incomes that loans are paid back quickly—the industry average is 3-6 months—with fewer than 3 percent of all loans defaulting. Such repayment rates and the success of microloans in stimulating microeconomic activity and helping people climb out of poverty have made them a favorite of development organizations.

Minority community-based organization

A public or private nonprofit community-based minority organization or a local affiliate of a national minority organization that has a governing board composed of 51 percent or more racial/ethnic minority members, a significant number of minorities in key program positions, and an established record of service to a racial/ethnic minority community.

Minority groups

In the United States, traditionally discriminated-against racial or ethnic groups, as opposed to the predominant or dominant group. United Nations intergovernmental bodies have been unable to define a "minority" population group. The most obvious way of defining a minority is in terms of numbers. A minority could be defined as a numerically inferior group living within a larger population (and territorial state) which seeks to preserve the ethnic, linguistic, cultural (including religious) and, perhaps, political characteristics that distinguish it from the larger population. A minority group may be discriminated against on the basis of one characteristic, such as religion or language, or several characteristics (as in the case of indigenous peoples). Adding to the definitional problem is the concept that minorities include groups such as nomads and migrant workers. Some minorities seek political self-determination as a way of liberation from discrimination and oppression; others willingly or grudgingly accept a politically assimilated status within the territory or state controlled by an ethnically different majority.

Minority populations

In the United States, American Indian or Alaska Native, Asian, Black or African American, Hispanic or Latino, and Native Hawaiian or Other Pacific Islander (Revision to the Standards for the Classification of Federal Data on Race and Ethnicity, *Federal Register 62*(210), p. 58782, October 30, 1997).

Mistrust

Not having confidence that the dominant population group (or individuals in that group) will do the right thing, morally, ethnically, or economically. For some minority groups, this results is seeking less help. For example, African Americans often give the following reasons for not seeking professional help with depression: lack of time, fear of hospitalization, and fear of treatment (Sussman et al., 1987). Mistrust among African Americans may stem from their experiences of segregation, racism, and discrimination (Primm et al., 1996; Priest, 1991). African Americans have experienced racist slights in their contacts with the mental health system, called "microinsults" by Pierce (1992). Lack of trust is likely to operate among other minority groups. This is particularly pronounced for immigrant families with relatives who may be undocumented, and hence are less likely to trust authorities for fear of being reported and having the family member deported. Within the Asian community, previous refugee experiences of groups such as Vietnamese, Indochinese, and Cambodian immigrants parallel those experienced by Salvadoran and Argentine immigrants. They, too, experienced imprisonment, death of family members or friends, physical abuse, and assault, as well as new stresses upon arriving in the United States (Cook & Timberlake, 1989; Mollica, 1989). American Indians' past experience in this country also imparted lack of trust of government. Those living on Indian reservations are particularly fearful of sharing any information with whites employed by the government. As with African Americans, the historical relationship of forced control, segregation, racism, and discrimination has reduced their ability to trust a white majority population (Herring, 1994; Thompson, 1997).

Mitigation

Making changes to a transportation project that will correct, eliminate, or alleviate aspects that have disproportionate adverse effects on protected demographic groups or communities. Mitigation includes *avoiding* the impact by not taking or modifying an action; *minimizing, rectifying,* or *reducing* the impacts through redesign or operation of the project or policy; or *compensating* for irreversible impacts by providing substitute facilities, resources, or opportunities (*see* 40 C.F.R. § 1508.20). Ideally, mitigation measures are built into the selected alternative, but it is appropriate to identify mitigation measures even if they are not immediately adopted or if they would be the responsibility of another organization or government unit.

Mobility

The ability to get from here to there with reasonable convenience. In a motorized society, the primary determinants of mobility are:

1. Vehicle ownership
2. Quality and affordability of the travel options available to those who do not own a car or are unable to drive
3. Ease of movement
4. Accessibility built into settlement patterns and reflected in household location choices and regional travel patterns.

Speed is the primary determinant of the mobility that users can derive from an interregional transportation system. Accessibility is the primary determinant of the mobility that users can derive from an urban transportation system, and ease of movement and ease of access both contribute to metropolitan mobility. There are seven key mobility objectives:

1. Convenient commute
2. Convenient transit access to the job centers of the urban core
3. Consistent and dependable level of service on major streets and highways during peak commute hours
4. Smooth and reliable flow of traffic on primary freight routes during midday hours
5. Convenient access and continuity of service to the region's primary activity centers including airports, universities, hospitals, and primary governmental centers
6. Dependable level of transit service for the urban carless
7. Mobility lifeline for the suburban carless

Performance measures for mobility include:

1. For most commuters, the critical descriptor of convenience is the time spent commuting.
2. For downtown commuters, the critical variable is the door-to-door convenience of travel by transit.
3. For highway users, the critical variable is the consistency and dependability of travel times.
4. For present and potential transit users, the critical variable is the convenience of service to primary activity centers such as the region's commercial business districts, airports, universities, and medical centers where parking is scarce or inconvenient.
5. For trucking companies, critical variables include reliable travel times during peak commute hours and the ability to avoid congestion-related delays during midday hours.
6. For the urban carless, the most critical variable is the continuing availability of frequent and reliable transit service.
7. For the suburban carless, the critical variable is the availability of transit and paratransit services that effectively complement and supplement the mobility provided by ridesharing.

Mobility needs and pure mobility do not always coincide because of several factors: lack of revenue, lack of time, lack of means, and lack of access. People's mobility and transport demand thus depend on their social situation. The most mobile are most often wealthier people occupying positions of superior responsibility and belonging to the most educated strata of population. Their mobility is attributed to variable characteristics related to the motive, the method, the origin and destination, the length and duration as well as the moment and the frequency.

Moral indignation
Inequalities often persist because both the advantaged and the disadvantaged stand to lose from change. Moral indignation can lead the disadvantaged to seek to alter the status quo by encouraging them to sacrifice their material self-interest for the sake of equality. Experimental research shows that moral indignation, understood as a willingness to suffer in order to punish unfair treatment by others, is widespread. It also indicates that a propensity to apparently self-defeating moral indignation can turn out to promote people's material self-interest if and because others will anticipate their actions. But potential rebels face collective action problems. Some of these can be reduced through the acts of "indignation entrepreneurs," giving appropriate signals, organizing discussions by like-minded people, and engaging in acts of self-sacrifice. The concept is developed by Edna Ullmann-Margalit and Cass R. Sunstein in "Inequality and Indignation," published in *Philosophy and Public Affairs*, February 2002.

Mortgage-transit program

In May 2002, the Massachusetts Housing Finance Agency, a state affordable housing agency, and the Massachusetts Bay Transportation Authority ("the T") entered into an agreement to launch a transit-related mortgage program. The "Take the T Home Mortgage Program" makes low- and median-income T commuters eligible for zero-down, below-market 6.6 percent mortgages. Area banks administer the loans and MassHousing, the state's affordable housing bank, insures them. Authorities hope that in addition to facilitating home purchase by low-income families, participants will choose to purchase homes near public transit, eliminating the need for a car. For more information, search for "mortgage program rewards" at www.knowledgeplex.org/fmfportal/.

New urbanism

In the early 1990s, the Congress for the New Urbanism was formed to re-establish the relationship between the art of city building and the conservation of the natural environment. New urbanists view "the divestment in central cities, the spread of placeless sprawl, increasing separation by race and income, environmental deterioration, loss of agricultural lands, and the erosion of society's built heritage as one interrelated community-building challenge." They call for reducing reliance on cars and bringing a wide range of amenities within a 10-minute walk of home and work. They advocate pedestrian-friendly design, including front porches and tree-lined streets, with parking hidden from view. Every neighborhood would be a mix of shops, offices, apartments, and homes, including people of diverse ages, classes, cultures, and races, with higher density in urban centers, and a celebration of rural life at the clearly marked edge of the city. Such cities, they argue, would result in greater sustainability and a higher quality of life for everyone. Despite the appeal of this vision, new urbanists have been slow to engage advocates of social and racial justice, civil rights, labor, housing, and faith-based leaders concerned about the challenges facing traditionally discriminated against groups, and are accused of creating phony white enclaves.

National Consortium on the Transportation of Human Services Coordination

A means for collaboration among the state and local organizations that administer and deliver human service transportation programs. The consortium includes state organizations, such as the National Governors Association and the National Conference of State Legislators; associations of transportation providers, such as the American Public Transportation Association, the Community Transportation Association of America, and the Taxicab, Limousine and Paratransit Association; human service organizations, such as the American Public Human Services Association and the National Association of Area Agencies on Aging; and several human service advocacy groups, such as the American Association of Retired Persons, National Easter Seals Project ACTION, and the Children's Health Fund. The consortium is working with the DOT/HHS Coordinating Council to accomplish particular components of the Council's Action Plan, and reaching out to its own constituents to promote further efforts to coordinate human service transportation at the local level.

National Environmental Policy Act (NEPA)
Established by Congress in 1969 to address issues of environmental protection and sustainable development. NEPA requires that an Environmental Impact Statement (EIS) be prepared for all federally funded transportation actions that significantly impact the human or natural environment, and also emphasizes the importance of community involvement in this process. It provides a framework for considering impacts of federally aided projects and the creation of a Council on Environmental Quality (CEQ).

Necessities
The Bureau of Labor Statistics tracks three goods as basic necessities—food, apparel, and housing. National and state policies should work to keep these items affordable. Transportation—an obligatory expense to get to and from work, home, school, and shopping—is not categorized as a basic necessity, even though it is the second highest household expenditure and continues to rise in price. For example, from 1992 to 2003, as a percent of expenditures, housing rose by 3.6 percent, but transportation rose by a huge 8.8 percent.

Needs
Products and services that people must have to maintain a basic quality of life. Demands on natural and human resources required to sustain individual and community values or standards of living (e.g., a safe, secure water supply, protection of ecosystem or species, environmental stability, appropriate economic development, and community viability).

Needs assessment
A systematic procedure for determining community issues and ranking their importance as a component of program development. Needs assessments were the forerunners of modern day public involvement programs.

Negative externalities
An economics term that refers to a bundle of bad effects that are by-products of a benefit enjoyed by those who use a service. Drivers, for example, enjoy the accessibility of major highways. Those living near the highways, however, experience the pollution and the noise of traffic.

Neighborhood development plan
Comprehensive urban planning that is sensitive to the needs of the local residents through use of a study of a specific area which assesses the potential

value of land and its uses, and incorporates the values and concerns of the people living in the area. It includes such facets of an area as parks, transportation, sewer and water infrastructure, resident income, densities, and potential zoning changes and overlays. It looks at various aspects of land-use and transportation relationships in a neighborhood, including mixed development, trip generation, land-use patterns, pedestrians, bicycles, transit, and vehicle traffic movements. Many such studies use focus groups and steering committees to gather information and formulate recommendations. (Also called Small Area Development Study.)

NEPA process

The process for preparing, for a highway project or transit project, (1) an environmental impact statement or (2) any other document required to be prepared under the National Environmental Policy Act of 1969 (42 U.S.C. § 4321 *et seq.*). It includes the process for and completion of any environmental permit, approval, review, or study required for a highway project or transit project under any federal law other than the National Environmental Policy Act of 1969.

Nonattainment area

Any geographic region of the United States that the U.S. Environmental Protection Agency (EPA) has designated as not attaining the federal air quality standards for one or more air pollutants, such as ozone and carbon monoxide. Some equity advocates have tried to make the case that governance structures in nonattainment areas have a special duty to serve the needs of low-income and minority people through transit services.

National Urban Sustainable Employment and Training Initiative

Includes workforce development and youth transportation career education by the National Urban League, funded by the Federal Highway Administration.

Office of Federal Contract Compliance Programs (OFCCP)

A component of the U.S. Department of Labor that compiles information relating to discrimination in employment and occupation concerning federal contractors and subcontractors, and enforces certain affirmative action laws. Such information includes a contractor's affirmative action plan, as well as summary data on personnel activity and compensation. Federal contractors and subcontractors also are required to provide OFCCP with general information on an establishment's equal employment opportunity program activities and similar programs and information concerning personnel activity; information by gender, race, and ethnicity; and compensation data for minorities and non-minorities by gender. OFCCP analyses the data it compiles and uses the results of that analysis, as well as other information, to assist in identifying establishments for compliance evaluation.

Offices of Small and Disadvantaged Business Utilization (OSDBUs)
Each major federal department and agency has an office that ensures uniform implementation of small business programs. OSDBUs are responsible for ensuring that small businesses have the maximum practicable opportunity to participate in the performance of federal contracts as both prime contractors and subcontractors. Certain businesses are presumed to have owners who are disadvantaged because of their membership in a racial or ethnic group, or because the owners are women.

Older Americans Act (OAA)
Federal law first passed in 1965. The act established a network of services and programs for older people. This network provides supportive services, including transportation and nutrition services, and works with public and private agencies that serve the needs of older individuals.

Outreach
Programs designed by an organization or institutional entity to seek out individuals, groups, and communities. Outreach can encompass both obtaining information from and providing services to these groups. These programs often rely upon the reports of family, neighbors, and community workers. Public outreach has long functioned as a desirable part of transportation planning in the United States. The process is well-known among DOTs and metropolitan planning organizations. Following mandates initially established under the National Environmental Policy Act (NEPA) in the 1970s and strengthened under the Statewide and Metropolitan Joint Planning Regulations of October 1993, departments of transportation around the country must provide the public with information on transportation improvements under consideration in their jurisdictions. The feedback they receive from the public is supposed to be used to refine their plans and ultimately create more effective projects. Information and feedback are exchanged through a variety of ways, including public meetings, focus groups, newsletters, Web sites, and formal hearings. Some definitions stress the underserved nature of the targeted group. Outreach has also been defined in terms of reaching out and assisting through personal contacts with people excluded from, unaware of, or unreceptive to certain information or services (Bannon, 1973). Advocacy can be an essential component of outreach. Through advocacy, outreach programs can extend the endeavors of community services to eradicate the problem, or at least ameliorate the situation. Components of outreach can include research, education, and service. Service outreach focuses on performing a function that benefits the targeted population. According to Edwards and Livingston, a comprehensive outreach approach has 11 features:

1. Target audience(s)
2. Needs assessments of the target audience(s)

3. Short- and long-term goals and objectives for responding to the needs
4. Outreach activities that address those needs
5. A timetable
6. A coordinator of outreach activities
7. Accurate, updated mailing lists
8. An evaluation plan to monitor success
9. Outreach messages and materials that are current, easily understood, positive, structured in such a way as to lead the receiver to "the next level" of information, need or services, and that highlight something unique and realistic
10. Repetition of distinct messages in varied forms to maximize outreach to the targeted audience
11. Ongoing research, both formal and informal, for effective outreach (Edwards and Livingston, 1990)

The particular population for whom the outreach program is intended must be aware that efforts are made to welcome and include their perspectives and respect their customs. From the outset, the organization conducting the outreach typically has a special interest in the population and believes that the population is a valued constituency. Bannon (1973) states that advocacy serves as the distinguishing factor between "benign forms of community help" and outreach. The goal of many outreach projects is to transform social behaviors and/or attitudes of the target population. Local organizational newsletters, community calendars of events, print media, radio and TV shows, and public service announcements are some of the commonly used venues that organizations have found to be successful for spreading information widely about an outreach project (Edwards and Livingston, 1990). For the distribution of information to be effective, attention to language and the cultural relevance of the materials is crucial to the perceived value of the information. Even when the information is current and accurate, it may be considered useless if it does not adhere to the cultural and social context of the audience.

People of color

While not universally accepted, this description is more accurate and preferred by many over "minority." In a numeric sense, people of color are rapidly becoming the majority in the United States, as in most of the world. The term "people of color" is a self-given description initially used in educational and academic circles in the early 1980s. The media rarely use the term, and the federal government sometimes uses the term "minority."

Perceived discrimination

The term used by researchers in reference to the self-reports of individuals about being the target of discrimination or racism. The term is not meant to imply that racism did not take place.

Persistently poor
Exhibiting poverty rates of 20 percent or more.

Personal mobility
The ease with which people are able to satisfy their transportation needs. Personal mobility includes vehicular mobility, but also includes transit, bicycle, and pedestrian transportation.

Personal Responsibility and Work Opportunity Reconciliation Act (PRWORA)
Welfare reform; welfare to work. A comprehensive bipartisan welfare reform bill in 1996 that established the Temporary Assistance for Needy Families (TANF) program. TANF block grants to states were created, changing the nature and provision of federal welfare benefits in America. This legislation dramatically changed the nation's welfare system into one that requires work in exchange for time-limited assistance and provides some support for families moving from welfare to work. The legislation provides a limit on the amount of time an individual can receive welfare benefits and, with limited exceptions, welfare recipients are expected to engage in work activities to move from welfare assistance to permanent employment.

Planning process participants
The parties responsible for conducting the planning process and for decision making, i.e., the state for statewide planning, and the state, MPO, and transit operator for metropolitan planning. However, TEA-21 emphasized the importance of involving a wider range of persons and groups in the transportation-planning process. Early consideration of environmental issues in planning are enhanced if resource and permit agencies have a meaningful role. Additionally, Indian tribal governments have a unique role that must be addressed in transportation planning. TEA-21 emphasizes the participation of non-metropolitan local officials and other key stakeholders in the development of transportation plans. Nonetheless, decision making still rests with the same parties, the planning process participants, as prior to TEA-21.

Potential environmental justice area
A minority or low-income community that may bear a disproportionate share of the negative environmental consequences resulting from industrial, municipal, and commercial operations or the execution of federal, state, local, and tribal programs and policies.

Poverty (*See also "Low income"*)
The United States was one of the first countries to establish an official definition of poverty. There are many different definitions. An economist's concept of "income poverty" compares cash income with an assessment of income needs, and has been used to track the nation's poverty rate and the characteristics of

people identified as poor (Fisher, 1992; Ruggles, 1990). The official measure identifies poor families and the individuals living in them by comparing two numbers: the current annual cash income of the family unit and an estimate of the income necessary for a family of a particular size and composition to meet a minimum level of consumption. This second number is the family's "poverty threshold" or "poverty line." If the income of the family does not exceed its poverty line, the family is defined as "poor." The nation's "poverty rate" is the percentage of its population who live in poor families. The official measure is open to many criticisms, both conceptual and practical. One important source of dissatisfaction is its lack of measurement of permanent family characteristics; it relies on a single year of cash income of a family, while for many families annual income fluctuates. It also does not necessarily measure social welfare benefits received. The concept of what a person and family need to be part of mainstream American life changes also. Unemployment, layoffs, the decision to undertake mid-career training or to change jobs, divorce, single parenthood, health considerations, barter, incarceration, and income from self-employment may cause the money income of a household to change substantially from one year to the next.

Poverty gap
The total amount by which the income of all poor households falls below the poverty line, reflecting both the extent of poverty (i.e., how many poor people there are) and the depth of poverty (how far below the poverty line these people fall). This topic is often discussed in terms of racial justice because people of color, especially African Americans, Hispanic Americans, and Native Americans, disproportionately fall below the poverty line. For instance, though poverty rates were in decline, "one-third of African American children (33.1 percent) and nearly one-third of Hispanic children (30.3 percent) were still poor in 1999" (Center on Budget & Policy Priorities: www.cbpp.org/9-26-00pov.htm).

Precautionary principle
This emerging principle of international law and environmental thinking is used to justify taking protective action when serious harm might occur due to a plan or action. It is a measure to slow development of a new technology, such as genetically engineered crops, until more is known about its side effects; or to bar imports of substances over which there is scientific controversy, such as beef containing hormone residues. The precautionary principle seeks to prevent harm before it happens by urging protective measures when there is reasonable or some evidence of possible harm. While our current regulations and laws ask "How much harm is allowable?", the precautionary principle asks, "How little harm is possible?" The precautionary approach is that if any possibility of a link exists, then action should be taken to reduce the risk. It is a tool for making better health and environmental decisions and aims to prevent harm from the

outset rather than manage it after the fact. One useful way to define the precautionary principle was developed in 1998 by a group of scientists, environmental activists, government officials, lawyers, and labor representatives at the Wingspread conference center in Wisconsin: "When an activity raises threats of harm to human health or the environment, precautionary measures should be taken even if some cause and effect relationships are not fully established scientifically." In common language, this means "better safe than sorry." The precautionary principle asks "How little damage is possible?" There are five primary pieces that make up a precautionary approach:

1. *Alternatives Assessment*. An obligation exists to examine a full range of alternatives and select the alternative with the least potential adverse impact on human health and the ecological systems, including the alternative of doing nothing.
2. *Anticipatory Action*. A duty to take anticipatory action to prevent harm.
3. *Right to Know*. The community has a right to know complete and accurate information on potential human health and environmental impacts associated with the selection of products, services, operations, or plans. The burden to supply this information lies with the proponent, not with the general public.
4. *Full Cost Accounting*. When evaluating potential alternatives, there is a duty to consider all the costs including raw materials, manufacturing, transportation, use, cleanup, eventual disposal, and health costs even if such costs are not reflected in the initial price.
5. *Thoughtful Decision Process*. Decisions applying the precautionary principle must be transparent, participatory, democratic, and informed by the best available independent science.

Racial profiling

The alleged practice by police officers of stopping African American and Hispanic drivers because of their color, using legitimate law enforcement goals as a pretext. U.S. DOT became involved in racial profiling, or "Driving While Black/Brown (DWB)," because of its efforts to encourage primary seatbelt laws and because of airport security screening efforts. Primary seatbelt laws permit police officers to stop and ticket drivers because they are not wearing seatbelts. There is fear in some parts of the African American and Hispanic communities that such laws will permit more racial profiling under color of law. There are also allegations that airport security screeners select an unduly high percentage of air travelers of color and of Arab descent or appearance or Arabic accent for additional bag searches and screening at terminal security stations. Bias-based traffic law enforcement may include differential treatment based solely on any number of personal attributes. This would include the stopping of motorists, the detention of a person, and/or the searching of a vehicle based on the individual's race, ethnic origin, gender, age, or income status. Some law enforcement officers engage in this practice on a regular basis.

Profiling data collection

Essential elements:

1. *Race/Ethnicity of Motorist.* It is critical to obtain information about the race/ethnicity of motorists stopped by police. Without this information, it is impossible to determine whether and to what extent people of color are stopped at a disproportionate rate.

2. *The Reason for the Stop.* People of color are often stopped for extremely minor traffic violations, such as burned out license plate lights, overly worn tire tread, failure to use turn signals properly, etc. These violations are often ignored when committed by white motorists, but when they are committed by people of color, law enforcement officers sometimes use these minor traffic violations as an excuse to conduct a stop, interrogation, and a search. Without information about the reason for the stop, it is impossible to know whether motorists of color are being singled out and stopped for minor violations that are ignored when committed by whites.

3. *Whether a Search Was Conducted.* Search data is essential. In some jurisdictions, people of color may be stopped at similar rates as whites, but people of color are searched at dramatically higher rates. If data are collected only about who is stopped, it may seem that no discrimination is occurring. In Maryland, for example, a study of traffic stops revealed that although African Americans composed only 17 percent of the drivers on the road, they accounted for nearly 75 percent of people who were stopped and searched.

4. *Whether Drugs or Other Evidence of Illegal Activity Were Found.* It is not enough simply to learn that a search was conducted. Without information about whether drugs or other evidence of illegal activity were found during the search, it is impossible to rebut the argument often made by law enforcement that it makes sense to target people of color because they are the ones most likely to be engaged in criminal activity. Studies of racial profiling have demonstrated that the "hit rate" for people of color and whites is nearly identical. Despite the widespread belief to the contrary, people of color are no more likely than whites to be carrying drugs in their cars. These data are necessary to eliminate racial stereotypes within and outside law enforcement about who the likely criminals are.

5. *Whether a Citation Was Issued or Arrest Was Made.* People of color regularly complain that they are often stopped and questioned about who they are, where they are going, what they are doing in a particular neighborhood, are sometimes searched and then released without a ticket or citation of any kind. The reason no citation is issued is because the supposed traffic

violation was not the real reason for the stop. Indeed, the classic "DWB" stop is one in which the driver is stopped, questioned, and/or searched, and no citation is issued.

Public Involvement (*See also "Outreach"*)

People want to have a voice in transportation decision making. Their communities and agencies must have public involvement to create a successful planning or project development process. A public involvement program:

- Informs people through outreach and participation (including people who are underserved by transportation).
- Involves people "face to face" through meetings.
- Gets feedback from participants.
- Uses special techniques to enhance participation.

For long-range transportation planning, public involvement is important to help articulate the community's/state's vision and goals, provide the public with the opportunity to champion a variety of transportation interests, and receive valuable input into the planning process. For transportation planning, public involvement can include regional agencies, local government, user/special interest groups, tribal governments, and states, as well as the private sector, legal system, and federal government. The seven basic functions for effective public involvement in any decision or activity are:

1. Plan and budget for public involvement activities
2. Identify the interested and potentially affected public
3. Consider providing technical or financial assistance to the public to facilitate involvement
4. Provide information and outreach to the public
5. Conduct public consultation and involvement activities in culturally sensitive ways, in languages people understand
6. Review and use input and provide feedback to the public
7. Evaluate the public involvement

Public involvement plan

Provides a systematic approach to linking between what needs to be done and what needs to be communicated through the people involved.

Public participation

The active and meaningful involvement of the public in the development of transportation plans and improvement programs. ISTEA and subsequent regulations require that state departments of transportation and metropolitan planning organizations (MPOs) proactively seek the involvement of all interested parties, including those traditionally underserved by the current transportation system.

Public Participation GIS

Covers the range of topics raised by the intersection of community interests and Geographic Information System (GIS) technology. This is concerned with the social, political, historical, and technological conditions in which GIS both empowers and marginalizes individuals and communities. Included in this list of research agendas are the following potential topics:

- "Successful" implementations of a public participatory GIS.
- Changes in local politics and power relationships resulting from the use of GIS in spatial decision making.
- What community groups need in the way of information and the role GIS plays or could play in meeting this need.
- Current attempts to use GIS to "empower" communities for spatial decision making.
- Impacts on communities of differential access to hardware, software, data, and expertise in GIS production and use.
- Educational, social, political, and economic reasons for lack of access and exemplary ways communities have overcome these barriers.
- The implications of map-based representations of information for community groups.
- Nature of GIS knowledge distortion from grassroots perspectives.
- Value of sophisticated analyses for understanding key issues, as opposed to the negative impact of such analyses in confusing and marginalizing individuals and groups.
- Implications of conflicting knowledge and multiple realities for spatial decision making.
- Ways in which socially differentiated communities and their local knowledge are or might be represented within GIS.
- GIS as local surveillance.
- Identify which public data policies have positive influences on small neighborhood businesses and which are negative.
- Develop prospective models (economic, organizational, legal, and technological) that might result in increased and more equitable opportunities among the diverse segments of society in accessing geographic information and tools.
- New issues, such as collaborative decision making involving the public.

Race

When defined as a social category, may overlap with ethnicity, but each has a different social meaning. For example, in many national surveys and in the 1990 U.S. census, Native Hawaiians and Vietnamese Americans are classified together in the racial category of "Asian and Pacific Islander Americans." Native Hawaiians, however, have very little in common with Vietnamese Americans in terms of their heritage. Similarly, Caribbean blacks and Pacific Northwest Indians have different ethnicities than others within their same racial category. Because Hispanics are an ethnicity, not a race, the different Latino American ethnic subgroups such as Cubans, Dominicans, Mexicans, Puerto Ricans, and Peruvians include individuals of all races. Race is not a biological category, but it does have meaning as a social category. Different cultures classify people into racial groups according to a set of characteristics that are socially significant. The concept of race is especially potent when certain social groups are separated, treated as inferior or superior, and given differential access to power and other valued resources.

Racially fragmented American cities

The role of race in the history of public policies in American cities (for a recent contribution, see Nancy Burns [1994]) has been studied extensively. Many of these studies have shown the provision and distribution of public goods in such cities is lower or less efficient than in whiter and more homogeneous cities. Alesina, Baqir, and Easterly (1999, 2000) show that in more fragmented cities the provision of "productive" public goods (roads, hospitals, schools, etc.) is lower. In more fragmented communities, public budgets are tilted away from "productive" public goods. Public employment as a share of the population is higher in more racially fragmented cites. Racial divisions have stronger effects than ethnic ones.

Real Accessibility Index (RAI)

A tool designed to score access to services by determining the extent and condition of transportation infrastructure. It was created at the University of Virginia with the intention of becoming a standard method of determining how balanced a system of transportation infrastructure is, where access to services is lacking, and how limited resources can best be used to improve the situation. Target areas receive points based on the availability of various modes of travel and connections made between services and residential areas. The more options that are available to an area, the higher its score will be. Scores reflect connectivity, continuity, ease of use, safety, integration of modes, and pleasantness of travel.

Redlining

The definition of geographic areas based primarily on racial/ethnic and/or socioeconomic factors, resulting in lack of services or benefits to people who fall on the "wrong" side of the red line. A group of advisory committees to the United States Commission on Civil Rights has defined insurance redlining as "canceling, refusing to insure or to renew, or varying the terms under which insurance is available to individuals because of the geographic location of a risk." Similarly, redlining within the home mortgage industry has been defined as "the process of drawing or outlining a geographic area within which lending will be denied due to the composition or characteristics of the area." Redlining dates to the Depression and refers to the map color used to denote urban areas where housing loans were not to be made, under Federal Housing Administration instructions, as these areas were full of immigrants and people of color.

Regressive

An economic concept meaning that lower-income consumers pay a greater share of their budget or income, or receive less benefit than consumers with higher income from a given initiative. A tax (or subsidy) is regressive if its application results in a less egalitarian distribution of income. A regressive tax falls more heavily on low-income taxpayers, taking a larger percentage of their income than it takes from those with higher earnings. A flat-rate general sales tax will be regressive if low-income consumers spend a greater percentage of their incomes on taxable purchases than do wealthier households able to save and invest more. A progressive tax, by contrast, constitutes a higher percentage of income as income rises, and a proportional tax remains a constant percentage of income across different income levels. A regressive tax or charge may be balanced by other methods of addressing income inequality, including subsidies and progressive taxes. Sales taxes are generally labeled regressive because they fall on many items considered necessities, which the rich and the poor use in equal amounts. The example often given is toilet paper. Although the rich and the poor theoretically use equal amounts of this good, the percent of discretionary income spent by the poor is much higher than the percent spent by the rich. A state that relies on regressive taxes and fees, such as tolls on roads, is providing a subsidy to those with high incomes and large property holdings, a subsidy paid by those with low incomes and few property holdings.

Residential security maps

In the 1930s, in the U.S. Home Owners Loan Corp., a program to provide federal guarantees for home mortgages opened up the possibility of owning a home for millions of Americans and created the long-term, guaranteed mortgages we know today. These are samples of phrases they used:

- Grade A neighborhood: Up and coming. In demand. Well-planned. Green.
- Grade B: Completely developed. Still good but not what people who can afford more are buying. Blue.
- Grade C: Buildings aged and obsolete. "Infiltration of lower grade populations." Experts say "lower grade," citizens were blacks (called "Negroes" by surveyors), Jews, and foreign-born whites. C neighborhoods "lack homogeneity." Yellow.
- Grade D: Detrimental influences. Undesirable population. Mostly rented homes with poor maintenance, vandalism, unstable families. Red.

Copies were distributed to banks, where residents would go for mortgages. Residents of green and blue districts had no trouble getting loans. In yellow areas, federal officials listed "lower loan commitments." Thus, minorities were denied home ownership and the ability to build wealth.

Ridesharing

The simultaneous use of a passenger road vehicle by two or more unrelated persons, usually for a trip from home to work.

Right to travel

Before the Bill of Rights, in Anglo-Saxon law the right to travel emerged at least as early as Magna Carta. Article 42 reads: "It shall be lawful to any person, for the future, to go out of our kingdom, and to return, safely and securely, by land or by water, saving his allegiance to us, unless it be in time of war, for some short space, for the common good of the kingdom: excepting prisoners and outlaws, according to the laws of the land, and of the people of the nation at war against us, and Merchants who shall be treated as it is said above."

The right to travel (or right to interstate mobility) protects U.S. citizens when they move interstate. States may try to discourage interstate movement by denying new residents certain benefits they grant tenured residents, such as the right to vote or receive public benefits. They do this by imposing durational residency requirements (e.g., only persons who have lived in the state for a year or more can vote). It is this type of discrimination (between previous and new residents) that triggers the right-to-travel doctrine. This doctrine does not prohibit states from imposing bona fide residency standards (such as mailing address or home in the jurisdiction) that confirm that persons are in fact residents. The doctrine is concerned only with laws that discourage or prevent people from obtaining residence if they want to do so (e.g., durational residency requirements).

Road pricing

Usage-based vehicle charges such as tolling lanes and roads, pay-as-you-drive insurance, "cash out" strategies such as parking cash out, and other pricing strategies that seek to affect road demand and use. Pricing generates revenue, affects congestion, travel demand, and emissions. It also alters the management and efficiency of the transportation system, redistributes the cost burden, and incurs administrative and compliance costs. Road pricing offers the potential to generate extra transportation revenue, while simultaneously managing demand. Recent advances in technology such as electronic toll collection (ETC) and global positioning systems (GPS), can reduce the cost of pricing systems, increasing the potential for pricing over time. On the other hand, there continue to be environmental and community impact limitations on the ability of metropolitan areas to expand their roadway systems, increasing the need for effective methods to manage increasing travel demand. Traffic congestion continues to be a serious problem facing drivers in many urban areas in the United States. Road pricing can be a tool in the process of operating and managing a highway system. It has been in existence for centuries, and was critical in the late 1700s and 1800s, as well as the period between 1940 and 1956, in financing new infrastructure in the United States. Modern implementations of road pricing include congestion pricing or value-priced tolls collected electronically that vary with the level of congestion. It can encompass a variety of market-based approaches to respond to congestion problems and subsequent regressive effects on low-income potential users.

Safety net
The network of policies and public services designed to provide low-wage and no-wage workers (stay-at-home mothers, people with disabilities, people on unemployment, social welfare recipients and others) access to health care and other social services.

Service routes
Combining the scheduling efficiencies of fixed routes and the enhanced accessibility features of paratransit, they seemed a way to achieve lower service costs and, at the same time, "bridge the gap" between accessibility and mobility for elderly and disabled persons. The service route network places priority on bringing bus service as close as possible to the user. Service routes try to offer the benefits of both paratransit (less walking to get to a bus stop) and fixed route (riders do not have to call ahead to reserve a trip) service.

Set-asides
A U.S. federal budget term, specific programs for which jurisdictions or non-profits must apply. In regard to Disadvantaged Business Enterprise (DBE) programs, the DBE rule defines a set-aside as "a contracting practice restricting eligibility for the competitive award of a contract solely to DBE firms." The rule limits set-asides, defined in this way, to "limited and extreme circumstances, when no other method could be reasonably expected to remedy egregious instances of discrimination." Set-asides have been criticized as a form of affirmative action.

Social adversities
Chronic social conditions that disproportionately affect America's poor and its racial and ethnic minority groups. These conditions include poverty, community violence, racism, and discrimination. The reduction of social adversities, while a formidable task, may be vital to improving the mental and physical health and the education and job outlook of racial and ethnic minorities. Although there is substantial literature on the damaging effects of poverty on these areas, there is less empirical evidence for the effects of exposure to racism, discrimination, and community violence.

Social capital

Those stocks of social trust, norms, and networks that people can draw upon to solve common problems. Networks of civic engagement, such as neighborhood associations, sports clubs, and cooperatives, are an essential form of social capital, and the denser these networks, the more likely that members of a community will cooperate for mutual benefit. This is so, even in the face of persistent problems of collective action (tragedy of the commons, prisoner's dilemma, etc.), because networks of civic engagement:

- Foster sturdy norms of generalized reciprocity by creating expectations that favors given now will be returned later;
- Facilitate coordination and communication, and thus create channels through which information about the trustworthiness of other individuals and groups can flow, and be tested and verified;
- Embody past success at collaboration, which can serve as a cultural template for future collaboration on other kinds of problems;
- Increase the potential risks to those who act opportunistically that they will not share in the benefits of current and future transactions.

In racially fragmented communities, social capital is lower. Two key aspects of social capital are participation in social activities or groups and trust.

Social equity

Implies a fair and equitable distribution of resources among the current generation. In terms of the urban environment, the city should provide a place of equal opportunity and not be an agent of segregation.

Social exclusion (British term)

Social exclusion refers to external constraints that prevent people from participating adequately in society, including education, employment, public services and activities. Inadequate transport sometimes contributes to social exclusion, particularly for people who live in an automobile-dependent community and are physically disabled, low income, or unable to own and drive a personal car. A name more common in England than in the U.S. (www.cabinetoffice.gov.uk/social_exclusion_task_force/). Social exclusion is due to the interplay of a number of factors, whose consequence is the denial of access, to an individual or group, to the opportunity to participate in the social and economic life of the community, resulting not only in diminished material and nonmaterial quality of life, but in tempered life chances and choices and reduced citizenship.

Dimensions of exclusion include:

1. economic
2. societal
3. social networks

4. organized political
5. personal political
6. personal
7. living space
8. temporal
9. mobility

Social impacts

The consequences to human populations of any public or private actions that alter the ways in which people live, work, play, relate to one another, organize to meet their needs, and generally cope as members of society. The term also includes cultural impacts involving changes to the norms, values, and beliefs that guide and rationalize their cognition of themselves and their society. Changes in people's lives resulting from a proposed public or private action (planned or unplanned). Consequences of an agency's actions that change the way people live, interact in groups (e.g., families, organizations, and communities), think, and feel.

Social impact assessments (SIA)

Efforts to assess or estimate, in advance, the social consequences that are likely to follow from specific policy actions (including programs and the adoption of new polices), and specific government actions (including buildings, large projects, and leasing large tracts of land for resource extraction). A subfield of several social science disciplines (mainly, rural and community sociology, applied anthropology, human geography, and social psychology). Developing a knowledge base for systematic appraisals of the impacts on the day-to-day quality of life of individuals, organizations, institutions, and communities whose environment is affected by a proposed project or policy change. The social science components of environmental impact statements, examining social or socioeconomic impacts of projects under review. They are useful for economic justice analyses. They are oriented toward predicting the social consequences that are likely to follow from specific policy actions and programs.

Socially disadvantaged

According to the Small Business Administration, under 13 C.F.R. § 124 (www .sba.gov) Sec. 124.103: "Those individuals who have been subjected to racial or ethnic prejudice or cultural bias within American society because of their identities as members of groups and without regard to their individual qualities. The social disadvantage must stem from circumstances beyond their control. There is a rebuttable presumption that the following individuals are socially disadvantaged: African Americans; Hispanics; Native Americans (American Indians, Eskimos, Aleuts, or Native Hawaiians); Asian–Pacific

Americans (persons with origins from Burma, Thailand, Malaysia, Indonesia, Singapore, Brunei, Japan, China [including Hong Kong], Taiwan, Laos, Cambodia [Kampuchea], Vietnam, Korea, the Philippines, U.S. Trust Territory of the Pacific Islands [Republic of Palau], Republic of the Marshall Islands, Federated States of Micronesia, the Commonwealth of the Northern Mariana Islands, Guam, Samoa, Macao, Fiji, Tonga, Kiribati, Tuvalu, or Nauru); Subcontinent Asian Americans (persons with origins from India, Pakistan, Bangladesh, Sri Lanka, Bhutan, the Maldives Islands or Nepal); and members of other groups designated from time to time by SBA."

Social overhead capital

Items of essential economic infrastructure required in the production of goods and services. Transportation, communication, and other such sectors can be included. The problem in such sectors is that it is difficult to quantify the contribution of the sector to the economy.

Social service program

A program administered by the federal government, or by a state or local government using federal financial assistance, that provides services directed at reducing poverty, improving opportunities for low-income people, revitalizing low-income communities, empowering low-income families and low-income individuals to become self-sufficient, and otherwise helping people in need. Such programs include, but are not limited to:

1. child care services, protective services for children and adults, services for children and adults in foster care, adoption services, services related to the management and maintenance of the home, day care services for adults, and services to meet the special needs of children, older individuals, and individuals with disabilities (including physical, mental, or emotional disabilities);
2. transportation services;
3. job training and related services, and employment services;
4. information, referral, and counseling services;
5. the preparation and delivery of meals and services related to soup kitchens or food banks;
6. health support services;
7. literacy and mentoring programs;
8. services for the prevention and treatment of juvenile delinquency and substance abuse, services for the prevention of crime and the provision of assistance to the victims and the families of criminal offenders, and services related to intervention in, and prevention of, domestic violence; and
9. services related to the provision of assistance for housing under federal law.

Spatially based analysis

Comparing the distribution of impacts among spatial units such as traffic analysis zones (TAZs) or census tracts, which can be classified by characteristic (low-income, predominantly minority, etc.). A general procedure is as follows:

1. Classify the spatial units according to the characteristic(s) across which the impacts are to be compared. For example, identify TAZs corresponding to census tracts with greater than X percent population in poverty or racial minority population.
2. Identify the magnitude of transportation project impacts for each spatial unit. For example, measure the change in accessibility, total emissions, or the concentration of emissions for each TAZ in the analysis area.
3. Compare the magnitude of impacts among the population groups of interest. For example, compare the average change in accessibility as a result of the regional transportation plan for TAZs with a higher racial minority population with the average change for TAZs with a lower minority population.
4. If appropriate, apply statistical tests to determine whether differences between alternatives and population groups are statistically significant.

Spatial mismatch

A barrier to employment, referring to the location of suitable jobs in areas that are inaccessible by public transportation (Coulton et al., 1996). This is a result of the growth of new jobs in areas outside the city. There is concentrated poverty in the historic center of cities, but deconcentrated opportunity in the form of job suburbanization toward the metropolitan periphery. This phenomenon is most prevalent in larger metropolitan areas that tend to be fragmented by multiple political jurisdictions, because that fragmentation helps to create disequilibrium, a market failure, in the labor market. Specifically, there is spot excess labor demand in the suburbs, and spot excess labor supply in the inner city. In addition to the problem of greater discrimination against African Americans by suburban employers, they may face limited physical access to these jobs. Poor people and blacks are generally located farther from areas of net employment growth. Job vacancy rates and wages are also higher in less-skilled jobs that are located in predominantly white suburbs rather than cities or racially mixed suburbs, suggesting better labor market opportunities for those with access to the former. For instance, inner-city black workers without cars have more difficulty gaining suburban employment than do black workers with cars, and employers located near public transit stops attract more black applicants and new employees than do those located further away. Presumably, the access of low-income inner-city residents to suburban employers depends not only on the proximity of employers to mass transit stops, but also on the distance of various employers from low-income neighborhoods and the extent to which direct public transit routes are available between these sites (i.e., without the need to change buses or trains one or more times).

Spatial responsibility
Suggests that the city has a "footprint" which is considerably larger than the area it occupies. Supply of resources, together with wastes and their impacts, are considered in the total space a city occupies.

Stafford Act
The Robert T. Stafford Disaster Relief and Emergency Assistance Act, P.L. 93-288, as amended, authorizes the president to provide financial and other forms of assistance to state and local governments, certain private nonprofit organizations, and individuals to support response, recovery, and mitigation efforts following presidentially declared major disasters and emergencies. This act concerns post-disaster federal assistance to communities. It was passed after allegations that poor people were not being helped as much as higher-income people after earthquakes, floods, hurricanes, and tornados. Section 308 of the act requires the president to publish regulations "for insuring that the distribution of supplies, the processing of applications, and other relief and assistance activities shall be accomplished in an equitable and impartial manner, without discrimination on the grounds of race, color, religion, nationality, sex, age, or economic status."

Statewide transportation improvement program (STIP)
A staged, multi-year, statewide, intermodal program of transportation projects that is consistent with the statewide transportation plan and planning processes, metropolitan plans, TIPs, and processes pursuant to 23 U.S.C. § 135.

Statewide transportation plan
The official statewide, intermodal transportation plan that is developed through the statewide transportation planning process pursuant to 23 U.S.C. § 135.

Steering
Conduct that may influence a person's choice of a housing location on the basis of his or her race, creed, color, national origin, ancestry, sex, marital status, familial status, and physical or mental handicap. Both private and public housing agencies and realtors may illegally engage in steering.

Sustainability
A concept that first arose at the turn of the century in utilitarian conservation movements (Schnaiberg and Gould, 1994). The idea resurfaced with the environmental movement of the 1960s, in part generated by the work of biologist Rachel Carson's book *Silent Spring*, which foretold the effects of chemical hazards and pesticides on future generations of plant, animal, and human life (Carson, 1962). In the 1980s, we saw a renewed emphasis on sustainability, linking

economics, development, equity, and social institutions such as religion, political systems, and local cultures (Omo-Faduka, 1993; Omari, 1993). Sustainability has been invoked to reassess socioeconomic and technological systems in terms of their long-term viability within the constraints of ecological limits (Schnaiberg and Gould, 1994, p. 205). Sustainable recovery has been promoted as holistic, involving environmental integrity, economic vitality, social and intergenerational equity, and disaster resilience as promoted through a participatory process (Natural Hazards Research and Applications Information Center, 2002).

Measures of sustainability include imputed costs of depletion of natural resources and environmental degradation. Sustainability identifies and incorporates activities and actions to meet the following goals: (1) Consume less energy and natural resources; (2) ensure that resources such as water, air, and land are as clean or cleaner at the end of use as at the beginning; (3) ensure that the viability, integrity, and diversity of natural systems are protected, undiminished, and maintained; (4) ensure that natural soundscape and dark skies are undiminished; (5) use green technologies and products that have less negative impacts on human health and the environment; (6) reduce the material entering landfills; and (7) ensure compliance with all natural and cultural requirements. In the funding context, sustainability often refers to the ability of a demonstration project to continue beyond an initial period of startup funding.

Sustainable development
Qualifies legitimate growth to have minimum negative impact and use resources at maintainable levels. Development that meets the needs of the present without compromising the ability of future generations to meet their own needs. While economic growth remains essential, development must not only meet present concerns for growth, it must also do so in a context that includes the long-term safeguarding of social and environmental resources. Sustainable development policies should include the preservation, maintenance, and strengthening of communities and their overall quality of life through a variety of community services and infrastructures. Sustainable development elements include quality education and safe streets; public transportation; adequate water, sewer, and other community facilities; and a clean, protected environment. Wasteful land use is antithetical to sustainable development. Preservation of land, the reduction of sprawl, and redevelopment of established urban areas are essential to sustainable development. Advocates wish to leave the next generation with a stock of capital no less than the present generation. They worry about the carrying capacity of the earth. The Three Es of sustainable development are prosperous economy, quality environment, and social equity. The ethical principle of equity, particularly intergenerational equity, is central to the concept of sustainable development, though it is often ignored. It refers to the durability or permanence in time of social and economic activities which improve and sustain

quality of life, foster economic growth, preserve the environment, and properly manage renewable resources. Recommended policies often include transit-oriented development; mixed-use developments; urban infill; brownfields redevelopment; encouragement of more transit use, biking, and walking; and better transportation information.

Sustainable transportation

The basic concept is to make transportation, land-use, and resource decisions in a manner that do not preclude options for future generations. The scope of transportation decisions are balanced in economic, environmental quality, and social equity considerations in the short and very long term. Many advocates have determined that promoting a sustainable environment and sustainable communities is a key objective. A sustainable transportation system is one that:

- allows the basic access needs of individuals and societies to be met safely and in a manner consistent with human and ecosystem health, and with equity within and between generations.
- is affordable, operates efficiently, offers choice of transport mode, and supports a vibrant economy.
- limits emissions and waste within the planet's ability to absorb them, minimizes consumption of nonrenewable resources, reuses and recycles its components, and minimizes the use of land and the production of noise.
- reduces greenhouse gas emissions;
- reduces health costs from increased level of physical activity in the community;
- increases life expectancy from increased physical activity and better air quality;
- increases public transport fare revenue;
- increases use of pedestrian and cycle infrastructure;
- reduces impacts resulting from local traffic;
- increases fare revenue for private-public transport operators;
- increases customers for local businesses as people walk to local shops rather than drive to large shopping centers;
- brings savings in travel costs;
- increases opportunities for social interaction with other members of the local community through more walking.

Systemic discrimination

A pattern of discrimination throughout a place of transportation employment, education, housing, or other social infrastructure that is a result of pervasive, interrelated actions, policies, or procedures. Policies or practices that serve to differentiate or to perpetuate a differentiation in terms or conditions of service status as members of a particular group. Such policies or practices may or may not be facially neutral, and intent to discriminate may or may not be involved. Systemic discrimination, sometimes called class discrimination or a pattern or practice of discrimination, concerns a recurring practice or continuing policy rather than an isolated act of discrimination.

Tax base sharing
Especially among suburbs and inner cities, equalizing resources in recognition of regional connections and interdependencies, both physical and economic, and minimizing parochial political actions.

Tax incentive
Tax code provisions (forgiveness of levy or reduction of taxes owed) that encourage private investment and lending at sites, particularly in situations where it might not ordinarily happen. Tax incentives often are used to help address market imperfections that are in the public interest.

Temporary Aid to Needy Families (TANF)
Created by the 1996 welfare reform law, TANF is a program of block grants to states to help them meet the needs of families with no income or resources. It replaces AFDC, JOBS, Emergency Assistance, and some other preceding federal welfare programs. Because of TANF-imposed time limits, states try to place recipients in jobs as quickly as possible, often using program funds to pay for transportation, childcare, and other barriers to workforce participation.

Transportation and Community and System Preservation Pilot program (TCSP)
A key component of the Clinton administration's livability agenda. Helping make communities more livable by preserving green space, easing traffic congestion, and employing smart growth strategies. Protecting the environment while growing the economy. Strengthen the government's role as a partner with state and local efforts to build livable communities for the 21st century. TCSP consists of research and grants that assist communities as they work to solve interrelated problems involving transportation, land development, environmental protection, public safety and economic development, under TEA-21. TCSP funds are used to help achieve locally determined goals such as improving transportation efficiency; reducing the negative effects of transportation on the environment; providing better access to jobs, services, and trade centers; reducing the need for costly future infrastructure; and revitalizing underdeveloped and brownfield sites. Grants also can be used to examine urban development patterns and create strategies that encourage private companies to work toward these goals in designing new developments.

Transit-dependent individuals
Those who are dependent on public transit for their local transportation needs, including low-income individuals, older adults, and persons with disabilities.

FTA estimates that transit-dependent persons compose 30 to 40 percent of the ridership on public transportation systems in urbanized areas.

Transit-oriented development (TOD)
Developing the land around public transit stations into housing, shopping, and services. Its advocates tout benefits ranging from more compact development and less automobile dependence to new retail opportunities and improved quality of life. TODs often have conventional suburban single-use development patterns, with conventional parking requirements, so that the development is actually transit-adjacent, not transit-oriented. Instead of branding anything that is built near transit a TOD, projects should be judged against specific desired outcomes: choice (for example, diverse housing and transportation); livability (less pollution per capita); and financial return (for instance, to developers and transit agencies). Three Ds, or three dimensions (density, design, and diversity), are needed for a TOD to work. Because low-income households tend to own fewer cars and are more likely to use transit, an affordable housing component of a transit-oriented development can add more riders, as well as furthering other public policy objectives. TOD can have the negative effect of lowering the quality of life along transit strips and destroying the better aspects of suburban development, such as open and green space.

Transportation barriers
Inadequate public transportation, lack of personal transportation, and spatial mismatch; issues of affordability underlie all three. Inadequate public transportation means limited, infrequent, or unaffordable transit service; limited routes covered by transit operation; and safety or security concerns on vehicle and at transit stations during off-peak hours. A lack of personal transportation means there is no privately owned car available for travel to work. This creates a problem, particularly for people in areas with limited public transportation. Welfare recipients without cars often face unreliable or untenable alternatives, such as having to rely on rides provided by a neighbor or having to take three or four buses each way to work.

Transportation conformity
A requirement of the Clean Air Act (CAA) that is designed to ensure that federal and federally assisted projects conform to the air quality objectives established in a state's air quality implementation plan (SIP) for attaining the national air quality standards. The transportation conformity rule was promulgated in 1993 by the Environmental Protection Agency (EPA), with the most recent major revisions to the rule in 1997. EPA issued its conformity regulation with USDOT's concurrence. Its implementation and regulatory approach continues to be controversial, with legislative provisions introduced and lawsuits filed frequently. In the FHWA and FTA programs, a conformity determination is accomplished

by ensuring that the expected motor vehicle emissions from planned transportation investments are within the emissions "budget" of the SIP—the "carrying capacity" of an area's emissions. A failure or inability to make a conformity determination is referred to as a "conformity lapse" and causes a halt in the flow of federal transportation funding to proposed highway and transit projects in the area, except for certain categories of projects.

Transportation control measures (TCMs)
Local actions to adjust traffic patterns or reduce vehicle use to lower air pollutant emissions. These may include HOV lanes, provision of bicycle facilities, ridesharing, telecommuting, etc.

Transportation data
Data used to model the geographic locations, interconnectedness, and characteristics of the transportation system within the United States. The transportation system includes both physical and nonphysical components representing all modes of travel that allow the movement of goods and people between locations.

Transportation demand management (TDM)
Plans to achieve increases in public transit use and reduce congestion and pollution. To achieve the greatest success in reducing vehicle trips, projects need to encompass TOD + TDM, that is, both transit-oriented development and transportation-demand management. Perhaps the most critical element of a TDM package is parking management. TOD and parking are inextricably entwined. Most conventional development uses parking ratios derived from suburbs that have little or no transit and where everyone is assumed to have a car. Walkability is maximized when streets are designed to accommodate lower traffic volumes in the first place. The key, then, is to factor the reduced trip-making benefits of TOD back into the street design.

Transportation disadvantaged
A term used to describe those persons who have little or no access to meaningful jobs, services, shopping, and recreation because a transportation system that does not meet their needs. Often refers to those individuals who cannot drive a private automobile because of age, disability, or lack of resources.

Transportation enhancement
Part of gasoline tax funding that provides funds to the states for activities designed to strengthen the cultural, aesthetic, and environmental aspects of the nation's intermodal transportation system. Funding is directed at nontraditional projects such as bike and pedestrian facilities, landscaping, and beautification. Up to 10 percent of Surface Transportation Program funds are available for enhancements. States often do not use the full amount for which they are authorized.

Transportation final demand

This measures not just the value-added of the transportation industry, but also the value of production that has a transportation purpose, even if it is not part of the transportation industry. For example, a great deal of transportation is carried out by households—people driving their own cars. That activity is not counted as gross domestic product at all. The value of the cars and gasoline that those people buy is counted as part of the output of the auto manufacturing industry, the petroleum refining industry, etc. If one concludes that the production of cars and gasoline has a transportation purpose, and count it as part of transportation rather than as part of auto manufacturing or petroleum refining, then one has the total of transportation final demand. Transportation final demand was 11.2 percent of GDP in 1997.

Transportation planning

The development of strategies for the design, construction, operation, and maintenance of transportation facilities for moving people and goods in a village, town, pueblo, rancheria, city, borough, county, township, parish, metropolitan area, Indian reservation, state, multistate region, or country. The transportation planning process is continuing and comprehensive and is based on the complexity of the transportation problems. There are certain characteristics of the transportation planning process that need to be emphasized:

- The planning process is linked to land-use, cultural preservation, culture, social, economic, environmental, and quality-of-life goals of the area covered by the plan (e.g., reservation, region, or state).
- The planning process examines current transportation operations and identifies future transportation needs (both physical and financial).
- The transportation planning process facilitates transportation investment decision making with multiple demands on limited resources.
- The planning process involves a variety of participants with an interest in transportation decision making. These include Indian tribal governments, federal agencies, states, local governments, metropolitan planning organizations (MPOs), regional planning organizations (RPOs), special interest groups, and others.
- The planning process results in the development of workable strategies to achieve optimum transportation investment over both the short-range (3–5 years) and long-range (20 years or more) planning periods.

In summary, transportation planning uses an analytical process to develop realistic priorities for the service population. It encourages community, tribal, and local involvement to increase community awareness.

Travel-time budget

People devote on average a constant fraction of their daily time to travel. The travel-time budget is typically between 1 and 1.5 hours per person per day in a wide variety of economic, social, and geographic settings. Residents of African villages have a travel-time budget similar to those of Japan, Singapore, Western Europe, and North America. Small groups and individuals vary in their behavior, but at the level of aggregated populations, a person spends an average of 1.1 hours a day traveling. If people hold their time for travel constant but also demand more mobility as their income rises, they must select faster modes of transport to cover more distance in the same time. The research suggests that the variable that most closely correlates to travel time budget is city size. A person's daily travel budget is not measured in miles, but in minutes. Travel habits of people are not determined as much by congestion as by their personal travel time budget. Time spent traveling in excess of the budget is more of a factor influencing habits than congestion experiences. In other words, people will more readily adjust their travel behaviors to seek compliance with their desired travel budget than they will in response to congestion issues.

Trickle out theory

Particular urban amenities (e.g., transit stops, convenient location) create significant influx of private investment to neighborhoods predominated by low-income renters who are unable to pay the inevitable increase in rental and housing prices. prices. *(See also "Gentrification")*

Twenty-year planning horizon

A forecast period covering 20 years from the date of plan adoption, reaffirmation, or modification in attainment areas and subsequent federal conformity finding at the time of adoption in nonattainment and maintenance areas. The plan must reflect the most recent planning assumptions for current and future population, travel, land use, congestion, employment, economic activity, and other related statistical measures for the metropolitan planning area.

Undercounting

Census data have long been recognized as inaccurate, often resulting in a net undercounting of the actual population. Minority communities are most frequently undercounted, especially those with higher levels of lack of English proficiency, disability, and uncertain immigration status. A 1999 study by the General Accounting Office found that because of undercounting in the 1990 census, states and localities with the largest undercount failed to get about $450 million from 15 federal programs. To compensate for undercounting, the Census Bureau conducts a statistical sampling to come up with an adjusted count. The Secretary of Commerce then decides which are more reliable—the adjusted or unadjusted data. In the 2000 census, the administration went with the unadjusted data and never released the adjusted count. Some advocates feel that under-counts are not an accident or a statistical anomaly.

Underrepresented population

The Tech Act Amendments of 1994 (Pub. L. 103–218) define an underrepresented population as "a population such as minorities, the poor, and persons with limited English proficiency." The Rehabilitation Services Administration (RSA), which administers the state-federal vocational rehabilitation program, defines "unserved and underserved" populations as groups of individuals who are not served or are inadequately served as the result of a variety of policy, practice, and environmental barriers.

Underserved populations

Individuals who fall within one or more of the categories protected under the Fair Housing Act who are also (1) of a immigrant population (especially ethnic minorities who are not English speaking); (2) in rural populations; (3) among the homeless; and (4) among persons with disabilities who can be historically documented to have been subject to discriminatory practices that were not the focus of federal, state, or local fair housing enforcement efforts.

Underutilization / Underrepresentation

A situation wherein a lower number of protected class employees are represented than parity would predict. Once underutilization is quantitatively established, an employer must (1) demonstrate that the underutilization is the legitimate effect of a bona fide occupational qualification (BFOQ) or results from business necessity; or (2) develop an affirmative action program with specific, action-oriented steps to overcome this underutilization. Having materially fewer minorities or women in a particular job group than reasonably would be expected based upon their availability is an example of underrepresentation.

User-side subsidy

A transportation funding structure in which qualified users (usually economically disadvantaged persons) are able to purchase vouchers for transportation services at a portion of their worth. The users may then use the vouchers to purchase transportation from any participating provider; the vouchers are redeemed by the provider at full value, and the provider is reimbursed by the funding agency for the full value.

Zoning

Local governmental designation of certain land parcels for particular uses. The authority to control land use through zoning is passed from the state to the municipality or county through enabling legislation. Since the 1926 inception of zoning as an acceptable use of police power to control land use in *Village of*

Euclid v. Ambler Realty Co., there has been an undercurrent of conflict between expectations of individual property use and protection of the public welfare.

The original intent of zoning was to protect property owners from harm or nuisance created by other public or private activities. Zoning is, by its nature, exclusionary. Many of the exclusionary practices in zoning have been brought to the forefront on the basis of racial discrimination, provision of affordable housing, and urban growth control. Three main reasons have been identified as the basis for exclusion. First, is the intent of preserving the status quo. Second, are economic reasons that include concerns of reduced property values or increased taxes required to support the community? The third reason is the unfortunate mix of bias and prejudice towards people who are not the same as the existing dominant group. It is argued that the same motives used to exclude people based on race, religion, and class differences are evident in the attempts to exclude people with disabilities, especially in residential areas.

A land-use plan for a city shows the different uses of land now and the projected uses in the future. Such uses might include single-family residential uses, multifamily residential uses, intense commercial, light commercial, industrial uses, and so forth. These uses are designated as zones, hence the term zoning. By using zoning, cities attempt to influence what use can be made of property in different parts of the community.

II

Executive Order No. 13007

Indian Sacred Sites

May 24, 1996

By the authority vested in me as President by the Constitution and the laws of the United States, in furtherance of Federal treaties, and in order to protect and preserve Indian religious practices, it is hereby ordered:

Section 1. *Accommodation of Sacred Sites*. (a) In managing Federal lands, each executive branch agency with statutory or administrative responsibility for the management of Federal lands shall, to the extent practicable, permitted by law, and not clearly inconsistent with essential agency functions, (1) accommodate access to and ceremonial use of Indian sacred sites by Indian religious practitioners and (2) avoid adversely affecting the physical integrity of such sacred sites. Where appropriate, agencies shall maintain the confidentiality of sacred sites.

  (b) For purposes of this order:

   i. "Federal lands" means any land or interests in land owned by the United States, including leasehold interests held by the United States, except Indian trust lands;

   ii. "Indian tribe" means an Indian or Alaska Native tribe, band, nation, pueblo, village, or community that the Secretary of the Interior acknowledges to exist as an Indian tribe pursuant to Public Law No. 103-454, 108 Stat. 4791, and "Indian" refers to a member of such an Indian tribe; and

   iii. "Sacred site" means any specific, discrete, narrowly delineated location on Federal land that is identified by an Indian tribe, or Indian individual determined to be an appropriately authoritative representative of an Indian religion, as sacred by virtue of its established religious significance to, or ceremonial use by, an Indian religion; provided that the tribe or appropriately authoritative representative of an Indian religion has informed the agency of the existence of such a site.

Section 2. *Procedures.* (a) Each executive branch agency with statutory or administrative responsibility for the management of Federal lands shall, as appropriate, promptly implement procedures for the purposes of carrying out the provisions of section 1 of this order, including, where practicable and appropriate, procedures to ensure reasonable notice is provided of proposed actions or land management policies that may restrict future access to or ceremonial use of, or adversely affect the physical integrity of, sacred sites. In all actions pursuant to this section, agencies shall comply with the Executive memorandum of April 29, 1994, "Government-to-Government Relations with Native American Tribal Governments."

(b) Within 1 year of the effective date of this order, the head of each executive branch agency with statutory or administrative responsibility for the management of Federal lands shall report to the President, through the Assistant to the President for Domestic Policy, on the implementation of this order. Such reports shall address, among other things,

  i. any changes necessary to accomodate access to and ceremonial use of Indian sacred sites;
 ii. any changes necessary to avoid adversely affecting the physical integrity of Indian sacred sites; and
iii. procedures implemented or proposed to facilitate consultation with appropriate Indian tribes and religious leaders and the expeditious resolution of disputes relating to agency action on Federal lands that may adversely affect access to, ceremonial use of, or the physical integrity of sacred sites.

Section 3. Nothing in this order shall be construed to require a taking of vested property interests. Nor shall this order be construed to impair enforceable rights to use of Federal lands that have been granted to third parties through final agency action. For purposes of this order, "agency action" has the same meaning as in the Administrative Procedures Act (5 U.S.C. § 551[13]).

Section 4. This order is intended only to improve the internal management of the executive branch and is not intended to, nor does it, create any right, benefit, or trust responsibility, substantive or procedural, enforceable at law or equity by any party against the United States, its agencies officers, or any person.

William J. Clinton
The White House
May 24, 1996
Updated April 30, 2002

Executive Order No. 12898

Federal Actions to Address Environmental Justice in Minority Populations and Low-Income Populations

February 11, 1994

By the authority vested in me as President by the Constitution and the laws of the United States of America, it is hereby ordered as follows:

Section 1-1. Implementation.

1-101. Agency Responsibilities. To the greatest extent practicable and permitted by law, and consistent with the principles set forth in the report on the National Performance Review, each Federal agency shall make achieving environmental justice part of its mission by identifying and addressing, as appropriate, disproportionately high and adverse human health or environmental effects of its programs, policies, and activities on minority populations and low-income populations in the United States and its territories and possessions, the District of Columbia, the Commonwealth of Puerto Rico, and the Commonwealth of the Mariana Islands.

1-102. Creation of an Interagency Working Group on Environmental Justice. (a) Within 3 months of the date of this order, the Administrator of the Environmental Protection Agency ("Administrator") or the Administrator's designee shall convene an interagency Federal Working Group on Environmental Justice

("Working Group"). The Working Group shall comprise the heads of the following executive agencies and offices, or their designees: (a) Department of Defense; (b) Department of Health and Human Services; (c) Department of Housing and Urban Development; (d) Department of Labor; (e) Department of Agriculture; (f) Department of Transportation; (g) Department of Justice; (h) Department of the Interior; (i) Department of Commerce; (j) Department of Energy; (k) Environmental Protection Agency; (l) Office of Management and Budget; (m) Office of Science and Technology Policy; (n) Office of the Deputy Assistant to the President for Environmental Policy; (o) Office of the Assistant to the President for Domestic Policy; (p) National Economic Council; (q) Council of Economic Advisers; and (r) other such Government officials as the President may designate. The Working Group shall report to the President through the Deputy through the Deputy Assistant to the President for Environmental Policy and the Assistant to the President for Domestic Policy.

(b) The Working Group shall:

(1) provide guidance to Federal agencies on criteria for identifying disproportionately high and adverse human health or environmental effects on minority populations and low-income populations.

(2) coordinate with, provide guidance to, and serve as a clearinghouse for, each Federal agency as it develops an environmental justice strategy as required by section 1-103 of this order, in order to ensure that the administration, interpretation and enforcement of programs, activities and policies are undertaken in a consistent manner;

(3) assist in coordinating research by, and stimulating cooperation among, the Environmental Protection Agency, the Department of Health and Human Services, the Department of Housing and Urban Development, and other agencies conducting research or other activities in accordance with section 3-3 of this order;

(4) assist in coordinating data collection, required by this order;

(5) examine existing data and studies on environmental justice;

(6) hold public meetings as required in section 5-502(d) of this order; and

(7) develop interagency model projects on environmental justice that evidence cooperation among Federal agencies.

1-103. Development of Agency Strategies. (a) Except as provided in section 6-605 of this order, each Federal agency shall develop an agency-wide environmental justice strategy, as set forth in subsections (b)-(e) of this section that identifies and addresses disproportionately high and adverse human health or environmental effects of its programs, policies, or activities on minority populations and low-income populations. The environmental justice strategy shall list programs, policies, planning and public participation practices, enforcement and/or rulemakings related to human health or the environment that should be revised to, at a minimum: (1) promote enforcement of all health and environmental statutes in areas with minority populations and low-income populations; (2) ensure greater public participation; (3) improve research and data collection relating to the health of and environment of minority populations and low-income populations; and (4) identify differential patterns of consumption of natural resources among minority populations and low-income populations. In addition, the environmental justice strategy shall include, where appropriate, a timetable for undertaking identified revisions and consideration of economic and social implications of the revisions.

(b) Within 4 months of the date of this order, each Federal agency shall identify an internal administrative process for developing its environmental justice strategy, and shall inform the Working Group of the process.

(c) Within 6 months of the date of this order, each Federal agency shall provide the Working Group with an outline of its proposed environmental justice strategy.

(d) Within 10 months of the date of this order, each Federal agency shall provide the Working Group with its proposed environmental justice strategy.

(e) Within 12 months of the date of this order, each Federal agency shall finalize its environmental justice strategy and provide a copy and written description of its strategy to the Working Group. During the 12-month period from the date of this order, each Federal agency, as part of its environmental justice strategy, shall identify several specific projects that can be promptly undertaken to address particular concerns identified during the development of the proposed environmental justice strategy, and a schedule for implementing those projects.

(f) Within 24 months of the date of this order, each Federal agency shall report to the Working Group on its progress in implementing its agency-wide environmental justice strategy.

(g) Federal agencies shall provide additional periodic reports to the Working Group.

1-104. Reports to the President. Within 14 months of the date of this order, the Working Group shall submit to the President, through the Office of the Deputy Assistant to the President for Environmental Policy and the Office of the Assistant to the President for Domestic Policy, a report that describes the implementation of this order, and includes the final environmental justice strategies described in section 1-103(e) of this order.

Sec. 2-2. Federal Agency Responsibilities for Federal Programs. Each Federal agency shall conduct its programs, policies, and activities that substantially effect human health or the environment, in a manner that ensures that such programs, policies, and activities do not have the effect of excluding persons (including populations) from participation in, denying persons (including populations) the benefits of, or subjecting persons (including populations) to discrimination under, such programs, policies, and activities, because of their race, color, or national origin.

Sec. 3-3. Research, Data Collection, and Analysis.

3-301. Human Health and Environmental Research and Analysis. (a) Environmental human health research, whenever practicable and appropriate, shall include diverse segments of the population in epidemiological and clinical studies, including segments at high risk from environmental hazards, such as minority populations, low-income populations and workers who may be exposed to substantial environmental hazards.

(b) Environmental human health analyses, whenever practicable and appropriate, shall identify multiple and cumulative exposures.

(c) Federal agencies shall provide minority populations and low-income populations the opportunity to comment on the development and design of research strategies undertaken pursuant to this order.

3-302. Human Health and Environmental Data Collection and Analysis. To the extent permitted by existing law, including the Privacy Act, as amended (5 U.S.C. section 552a): (a) each Federal agency, whenever practicable and appropriate, shall collect, maintain, and analyze information assessing and comparing environmental and human health risks borne by populations identified by race, national origin, or income. To the extent practicable and appropriate, Federal agencies shall use this information to determine whether their programs, policies, and activities have disproportionately high and adverse human health or environmental effects on minority populations and low-income populations.

(b) In connection with the development and implementation of agency strategies in section 1-103 of this order, each Federal agency, whenever practicable and appropriate, shall collect, maintain and analyze information on the race, national origin, income level, and other readily accessible and appropriate information for areas surrounding facilities or sites expected to have a substantial environmental, human health, or economic effect on the surrounding populations, when such facilities or sites become the subject of a substantial Federal environmental administrative or judicial action. Such information shall be made available to the public, unless prohibited by law; and

(c) Each Federal agency, whenever practicable and appropriate, shall collect, maintain, and analyze information on the race, national origin, income level, and other readily accessible and appropriate information for areas surrounding Federal facilities that are: (1) subject to the reporting requirements under the Emergency Planning and Community Right-to-Know Act, 42 U.S.C. section 11001-11050 as mandated in Executive Order No. 12856; and (2) expected to have a substantial environmental, human health, or economic effect on surrounding populations.

(d) In carrying out the responsibilities in this section, each Federal agency, whenever practicable and appropriate, shall share information and eliminate unnecessary duplication of efforts through the use of existing data systems and cooperative agreements among Federal agencies and with States, local, and tribal governments.

Sec. 4-4. Subsistence Consumption of Fish and Wildlife.
4-401. Consumption Patterns. In order to assist in identifying the need for ensuring protection of populations with differential patterns of subsistence consumption of fish and wildlife, Federal agencies, whenever practicable and appropriate, shall collect, maintain, and analyze information on the consumption patterns of populations who principally rely on fish and/or wildlife for subsistence. Federal agencies shall communicate to the public the risk of those consumption patterns.

4-402. Guidance. Federal agencies, whenever practicable and appropriate, shall work in a coordinated manner to publish guidance reflecting the latest scientific information available concerning methods for evaluating the human health risks associated with the consumption of pollutant-bearing fish or wildlife. Agencies shall consider such guidance in developing their policies and rules.

Sec. 5-5. Public Participation and Access to Information. (a) The public may submit recommendations to Federal agencies relating to the incorporation of environmental justice principles into Federal agency programs or policies. Each Federal agency shall convey such recommendations to the Working Group.

(b) Each Federal agency may, whenever practicable and appropriate, translate crucial public documents, notices and hearings relating to human health or the environment for limited English-speaking populations.

(c) Each Federal agency shall work to ensure that public documents, notices, and hearings relating to human health or the environment are concise, understandable, and readily accessible to the public.

(d) The Working Group shall hold public meetings, as appropriate, for the purpose of fact-finding, receiving public comments, and conducting inquiries concerning environmental justice. The Working Group shall prepare for public review a summary of the contents and recommendations discussed at the public meetings.

Sec. 6-6. General Provisions.
6-601. Responsibility for Agency Implementation. The head of each Federal agency shall be responsible for ensuring compliance with this order. Each Federal agency shall conduct internal reviews and take such other steps as may be necessary to monitor compliance with this order.

6-602. Executive Order No. 12250. This Executive Order is intended to supplement but not supersede Executive Order No. 12250, which requires consistent and effective implementation of various laws prohibiting discriminatory practices in programs receiving Federal financial assistance. Nothing herein shall limit the effect or mandate of Executive Order No. 12250.

6-603. Executive Order No. 12875. This Executive Order is not intended to limit the effect or mandate of Executive Order No. 12875.

6-604. Scope. For the purposes of this order, Federal agency means any agency on the Working Group, and such other agencies as may be designated by the President, that conducts any Federal program or activity that substantially effects human health or the environment. Independent agencies are requested to comply with the provisions of this order.

6-605. Petitions for Exemptions. The head of a Federal agency may petition the President for an exemption from the requirements of this order on the grounds that all or some of the petitioning agency's programs or activities should not be subject to the requirements of this order.

6-606. Native American Programs. Each Federal agency responsibility set forth under this order shall apply equally to Native American programs. In addition, the Department of the Interior, in coordination with the Working Group, and after consultation with tribal leaders, shall coordinate steps to be taken pursuant to this order that address Federally-recognized Indian tribes.

6-607. Costs. Unless otherwise provided by law, Federal agencies shall assume the financial costs of complying with this order.

6-608. General. Federal agencies shall implement this order consistent with, and to the extent permitted by, existing law.

6-609. Judicial Review. This order is intended only to improve the internal management of the executive branch and is not intended to, nor does it create any right, benefit, or trust responsibility, substantive or procedural, enforceable at law or equity by a party against the United States, its agencies, its officers, or any person. This order shall not be construed to create any right to judicial review involving the compliance or noncompliance of the United States, its agencies, its officers, or any other person with this order.

William J. Clinton
The White House
February 11, 1994

IV

Executive Order No. 13166

Improving Access to Services for Persons with Limited English Proficiency

August 11, 2000

By the authority vested in me as President by the Constitution and the laws of the United States of America, and to improve access to federally conducted and federally assisted programs and activities for persons who, as a result of national origin, are limited in their English proficiency (LEP), it is hereby ordered as follows:

Section 1. Goals.

The Federal Government provides and funds an array of services that can be made accessible to otherwise eligible persons who are not proficient in the English language. The Federal Government is committed to improving the accessibility of these services to eligible LEP persons, a goal that reinforces its equally important commitment to promoting programs and activities designed to help individuals learn English. To this end, each Federal agency shall examine the services it provides and develop and implement a system by which LEP persons can meaningfully access those services consistent with, and without unduly burdening, the fundamental mission of the agency. Each Federal agency shall also work to ensure that recipients of Federal financial assistance (recipients) provide meaningful access to their LEP applicants and beneficiaries. To assist the agencies with this endeavor, the Department of Justice has today issued a general guidance document (LEP Guidance), which sets forth the compliance standards that recipients must follow to ensure that the programs and activities they normally provide in English are accessible to LEP persons and thus do not discriminate on the basis of national origin in violation of title VI of the Civil Rights Act of 1964, as amended, and its implementing regulations. As described in the LEP Guidance, recipients must take reasonable steps to ensure meaningful access to their programs and activities by LEP persons.

Sec. 2. Federally Conducted Programs and Activities.

Each Federal agency shall prepare a plan to improve access to its federally conducted programs and activities by eligible LEP persons. Each plan shall be consistent with the standards set forth in the LEP Guidance, and shall include the steps the agency will take to ensure that eligible LEP persons can meaningfully access the agency's programs and activities. Agencies shall develop and begin to implement these plans within 120 days of the date of this order, and shall send copies of their plans to the Department of Justice, which shall serve as the central repository of the agencies' plans.

Sec. 3. Federally Assisted Programs and Activities.

Each agency providing Federal financial assistance shall draft title VI guidance specifically tailored to its recipients that is consistent with the LEP Guidance issued by the Department of Justice.

This agency-specific guidance shall detail how the general standards established in the LEP Guidance will be applied to the agency's recipients. The agency-specific guidance shall take into account the types of services provided by the recipients, the individuals served by the recipients, and other factors set out in the LEP Guidance.

Agencies that already have developed title VI guidance that the Department of Justice determines is consistent with the LEP Guidance shall examine their existing guidance, as well as their programs and activities, to determine if additional guidance is necessary to comply with this order. The Department of Justice shall consult with the agencies in creating their guidance and, within 120 days of the date of this order, each agency shall submit its specific guidance to the Department of Justice for review and approval. Following approval by the Department of Justice, each agency shall publish its guidance document in the Federal Register for public comment.

Sec. 4. Consultations.

In carrying out this order, agencies shall ensure that stakeholders, such as LEP persons and their representative organizations, recipients, and other appropriate individuals or entities, have an adequate opportunity to provide input. Agencies will evaluate the particular needs of the LEP persons they and their recipients serve and the burdens of compliance on the agency and its recipients.

This input from stakeholders will assist the agencies in developing an approach to ensuring meaningful access by LEP persons that is practical and effective, fiscally responsible, responsive to the particular circumstances of each agency, and can be readily implemented.

Sec. 5. Judicial Review.

This order is intended only to improve the internal management of the executive branch and does not create any right or benefit, substantive or procedural, enforceable at law or equity by a party against the United States, its agencies, its officers or employees, or any person.

William J. Clinton
The White House
August 11, 2000

References

Adarand Constructors, Inc. v. Peña (93-1841) 515 U.S. 200 (1995).

Alexander v. Sandoval, 532 U.S. 275 (2001); 121 S. Ct. 1511 (2001).

Almanza, S., & R. Alvarez. (1995). *Low-income communities and communities of color*. Background paper presented at the Transportation: Environmental Justice and Social Equity Conference, Washington, D.C.

American Academy of Pediatrics. (2003). *The prevention of unintentional injury among American Indian and Alaska Native children: A subject review*. Committee on Native American Child Health and Committee on Injury and Poison Prevention. Retrieved on March 27, 2005, from www.cdc.gov/mmwr/preview/mmwrhtml/mm5230a2.htm.

American Association of Community Colleges. (n.d.). *Student enrollment and characteristics*. Retrieved March 17, 2006, from www.aacc.nche.edu/Content/NavigationMenu/AboutCommunityColleges/Trends_and_Statistics/EnrollmentInfo/Enrollment_Info.htm.

American Lung Association. (2000). *Minority lung disease data 2000*. Retrieved May 2003 from www2.lungusa.org/pub/minority/mldd_00.html.

American Public Transportation Association. (n.d.). *Public transportation ridership statistics*. Retrieved on May 11, 2003, from www.apta.com/research/stats/ridershp/race.cfm.

American Public Transportation Association. (1991). *Effects of fare changes on bus ridership*. Washington, D.C.: Author.

American Public Transportation Association. (1992). *Americans in transit: A profile of public transit passengers*. Washington, D.C.: Author.

American Public Transportation Association. (2002). *Impact of the 2001–2002 economic slowdown on public transportation*. Washington, D.C.: Author.

Americans with Disabilities Act (1990).

Ammons v. Dade City, Florida, 783 F.2d 982, 11th Cir. (1986).

Association of the Bar of the City of New York (1996). Committees on Environmental Law and Civil Rights. (February 13).

Austin City Connection. (2001). *Environmental issues and concerns: Frequently asked questions*. Retrieved on June 17, 2006, from www.ci.austin.tx.us/news/pipe_environ_faq.htm.

Barnes, C. A. (1983). *Journey from Jim Crow: The desegregation of Southern transit*. New York: Columbia University Press.

Blumenberg, E. (2002). "On the way to work: Welfare recipients and barriers to employment." *Economic Development Quarterly, 16*(4), 314–325.

———. (January 2003). "Transportation costs and the American dilemma: Race, ethnicity and the costs of travel." Paper presented for the Civil Rights Project at Harvard roundtable Racial Equity in Transportation: Establishing Priorities for Research and Policy. Washington, D.C.: Brookings Institution.

Boarnet, M. G., J. F. DiMento, & G. P. Macey. (June 2002). "Toll-highway finance lessons from Orange County." *California Policy Research Center Brief, 14*, 3.

Bollens, S. A. (2003). "In through the back door: Social equity and regional governance." *Housing Policy Debate, 13*(4), 631–657.

Bostock, L. (2001). "Pathways of disadvantage? Walking as a mode of transport among low-income mothers." *Health and Social Care in the Community, 9*(1), 11–18.

Brock, W., B. Cunill, S. Dockter, J. Isom, G. King, J. Lindsey-Foster, D. Sparklin, & B. Stevens. (September 1996). *Community impact assessment: A quick reference for transportation* (No. FHWA-PD-96-036). Washington, D.C.: Federal Highway Administration.

Brown v. Board of Education of Topeka, 347 U.S 483 (1954).

Bryjak, G. A. (2004). "Outsourcing the American Dream." *Z Magazine, 17*, 4.

Bullard, R. D., & G. S. Johnson (Eds.). (1997). *Just transportation: Dismantling race and class barriers to mobility.* Gabriola Island, B.C.: New Society Publishers.

Bureau of Transportation Statistics. (1999). *Transportation Statistics Annual Report.* Washington, D.C.: Author.

Cabanatuan, M. (2001). "Poor kids' pleas for bus passes taken to heart." *San Francisco Chronicle*, p. A-19. Retrieved May 2003 from www.co.alameda.ca.us/board/carson/news/2001/kids.htm.

Campos-Outcalt, D., C. Bay, A. Dellapena, & M. K. Cota. (1999). "Motor vehicle crash fatalities by race/ethnicity in Arizona, 1990–96." *Pediatrics, 104*(6), 1397–1399.

Campos-Outcalt, D., D. Prybylski, A. J. Watkins, G. Rothfus, & A. Dellapena. (1997). "Motor-vehicle crash fatalities among American Indians and non-Indians in Arizona, 1979 through 1988." *American Journal of Public Health, 87*, 282–285.

Carter, D. J., S. M. Flores, & R. J. Reddick (Eds.). (2004). *Legacies of Brown: Multiracial equity in American education.* Cambridge, Mass.: Harvard Education Press.

Centers for Disease Control and Prevention. (n.d.). National Center for Injury Prevention and Control. *Injury fact book 2001–2002.* Retrieved May 2003 from www.cdc.gov/ncipc/fact_book/07_Different.htm.

Centers for Disease Control and Prevention. (2002a). "Barriers to children walking and biking to school—United States, 1999." *Morbidity and Mortality Weekly Report 51*, 701–704.

Centers for Disease Control and Prevention. (2002b). *Surveillance for asthma, United States, 1980–1999*. Retrieved May 2003 from www.cdc.gov/mmwr/preview/mmwrhtml/ss5101a1.htm

Centers for Disease Control and Prevention. (2003). "Injury mortality among American Indian and Alaska Native children and youth—United States, 1989–1998." *Morbidity and Mortality Weekly Report, 52*(30), 697–701.

Cherokee Nation v. Georgia, 30 U.S. (5 Pet.) 1, 17, (1831).

Civil Rights Act of 1964, 23 C.F.R. pt. 200, § 200.9.

Civil Rights Cases, 109 U.S. 3 (1883).

CNN Interview. (2001). Retrieved on June 9, 2005, from http://archives.cnn.com/2001/US/05/10/access.lewis.freedom.rides/.

Code of Federal Regulations, Title 20, § 645.220(f)(1).

Community Transportation Association of America. (n.d.). *A model for solving rural transportation issues*. Washington, D.C.: Author.

Community Transportation Association of America. (1998). *Access to jobs: A guide to innovative practices in welfare-to-work transportation*. Washington, D.C.: Author.

Congress for the New Urbanism. (2000). *Charter of the new urbanism*. Michael L. & K. McCormick (Eds.). New York: McGraw-Hill.

Coulton, C., L. Leete, & N. Bania. (1997). *Housing, transportation and access to suburban jobs by welfare recipients in the Cleveland area*. Center for Urban Poverty and Social Change: Mandel School of Applied Social Sciences, Case Western Reserve University.

Crain & Associates with R. Byrd & Omniversed International. (1999). *Using public transportation to reduce the economic, social, and human costs of personal immobility*. Washington, D.C.: Transit Cooperative Research Program.

DARE Seeds of Change. (2003). *No Education without transportation*. Providence, R.I.: Author.

Deka, D. (2004). "Social and environmental justice issues in urban transportation." In Susan Hanson & Genevieve Giuliano (Eds.), *Geography of urban transportation* (3rd Ed.). New York: Guilford Press.

Delucchi, M. A. (2002). *The social cost of transport: Efficient pricing of modes and benefit/cost analysis of transport alternatives*. Does Research and Institute of Transportation Studies, University of California. Retrieved on March 15, 2005, from www.sactaqc.org/plenaries/09-05-02/delucchi.ppt.

———. (1996). "The annualized social cost of motor-vehicle use in the U.S., 1990-1991: Summary of theory, data, methods, and results." ITS-Davis. Report #1 in the series: *The annualized social cost of motor-vehicle use in the United States, based on 1990-1991 data*. October 2004. Publication No. UCD-ITS-RR-96-3 (1) rev. 1.

Dill, J. (2001). "The design and administration of voluntary accelerated vehicle retirement programs in North America and abroad." *Transportation Research Record, 1750*: 32–39.

Dornan, D. L., & J. W. March (July/August 2005). "Direct user charges." *Public Roads, 69*(1).

Downs, A. (1971). "Suburban housing: A program for expanded opportunities." *Real Estate Review, 1*(1), 4–10.

Dred Scott v. Sandford, 19 Howard (1857).

Education Research Advocacy & Support to Eliminate Racism (2005). *Housing strategies*. Retrieved on April 5, 2006, from www.eraseracismny.org/strategies/housing/.

Eisenhower, D. D. (22 February 1955). Transmitting the Clay Committee's report "A Ten-Year National Highway Program" to Congress, quoted in Richard F. Weingroff, *The Man Who Changed America, Part I*, March/April 2003, 66(5), Public Roads, Federal Highway Administration.

Endangered Species Act of 1973, 16 U.S.C. § 1531.

Ernst, M. (2003). Unpublished analysis based on the Federal Highway Administration's 2001 Fiscal Management Information Systems data, Surface Transportation Policy Project.

Executive Order No. 12898, 3 C.F.R. §§ 6-608 and 6-609 (1998), 59 *Fed. Reg.* at 7632–7633.

Fichtenbaum, R., & J. P. Blair. (1989). "Regional differences in labor demand in the United States." *The Review of Regional Studies, 19*(1), 72–76.

Forkenbrock, D. J., S. Benshoff, & G. E. Weisbrod. (2001). Assessing the social and economic effects of transportation projects. National Cooperative Highway Research Program. Washington, D.C.: Transportation Research Board.

Forkenbrock, D. J., & L. A. Schweitzer. (1997). *Environmental justice and transportation investment policy*. Public Policy Center, University of Iowa.

Frankenberg, E., & C. Lee. (2003). *Charter Schools and Race: A Lost Opportunity for Integrated Education*. Cambridge, Mass.: The Civil Rights Project at Harvard University.

Frederickson, G. M. (2003). The historical origins and development of racism. Retrieved on June 17, 2006, from www.stanbridgeacademy.org/Classes/socialjustice/supportdocs/Race%20Readings/HistoricalOrigins.pdf.

Frey, W. (2001). *Melting pot suburbs: A Census 2000 study of suburban diversity*. Washington, D.C.: Brookings Institution. Retrieved April 2003 from www.brookings.org/es/urban/projects/census/freyexecsum.htm.

———. (2002). "Metro magnets for minorities and whites: Melting pots, the new sunbelt, and the heartland." *Population Studies Center Research Report No. 02-496*. Retrieved April 2003 from www.psc.isr.umich.edu/pubs/papers/rr02-496.pdf.

Friedman, M. S., K. E. Powell, L. Hutwagner, L. Graham, & W. G. Teague. (2001). "Impact of changes in transportation and commuting behaviors during the 1996 Summer Olympic Games in Atlanta on air quality and childhood asthma." *Journal of the American Medical Association, 285*(7), 897–905.

Frumkin, H. (2002). "Urban sprawl and public health." *Public Health Reports, 117*, 201–217.

Galbraith, J. K. (1998). *Created unequal*. New York: Free Press.

García, R., & M. Brenman. (2005). *Katrina and the Demographics of Destruction and Reconstruction*. Center for Law in the Public Interest (September 16).

Garcia, R., & T. A. Rubin. (2004). "Crossroad blues: The MTA consent decree and just transportation." In Karen Lucas (Ed.), *Running on empty: Transport, social exclusion and environmental justice*. London: Policy Press.

Giuliano, G. (1994). "Land use impacts of transportation investments: Highway and transit." In S. Hanson (Ed.), *The geography of urban transportation* (2nd Ed.). Guilford Press, New York.

Glaeser, E. L., & J. Vigdor. (2001). *Racial segregation in the 2000 Census: Promising news*. Center on Urban and Metropolitan Policy, Brookings Institution.

Gómez-Ibáñez, J. A. (1976). "Assessing the arguments for urban transit operating subsidies." *Transportation Research Record, 573*, 126–132.

Gordon, P., A. Kumar, & H. W. Richardson. (1989). "The spatial mismatch hypothesis: Some new evidence." *Urban Studies, 26*, 315–326.

Hagman, D. G. (1980). *Public planning and control of urban development: Cases and materials* (2nd Ed.). St. Paul, Minn.: West Publishing Company.

Haley, K. (2000). "Sisters acting up: Meet the sisters in action for power." *Wiretap*. Retrieved May 2003 from www.alternet.org/story.html?StoryID=9753.

Hill, E. W., B. Geyer, K. O'Brien, C. Robey, J. Brennan, & R. Puentes. (2003). *Slanted pavement: How Ohio's highway spending shortchanges cities and suburbs*. Washington, D.C.: Brookings Institution.

Hobbs, F., & N. Stoops. (2002). *Demographic trends in the 20th century: Census 2000 special reports at 100*. Washington, D.C.: U.S. Department of Commerce, U.S. Bureau of the Census.

Hodge, D. (1980). "Inner city revitalization as a challenge to diversity?" In S. B. Laska & D. Spain (Eds.), *Back to the city: Issues in neighborhood renovation*. New York: Pergamon Press.

Holzer, H. J. (1991). "The spatial mismatch hypothesis: What has the evidence shown?" *Urban Studies, 28*, 105–122.

Holzer, H. J., H. R. Ihlanfeldt, & D.L. Sjoquist. (1994). "Work, search, and travel among white and black youth." *Journal of Urban Economics, 35*, 320–345.

Iceland, J., D. H. Weinberg, & E. Steinmetz. (2002). *Racial and ethnic residential segregation in the United States: 1980–2000*. Paper presented at the annual meetings of the Population Association of America, Atlanta.

Ihlanfeldt, K. R., & D.L. Sjoquist. (1998). "The spatial mismatch hypothesis: A review of recent studies and their implications for welfare reform." *Housing Policy Debate, 9*(4), 849–892.

Indian Self-Determination Act, 25 U.S.C. § 450.

Indian Tribal Justice Support Act, 25 U.S.C. § 3601.

Interfaith Federation. (June 1, 1999). People's Re-certification Hearing on NIRPC, Gary, Indiana.

Intermodal Surface Transportation Efficiency Act of 1991, H.R. 2950, 102nd Cong., 1 sess. (1991). Title, I, § 1024, subsection 134 (b) 2.

Institute for Social and Economic Research. (1995). *Expanding Native employment in existing jobs and programs*. Retrieved on March 17, 2006, from www.iser.uaa.alaska.edu/publications/client/afnjobs/intchiii.pdf.

Institute on Race and Poverty. (1996). *Integration and regional and urban planning, institute on race and poverty, linking regional and local strategies to create healthy communities, April 12–13 1996*. Retrieved on December 10, 2005, from www1.umn.edu/irp/april1296/integration.htm.

Jackson, K. T. (1985). *Crabgrass frontier*. New York: Oxford University Press.

Jargowsky, P. A. (1997). *Poverty and place: Ghettos, barrios, and the American city*. New York: Russell Sage Foundation Publications.

Jefferson, T. (June 28, 1776). The rough draft of the Declaration of Independence, Department of Alfa-informatica, University of Groningen.

Journal of Mine Act (2002). *Breaking new ground: Assisting farmers with disabilities through the application of assistive technology, 6.3, victim assistance*. Retrieved on June 17, 2006, from maic.jmu.edu/journal6.3/focus/field/field.htm.

Kain, J. F. (1968). "Housing segregation, Negro employment, and metropolitan decentralization." *Quarterly Journal of Economics, 82*, 175–197.

Kain, J. F., & J. R. Meyer. (1970). "Transportation and poverty." *The public interest, 18*, 75–87.

Katz, B., & M. Muro. (2003). "The smart money is on smart growth." *The Hartford Courant* (June 8).

Kennedy, M., & P. Leonard. (2001). *Dealing with neighborhood change: A primer on gentrification and policy choices*. Washington, D.C.: The Brookings Institution and Oakland, California: Policy Link. Retrieved June 2003 from www.brookings.edu/dybodocroot/es/urban/gentrification/gentrification.pdf.

Kinsey, S. (2003). "Local control breeds local innovation: California's successful experiment with sub-allocation." *Progress*. Washington, D.C.: Surface Transportation Policy Project, p. 3.

Labor/Community Strategies Center, Bus Riders Union, et al. v. L.A. County Metropolitan Transportation Authority, Plaintiffs' Revised Statement of Contentions of Fact and Law, No. CV-945936 (C.D. CA, October 24, 1996).

Lamberth, J. (n.d.). *Racial profiling doesn't work*. Retrieved on June 19, 2006, from www.lamberthconsulting.com/about-racial-profiling/racial-profiling -doesnt-work.asp.

Lang, R. E. (2003). *Edgeless cities: Exploring the elusive metropolis*. Washington, D.C.: Brookings Institution Press.

Laska, S. B., & D. Spain. (1980). *Back to the city: Issues in neighborhood renovation*. New York: Pergamon Press.

Lee, B. L. (1997). "Civil rights and legal remedies: A plan of action." In R. D. Bullard & G. S. Johnson (Eds.), *Just transportation: Dismantling race and class barriers to mobility*. Gabriola Island, B.C.: New Society Publishers.

Lewis Mumford Center. (2005). *Metropolitan Racial and Ethnic Data—Census 2000*. Retrieved on June 18, 2006, from http://mumford.albany.edu/census/.

Lin, S., J. P. Munsie, S. Hwan, E. Fitzgerald, & M. R. Cayo. (2002). "Childhood asthma hospitalization and residential exposure to state route traffic." *Environmental Research, A(88)*, 73–81.

Lineberry, R. (1977). *Equality and urban policy: The distribution of municipal public services*. Beverly Hills: Sage.

Litman, T. (1996). "Using road pricing revenue: Economic efficiency and equity considerations." *Transportation Research Record, 1558*, 24–28.

———. (2005). *Evaluating transportation equity: Guidance for incorporating distributional impacts in transportation equity*. Victoria, B.C.: Victoria Transport Policy Institute.

Logan, J. R. (2001). *The new ethnic enclaves in America's suburbs*. Lewis Mumford Center. Retrieved April 2003 from http://mumford1.dyndns.org/cen2000/ suburban/SuburbanReport/page1.htm.

———. (2002a). *Separate and unequal: The neighborhood gap for blacks and Hispanics in metropolitan America*. Lewis Mumford Center for Comparative Urban and Regional Research, State University of New York at Albany.

———. (2002b). "The suburban advantage: New census data show unyielding city–suburb economic gap, and surprising shifts in some places." *Lewis Mumford Center Census 2000 Metropolitan Racial and Ethnic Change Series*. Retrieved April 2003 from http://mumford1.dyndns.org/cen2000/City Profiles/SuburbanReport/page1.html.

Luckett, S. (2001). "Did you know? Homes account for 44 percent of all wealth: Findings from the SIPP 1995." *U.S. Census Bureau current population reports*. Washington, D.C.: U.S. Government Printing Office.

Maantay, J. (2001). "Zoning, equity, and public health." *American Journal of Public Health, 91*, 1033–1041.

Mann, E. (1997). "Confronting transit racism in Los Angeles." In R. D. Bullard & G. S. Johnson (Eds.), *Just transportation: Dismantling race and class barriers to mobility*. Gabriola Island, B.C.: New Society Publishers.

Massey, D. S., & N. A. Denton. (1988). "The dimensions of residential segregation." *Social Forces, 67,* 281–315.

Mather, M., & K. L. Rivers. (February 2006). *The concentration of negative child outcomes in low-income neighborhoods.* Baltimore: Annie E. Casey Foundation and Population Reference Bureau.

McFate, K. (1991). *Poverty, inequality and the crisis of social policy.* Washington, D.C.: Joint Center for Political and Economic Studies.

Metropolitan Transportation Commission. (2001). Bus pass pilot program for low income students. Retrieved on May 11, 2003, from www.mtc.ca.gov/projects/rtp/bus_pass.htm.

Meyer, J. A. (1999). "Assessing welfare reform: Work pays." *The Public Interest, 136,* 113–120.

Meyer, J. R., & J. A. Gómez-Ibáñez. (1981). *Autos, transit, and cities.* Cambridge, Mass.: Harvard University Press.

Milton S. Eisenhower Foundation. (1998). *The millennium breach.* The Corporation for What Works. Washington, D.C.: Author.

Moore, A. (2005). "Telecommuting Outstrips Transit." Retrieved on July 17, 2007, from www.visaliaedc.com/developments/documents/telecommuting outstripstransit.doc.

Mortimer, K. M., L. M. Neasa, D. W. Dockery, S. Redline, & I. B. Tager. (2002). "The effect of air pollution on inner-city children with asthma." *European Respiratory Journal, 19,* 699–705.

Morton v. Mancari, 417 U.S. 535 (1974).

Murakami, E., & J. Young. (1997). "Daily travel by persons with low income." Paper presented at the Nationwide Personal Transportation Survey (NPTS) Symposium, Bethesda, Maryland.

National Advisory Commission on Civil Disorders. (1968). *Report of the National Advisory Commission on Civil Disorders.* Washington, D.C.: U.S. Government Printing Office.

National Association of County and City Health Officials. (2002). "Creating health equity through social justice." Draft Working Paper.

National Criminal Justice Reference Service. (1998). *Guidelines for the screening of persons working with children, the elderly, and individuals with disabilities in need of support* (NCJ 167248). Washington, D.C.: Author.

National Environmental Policy Act, 42 U.S.C. §§ 432–4347.

National Environmental Policy Act, 40 C.F.R. § 1508.20.

National Highway Traffic Safety Administration. (1997). *Initiative for increasing seat belt use nationwide.* Retrieved on March 16, 2006, from www.nhtsa.dot .gov/people/injury/airbags/Archive-04/PresBelt/fullreport.html.

National Highway Traffic Safety Administration. (2004). *2003 motor vehicle occupant safety survey* (Volume 5: Child Safety Seat Report), Washington, D.C.: Author.

National Safety Council. (2002). *Primary seat belt laws save kids, new messages that can redefine the debate.* Retrieved on March 17, 2006, from www.nsc.org/partners/primary.htm.

Native American Graves Protection and Repatriation Act, 25 U.S.C. § 3001.

Native American Languages Act, 25 U.S.C. §§ 2901–2905.

Nelson, A. C., & T. W. Sanchez. (2005). "The effectiveness of urban containment regimes in reducing exurban sprawl." *NSL Network City and Landscape, 160,* 42–47.

New York City Department of City Planning. (2002). *Bronx Community District 2 profile.* Retrieved May 2003 from www.ci.nyc.ny.us/html/dcp/html/lucds/bx2lu.html

New York City Department of City Planning. (2002). *Manhattan Community District 10 profile.* Retrieved May 2003 from www.ci.nyc.ny.us/html/dcp/html/lucds/mn10lu.html.

Nijkamp, P., & E. Blaas. (1994). *Impact assessment and evaluation in transportation planning.* Dordrecht: Kluwer Academic Publishers.

Niolet, B. (2003). "Transportation plan rejected." *The Birmingham News,* March 4.

Ong, P. (1996). "Work and car ownership among welfare recipients." *Social Work Research, 2*(4), 255–262.

Ong, P., & E. Blumenberg. (1998). "Job access, commute and travel burden among welfare recipients." *Urban Studies, 35*(1), 77–93.

Oosterlee, A., M. Drijver, E. Lebret, & B. Brunekreef. (1996). "Chronic respiratory symptoms in children and adults living along streets with high traffic density." *Occupational and Environmental Medicine, 53*(4), 241–247.

Orlandi, Mario A. (1992) *Cultural competence for evaluators: A guide for alcohol and other drug abuse prevention practitioners working with ethnic/racial communities.* Rockville, Md.: National Clearinghouse for Alcohol and Drug Information.

Overton, K. (1994). "Auto-dependence: A driving force for gender inequality." *Transportation Alternatives Magazine,* March/April, 6–7.

Perera, F. P., S. M. Illman, P. L. Kinney, R. M. Whyatt, E. Z. Kelvin, P. Shepard D. Evans, M. Fullilove, J. Ford, R. L. Miller, I. H. Meyer, & V. A. Rauh. (2002). "The challenge of preventing environmentally related disease in young children: Community based research in New York." *Environmental Health Perspectives, 100*(2), 197–204.

Plessy v. Ferguson, 163 U.S. 537 (1896).

powell, j. a., & K. M. Graham. (2002). "Urban fragmentation as a barrier to equal opportunity." In D. M. Piche, W. L. Taylor, & R. A. Reed (Eds.), *Rights at risk: equality in an age of terrorism.* Report of the Citizens Commission on Civil Rights, Washington, D.C.

powell, j. a. (2002). "How sprawl makes us poor." *The Albuquerque Journal,* March 22.

Proctor, B. D., & Dalaker, J. (2002). *Poverty in the United States: 2001*. Washington, D.C.: U.S. Census Bureau.

Public Law 104–193.

Public Law 105–178.

Public Law 107–110, § 1116.

Pucher, J., & J. L. Renne. (2003). "Socioeconomics of urban travel: Evidence from the 2001 NHTS." *Transportation Quarterly, 57*(3).

Puentes, R., & R. Prince. (2003). *Fueling transportation finance: A primer on the gas tax*. Washington, D.C.: Brookings Institution.

Puentes, R., & L. Bailey. (2005). "Improving metropolitan decision making in transportation: Greater funding and devolution for greater accountability." In B. Katz & R. Puentes (Eds.), *Taking the high road: A metropolitan agenda for transportation reform*. Washington: Brookings Institution Press.

Putnam, R. D. (1995). "Bowling alone: America's declining social capital." *Journal of Democracy, 6*(1), 65–78.

———. (2000). *Bowling alone: The collapse and revival of American community*. New York: Simon & Schuster.

Raphael, S., & L. Rice. (2002). "Car ownership, employment, and earnings." *Journal of Urban Economics, 52*, 109–130.

Raphael, S., & A. Berube. (2006). "Socioeconomic differences in household automobile ownership rates: Implications for evacuation policy." Berkeley Symposium on Real Estate, Catastrophic Risk, and Public Policy. Brookings Institution. Retrieved on January 5, 2006, from http://urbanpolicy.berkeley.edu/pdf/06symposium.abstracts.pdf.

Rice v. Cayetano, 528 U.S. 495, 519–20 (2000).

Rice, L. (2004). *Transportation spending by low-income California households: Lessons for the San Francisco Bay Area*. San Francisco: Public Policy Institute of California.

Rivara, F. P. (1999). "Pediatric injury control in 1999: Where do we go from here?" *Pediatrics, 103*(4), 883–888.

Roanhorse Jr., A. (2005). Written statement to the U.S. Senate Committee on Indian Affairs, Hearing on Indian Health, Washington, D.C. Retrieved on April 22, 2006, from http://indian.senate.gov/2005hrgs/041305hrg/roanhorse.pdf.

Rubin, T. A. (2000). "Environmental justice and transportation decisions—The Los Angeles experience." Paper presented at the Transportation Research Board Annual Meeting, Washington, D.C.

SAGE Council. (n.d.). *Protecting the petroglyphs*. Retrieved on July 10, 2004, from www.sagecouncil.org/petro.html.

Sanchez, T. W. (1998). "Equity analysis of personal transportation system benefits." *Journal of Urban Affairs, 20*(1), 69–86.

———. (2002). "The impact of public transportation on U.S. metropolitan wage inequality." *Urban Studies, 39*(3), 423–436.

Sanchez, T. W., R. Stolz, & J. S. Ma. (2003). *Moving to equity: Addressing inequitable effects of transportation policies on minorities.* Cambridge, Mass.: The Civil Rights Project at Harvard University.

Schulz, A. J. et al. (2002). "Racial and spatial relations as fundamental determinants of health in Detroit." *The Milbank Quarterly, 80*(4), 677–707.

Seminole Nation v. United States, 316 U.S. 286, 296–297 (1942).

Shapiro v. Thompson, 394 U.S. 618 (1969).

Spiller v. White, 352 F.3d 235 (5th Cir. 2003).

Stiglitz, J. E. (2005). *Public sector economics.* Upper Saddle River, N.J.: Prentice-Hall.

Stolz, R. (2001). "MOSES gathering power for transportation equity." *The Organizing Newsletter.* Washington, D.C.

———. (2002). "Transportation equity and environmental justice." In *Planners Network Magazine.* Fall.

Surface Transportation Policy Project. (2001). *Driven to spend: The impact of sprawl on household transportation expenses.* Washington, D.C.: Author.

Surface Transportation Policy Project. (2002). *Mean streets 2002.* Washington, D.C.: Author.

Talen, E. (2002). "The social goals of new urbanism." *Housing Policy Debate, 13*(1), 165–188.

Taylor, B. D., & P. M. Ong. (1995). "Spatial mismatch or automobile mismatch? An examination of race, residence, and commuting in U.S. metropolitan areas." *Urban Studies, 32*, 1453–1473.

Title VI of the Civil Rights Act of 1964, 42 U.S.C. § 2000d, *et seq.*

Transportation Research Board. (1996). *Transit Cooperative Research Program (TCRP) Report 19: Guidelines for the location and design of bus stops.* Washington, D.C.: National Academies.

Transportation Research Board. (2002). *The relative risks of school travel: A national perspective and guidance for local community risk assessment.* Washington, D.C.: National Academies.

Triangle Improvement Council v. Ritchie, 402 U.S. 497, 502 (1971).

United States v. Sandoval, 231 U.S. 28, 34 S. Ct. 1, 58 L.Ed. 107 (1913).

U.S. 437 F.2d 1286 (1971).

U.S. 468 F.2d 287 (1972).

U.S. Statutes at Large, Vol. XVIII, p. 335 ff.

U.S. Bureau of the Census. (2001a). Census 2000 data. Retrieved on March 15, 2005, from www.census.gov.

U.S. Census (2001b). Census 2000 commuting data. Retrieved on November 21, 2004, from www.census.gov/population/www/socdemo/journey.html and www.census.gov/population/www/cen2000/commuting.html.

U.S. Code 23 § 109(h).

U.S. Code 23 § 129.

U.S. Code 23 § (b)(1).

U.S. Code 25 § 2502(d).

U.S. Code 25 § 472 and 473.

U.S. Code 25 § 479a.

U.S. Code 42 § 3601–3631.

U.S. Department of Transportation's Federal Highway Administration. (n.d.). Transportation decision-making factors. Retrieved on March 6, 2005, from www.fhwa.dot.gov/environment/nepa/decision.htm.

U.S. Department of Transportation. (1997). Order to Address Environmental Justice in Minority and Low-Income Populations (62 FR 18377).

U.S. Department of Transportation. (1999). Memorandum re: action: implementing Title VI requirements in metropolitan and statewide planning. Washington, D.C.: Author.

U.S. Department of Transportation. (2001). Guidance to recipients of special language services to limited english proficient (LEP) beneficiaries, Washington, D.C.: Author.

U.S. Department of Transportation. (1993). On federal aid highway projects on and near Indian reservations (DOT Notice N 4720.7), Washington, D.C.: Author.

U.S. Department of Transportation. (2002). FY 2004 performance plan, transportation accessibility. Retrieved on June 17, 2006, from www.dot.gov/PerfPlan 2004/mobility_accessibility.html.

U.S. Environmental Protection Agency. (2000). America's children and the environment: A first view of available measures. Retrieved May 2003 from http://yosemite.epa.gov/ochp/ochpweb.nsf/content/ACE-Report.htm/ $file/ACE-Report.pdf.

U.S. Federal Highway Administration. (2003). Publication No. FHWA-PL-03-017. Retrieved on June 22, 2005, at www.fhwa.gov/ohim/tollpage.htm.

U.S. Federal Highway Administration. (2005). The Facts. Retrieved on March 15, 2005, from www.fhwa.dot.gov/environment/ejustice/facts/index.htm.

U.S. General Accountability Office. (1998). *Welfare reform: Transportation's role in moving from welfare to work.* (GAO/RCED-98-161).

U.S. General Accountability Office. (1999). *Transportation coordination: Benefits and barriers exist, and planning efforts progress slowly.* (GAO/RCED-00-1).

U.S. General Accountability Office (2005). *Transportation services: Better dissemination and oversight of DOT's guidance could lead to improved access for limited English-proficient populations.* (GAO-06-52)

Wachs, M. (2003). *A dozen reasons for raising gasoline taxes.* Institute of Transportation Studies, University of California at Berkeley. Retrieved on May 11, 2005, from www.its.berkeley.edu/publications/UCB/2003/rr/UCB-ITS-RR-1.pdf.

Wachs, M., & B. D. Taylor. (1998). "Can transportation strategies help meet the welfare challenge?" *Journal of the American Planning Association, 64*(1), 15–19.

Waller, M., & M. A Hughes. (1999). *Working far from home: Transportation and welfare reform in the ten big states*. Washington, D.C.: Progressive Policy Institute.

Washington v. Davis, 426 U.S. 229, 96 S.Ct. 2040, 48 L.Ed.2d 597 (1976).

Weiland, S. K., K. A. Mundt, A. Ruckmann, & U. Keil. (1994). "Self-reported wheezing and allergic rhinitis in children and traffic density on street of residence." *Annals of Epidemiology, 4*(3), 243–247.

Wernette, D. R., & L. A. Nieves. (1992). "Breathing polluted air: Minorities are disproportionately exposed." *EPA Journal, 18*, 16–17.

Wilson, W. J. (1987). *The truly disadvantaged: The inner city, the underclass, and public policy*. Chicago: University of Chicago Press.

Wjst, M., P. Reitmeir, S. Dold, A. Wulff, T. Nicolai, E. F. von Loeffelholz-Colberg, & E. von Mutius. (1993). "Road traffic and adverse effects on respiratory health in children." *British Medical Journal, 307*(6904), 596–600.

Index

Questions for Discussion

1. What are some of the most significant advances in civil rights related to urban transportation?

2. What changes in transportation or communications technology have the greatest potential to increase social and economic opportunity for low-income persons and persons of color?

3. As planners consider the importance of accessibility to jobs, what negative impacts can result from particular modes of travel (auto access, transit access, pedestrian access)?

4. As the U.S. population ages, what particular transportation and land-use issues will become priorities?

5. How can we provide for equitable levels of transportation accessibility? What about transportation mobility?

6. Some research has shown that immigrants may have particular transport accessibility handicaps. How does this group fit into the transportation equity framework discussed in this book?

7. Will current demographic trends lead to more pressure for equitable transportation systems—or less pressure?

8. What level of government should enforce civil rights and environmental justice laws related to transportation: local, metropolitan, state, federal, or some combination?

9. What particular lessons can grassroots advocacy groups learn from the early efforts of the Freedom Riders and Rosa Parks?

10. How do various types of infrastructure, such as housing, education, and transportation, interact to increase or maintain segregation?

11. How does transportation affect social mobility?

12. President Clinton's Secretary of Transportation, Rodney Slater, said, "Transportation is about more than concrete, asphalt, and steel." Do you agree? Why? What other factors should be considered?

13. Toll roads and toll lanes are becoming popular ways to decrease congestion. How important are the regressive economic effects of such a flat tax?

14. By definition, sustainable development includes equity considerations. Yet these issues are rarely discussed in the context of the environment and global warming. How should equity be included in that increasingly important conversation?

15. Studies of transportation projects are supposed to analyze the projects' cumulative impacts, including impacts on minority communities. Yet they rarely do so. What can be done to change that situation?

16. The U.S. is becoming increasingly diverse in population, culture, and religion. Do our transportation systems increase assimilation or separation? Further, can transportation decisions be made with or without such implied value judgments, or do all such decisions contain values, even if they are hidden?

17. Is using transportation to drive social equity a form of "social engineering"? Is this wrong?

18. Transportation infrastructure decisions are usually made by white men. Civil rights advocates sometimes call this a form of institutional racism. Is it? Should the system be changed, and if so how?